ENCYCLOPAEDIA OF INDIA, PAKISTAN AND BANGLADESH

ENCYCLOPAEDIA OF
INDIA, PAKISTAN
AND
BANGLADESH

(In 9 Volumes)

(Volume 3)

OM GUPTA

ISHA

ISHA BOOKS

Delhi-110033

Encyclopaedia of India, Pakistan and Bangladesh
(In 9 Volumes)

ISBN : 81-8205-389-7 (Set)
ISBN : 81-8205-392-7 (Vol. 3)

Rs. 6300 (Set)

Published in 2006 in India by
Isha Books
D-43, Prithviraj Road,
Adarsh Nagar, Delhi - 110033
e-mail : ishabooks@hotmail.com

Laser Typesetting : Vinayak Printers, Delhi
Printed at : Salasar Imaging Systam, Delhi

Preface

According to Oxford dictionary Encyclopaedia is a book or aset of books that gives information on many subjects or many aspect of one subject. This encyclopaedia does that on India, Pakistan and Bangladesh. It is the first work of its kind. There have been anthologies on India but there is no compendium of information in an alphabetical order. Even Britannica could go as far as four-volume encyclopaedia on Indian history.

Encyclopaedia is an extension of a dictionary. The latter gives you meanings of words while the former gives facts about people, places and events. No one can claim to compile all the facts and that of a sub-continent called India. But then it is the prerogative of the editor to pick up his entries that he considers would be useful to his reader. Generally we soon find our comfort levels in a language. And rarely consults a dictionary and lesser an encyclopaedia. But those who dare, find the experience worth it. It can be easily compared to a human body. In our daily life we tend to be our own quacks and medicate on the basis of common sense. If we refer to a doctor we come to know the actual cause of the symptom and get relieved on knowing the gravity of the situation or the absence of it. One would realize that encyclopaedia reveals the fundamentals of any situation, person or the event and we feel at home with that information.

A dictionary and an encyclopaedia can easily enlarge the process of learning even to an uninitiated person. It is truer in case of humanities. Popular myth about encyclopaedia is that it is meant to be referred to in a library only. The librarians, the world over keep encyclopaedia in such zealously guarded protection that the generally refrain from asking for it. Since the advent of internet in our life, the bulkiness of encyclopaedias has disappeared. That is why we have divided this enterprise in nine volumes. Encyclopaedias are generally global in its expanse. Even subject-related encyclopaedias give the global perspective.That is why country-specific encylopaedias have never been seriousy attempted. We hope that this effort will fill that volume. Traditionally encyclopaedias don't deal with factual data e.g. Indian exports, population figures, GDP. That is the job of annual reference books. They are also different from alamans in as much as that they don't give dated entries. That will become texts on history. Encyclopaedias need to be updated. A country is alive and kicking. People and events continue to play role in various aspects of life. Hence they need to be added. That is why either annual supplements or updation needs to be done in encyclopaedias. We would strive for that.

Regarding its contents only those entries have been included that continue to influence the life of a nation. There are historical figures who might have played a significant role in their times but if those deeds have no relevance to the present they have been excluded. Another example is literary awards. They always create controversies because their selection at times is subjective. Hence only universally accepted meritorious work has found place in these volumes. In this context a debatable point need to be stated. Who is more important book or the author. Conventionally work is an end product and only that is a measure of the author's importance but then a prolic writer might have produced a large body of creations. Hence to save space the author is entered with all his important work.That is also an international practice.

Lastly, why India, Pakistan and Bangladesh have been clubbed together. Before India's independence they were one nation. They share a common heritage and composite culture. Their post-independence history is different but 22their foundation is undivided. In order to appreciate the historical context better it is necessary to cross-refer and that was possible when they are juxtaposed.

Om Gupta

C

Cabinet Mission : The British Cabinet Mission of 1946 to India aimed to discuss and finalize plans for the transfer of power from the British Raj to Indian leadership, providing India with independence under Dominion status in the Commonwealth of Nations. Formulated the initiative of Clement Attlee, the Prime Minister of the United Kingdom, the mission consisted of Lord Pethick-Lawrence, the Secretary of State for India, Sir Stafford Cripps, President of the Board of Trade, and A. V. Alexander, the First Lord of the Admiralty. It was also supplemented by Lord Wavell, the Viceroy of India at the time.

Calangute : Once upon a time, Calangute was the it beach for hippies, where pujas, ganja, drug-addled musicians and other lost artistic souls predominated, a beach of the truly half-baked that modern Leonardo di Caprioan versions couldn't hold a psychedelic candle to. But alas for those who still seek the 'revolution', or the occasional naked group frolic, Calangute is no longer Hippy Central. The local people, who used to rent out rooms in their houses for a pittance, have moved on to more profitable things, and the place has undergone a metamorphosis to become the centre of Goa's rapidly expanding package-tourist market.

Calangute isn't one of the best Goan beaches: there are hardly any palms, the sand is contaminated with red soil and the beach drops rapidly into the sea. There is, however, plenty going on, especially if you don't mind playing a minor role in this stage-managed parody of what travelling is meant to be about. Try heading off the beaten track unless you need a bit of R 'n' R to recover from life on the road, or want to mix it with the Simons and Sandras of this world who are visiting India to pep up their winter suntans.

Calcutta Medical College : Calcutta Medical College, also known as Medical College Calcutta was established in 1835 as Medical College, Bengal in Kolkata, India as the first college of European medicine in Asia. The purpose of establishing this college was to train native youths irrespective of caste and creed in the principles and practices of medical science in accordance with the mode adopted in Europe. The college now imparts the degrees MBBS after completion of 5 and half years of medical training. Also specialization degrees like MD and MS are given to post-graduate students. Besides there are nursing and several para-medical courses. The hospital associated with the college is one of the largest hospitals in Kolkata and houses several speciality and super-speciality departments.

Calico Museum : The excellent Calico Museum of Textiles, is one of the finest textile museums in the world constructed in 1949. It houses the finest fabrics spun, woven, printed and painted in different parts of India during past five centuries. Also on display are old weaving machines. The museum is in Sarabhai House, a former mansion in the Shahi Bagh Gardens. Museum closed on Tuesdays.

Cambay : The old seaport of Ahmedabad is 92km to the south-west at the northern end of the Gulf of Cambay. At the height of Muslim Power in Gujarat, the entire region was known as Cambay and when the first ambassadors arrived from England in 1583, they bore letters from Queen Elizabeth addressed to Akbar, the 'King of Cambay'.

Canacona : Canacona is an administrative region in south Goa, in India. Canacona is one of the five talukas that constitute the South Goa district. It is bounded on the north by the taluka of Quepem, on the northeast by Sanguem, on the south by the state of Karnataka, and on the west by the Arabian Sea. The town of Chaudi is the administrative headquarters of the taluka of Canacona.

The name Canacona is a corruption of the name Konkan. The area was one of the districts of the former Kingdom of Soonda, itself a remnant of the former Vijayanagara Empire. When Soonda was invaded and partially occupied by Hyder Ali of Mysore, the heirless Raja ceded the remaining parts to Portugal and these were incorporated into Goa as the districts of Quepem, Sanguem and Canacona.

Canacona was incorporated into Goa in 1794. Like most of Goa, the culture of the district reflects an Indo-Portuguese fusion, yet Canacona experienced less Lusitanisation than the central Velhas Conquistas. The Canacona railway station of the Konkan Railways is located at the center of the district, close to the tourist attractions of the coast. The railway junction of Margao to the north is the closest major rail station. Buses from Bombay may terminate at Panaji (Panjim), but some go on to Margao. Highway Route NH17 from Bombay to Goa connects Chaudi to Margao and Panaji. The scenic coastal road connects Navelim, Chinchinim, Assolna, Betul, and Canaguinim.

Canara Bank : Canara Bank (BSE: 532483), established in 1906 with the name of Canara Bank Hindu Permanent Fund in Mangalore, India, by Ammembal Subba Rao Pai, is one of the oldest and major commercial bank of India. Its name was changed to Canara Bank Limited in 1910. The bank, along with 13 other major commercial banks of India, was nationalisd on 19th July, 1969, by the Government of India. In 2005, the bank has 2508 branches spread all over India. The bank also has international presence in several centers, including London, Hong Kong, Moscow, Shanghai, Doha, and Dubai. In terms of business it is the second largest nationalised commercial bank in India with a total business of about Rs.170000 crores.

Capital Development Authority : Capital Development Authority (CDA), Islamabad, Pakistan was established on June 14, 1960, first by an executive order issued on June 24, 1960 entitled the Pakistan Capital Regulation, to be superseded by the CDA ordinance issued on June 27, 1960.

Captain Karnal Sher Khan Shaheed : Captain Karnal Sher joined those eight legendary heroes who received the highest military award of Nishan-i-Haider for laying down their lives in defence of the beloved motherland.

Captain Karnal Sher Khan emerged as the symbol of mettle and courage during the Kargil conflict on the Line of Control (LoC). He set personal examples of bravery and inflicted heavy losses on the enemy. He defended the five strategic posts, which he established with his jawans at the height of some 17,000 feet at Gultary, and repulsed many Indian attacks.

After many abortive attempts, the enemy on July 5 ringed the post of Capt. Sher Khan with the help of two battalion and unleashed heavy mortar firing and managed to capture some part of the post. Despite facing all odds, he lead a counter-attack and re- captured the lost parts. But during the course he was hit by the machine-gun fire and embraced Shahadat at the same post. He is the first officer from the NWFP province to be awarded with Nishan-i-Haider.

Captain Lakshmi Sahgal : Captain Lakshmi Sahgal (or Sehgal) (born October 24, 1914 in Madras) served in the Indian National Army (Azad Hind Fauz) led by noted freedom fighter Subhash Chandra Bose, during the Second World War against the British in the early and mid 20th century.

She was born as Lakshmi Swaminathan, daughter of Dr S Swaminathan, a leading lawyer practising Criminal Law at Madras High Court (now Chennai). Her mother was A V Ammukutty, better known as Ammu Swaminathan, a social worker and freedom fighter. She decided to study medicine because she wanted to be of service to the poor, especially to poor women. As a result, she received an MBBS degree from Madras Medical College in 1938. A year later, she received her diploma in gynaecology and obstetrics.

In 1940, she left for Singapore where she established a clinic for the poor mostly migrant labour from India. She became one of the most popular and prosperous gynecologists in the city. She was not only a competent doctor but also played an active role in the India Independence League which contributed greatly to the freedom movement in India.

In 1942 during the historic surrender of Singapore by the British to the Japanese, she worked hard in serving the Prisoners of war who were hurt during the skirmishes. In the process she came in contact with many Indian Prisoners of War (POWs) who were thinking of forming a Indian liberation army. Subhas Chandra Bose arrived in Singapore on July 2, 1943. In the next few days, at all his public meetings, *Netaji* spoke of his determination to raise a women's regiment, the Rani of Jhansi Regiment, which would also "fight for Indian Independence and make it complete". She was given the rank of a Colonel.

She became the Minister in charge of Women's Organization in Arzi Hukumate Azad Hind (Provisional Government of Free India), led by Subhash Chandra Bose. She held this portfolio over and above her command of the Rani Jhansi Regiment. The unit had the strength of a Brigade. In a regular army, this women's army unit was the first of its kind in Asia. The army fought on the side of the Axis powers against the British.

She was active both militarily and on the medical front. She played a heroic role not only in the fighting but during the days that INA personnel were hunted by the victorious British troops and saved many lives. She was captured and brought to India on March 4, 1946 where she received a heroine's welcome. The British realised that keeping her a prisoner would prove counter-productive and she was later released.

Colonel Prem Kumar Sahgal was among those who were released from the Red Fort. In March 1947, Colonel Sahgal and Captain Lakshmi were married in Lahore. (Colonel Sahgal was the son of Justice Achhru Ram Sahgal) After their marriage, they settled down in Kanpur. In Kanpur she carried on with her medical profession and served the refugees who were arriving in large numbers during the partition. In 1971 she joined the Communist Party of India (Marxist), and became a leader of the All India Democratic Women's Association. In 1988, she was awarded the Padma Vibhushan by the President of India.

Car Nicobar : Car Nicobar (known as Malacca or Pu in the local language) is the northernmost of the Nicobar Islands, which in turn are the southern part of the Indian union territory of the Andaman and Nicobar Islands. It lies at 9°10′N 92°45′E and has an area of 127 km^2.

Although this is less than 7% of the area of the Nicobar group, in the census of 2001 its population of 29,145 was more than half of the total Nicobar population.

There were 16 villages, the largest being Malacca. Direct administration of the island is performed by the Car Nicobar tehsil, a local administratve division of the Nicobar district. A tehsil is roughly equivalent to a county in its administrative powers.

Cardamom Hills : The Cardamom Hills are hills in Kerala, India, named after the cardamom grown in the hill's cool regions, in addition to pepper and coffee. These hills are situated in south-central Kerala. The hills reach 2,000 to 2,500 metres above sea level.

Carnatic Music : Carnatic music, known as karnataka sangitam is the classical music that originated in Karnataka, South India. Lyrics in Carnatic music are largely devotional; most of the songs are addressed to the Hindu deities. There are, besides, a lot of songs emphasising love and other social issues which have been composed in Carnatic music, although some of them, especially with the 'Rasa' (emotion) of love, continue to be composed and are widely popular, that rest on the concept of sublimation of human emotions for union with the divine.

Thus, for instance, a young woman in a modern classical composition, will be yearning for one of the deities, such as Krishna, as her 'lover—the purpose of such musical pieces being at once to provide an outlet for human emotions and, unlike in the normal run of motion pictures, to address God rather than another human being. Carnatic music as a classical form is always thus required to be a culturally elevating medium. As with all Indian classical music, the two main components of Carnatic music are raga, a melodic pattern and tala, a rhythmic pattern.

Ceasefire : On September 22, the United Nations Security Council unanimously passed a resolution that called for an unconditional ceasefire from both nations. The war ended the following day. The Soviet Union, led by Premier Alexey Kosygin, brokered a ceasefire in Tashkent (now in Uzbekistan), where Indian Prime Minister Lal Bahadur Shastri and Pakistani President Ayub Khan signed an agreement to withdraw to pre-August lines no later than February 25, 1966. The battle remained largely inconclusive despite Pakistan suffering relatively more losses, and saw a six year period of relative peace between the two neighboring rivals before war broke out once again in 1971.

The war had created a tense state of affairs in its aftermath. Both India and Pakistan increased their defence spending and the Cold War politics had taken roots in the subcontinent. Partly as a result of the inefficient information gathering of India in the war, the Research and Analysis Wing was set up for external espionage and intelligence as a separate entity a few years later. India slowly started aligning with the Soviet Union both politically and militarily. This would be cemented formally years later before the Bangladesh Liberation War. It also showed that the numerically larger Indian Military—which was then undergoing massive changes in the armed forces—had been able to withstand an attack by a qualitative superior enemy. In light of the previous war against the Chinese, the performance in this war was viewed as a "politico-strategic" victory in India.

Pakistan's performance was hailed back home, especially the initial moves including Rann of Kutch and the defence of Sialkot. September 6 is celebrated as Defence Day in Pakistan in commemoration of that defence. Pakistan Air Force was also seen with pride for its performance against its numerically bigger counterpart. However, the end game left a lot to desire as Pakistan had lost more ground than gained and more importantly did not achieve the goal of occupying Kashmir. Many high ranking Pakistani officials and military experts later criticized the faulty planning in Operation Gibraltar that ultimately led to the war. The Tashkent declaration was further seen as a raw deal in Pakistan though few citizens realised the gravity of the situation that existed at the end of the war. This war also became a political liability for Ayub. Under the advice of his Foreign Minister (Zulfikar Ali Bhutto), he had raised very high expectations among the people of Pakistan about the superiority—if not invincibility—of its armed forces. The fighting also caused simmering resentment among East Pakistan whose security lay quite bare. Sheikh Mujibur Rahman was apprehensive of this situation and the need for greater autonomy for the east led to another war between India and Pakistan in 1971.

Cellular Jail : The Cellular Jail (also known as Kalapani) was built in 1906 on the Andaman and Nicobar Islands (India). It was called 'cellular' because its entire structure was made up of individual cells for the solitary confinement (and torture) of prisoners — Indian freedom fighters. Among the illustrious prisoners here has been Veer Savarkar.

Cemetery H Culture : The Cemetery H culture developed out of the northern part of the Indus Valley Civilization around 1900 BC, in and around the Punjab region. It was named after a cemetery found in "area H" at Harappa. The distinguishing features of this culture include:

—The use of cremation of human remains. The bones were stored in painted pottery burial urns. This is completely different to the Indus civilization where bodies were buried in wooden coffins. This burial practice is not vedic and may be Mazdean/Zoroastrian.

—Reddish pottery, painted in black with antelopes, peacocks etc., sun or star motifs, with different surface treatments to the earlier period.

—Expansion of settlements into the east.

—Use of new crops such as rice.

—Apparent breakdown of the widespread trade of the Indus civilization, with materials such as marine shells no longer used.

—Continued use of mud brick for building.

—The archaeologist Kenoyer noted that this culture "may only reflect a change in the focus of settlement organization from that which was the pattern of the earlier Harapppan phase and not cultural discontinuity, urban decay, invading aliens, or site abandonment, all of which have been suggested in the past."

Cenda : Chenda is a cylindrical wooden drum which is two feet in length and about a foot in diameter. Both sides of the chenda is covered with skin. Although the chenda has two faces, only one surface of it is beaten. The drummer suspends the chenda from his neck such that it hangs more or less vertically and with two sticks held in both the hands, he strikes the upper parchment.

It is an important percussion instrument used in 'Kathakali', 'Koodiyattam' and related forms of dances. The same instrument is known as the chende in certain areas of Karnataka and it is used in 'Yakshagana' which is a folk dance-drama. The sound produced by the chenda is very loud. There are many varieties of this drum like uruttu chenda (for playing variations), the veekku chenda (one which beats the basic rhythm), acchan chenda and so on.

Central Board of Secondary Education : The Central Board of Secondary Education (CBSE) is a board of school education in India.The CBSE prepares the syllabus for students from Lower Kindergarten(L.K.G) to Class 12, for schools affiliated with it. It conducts two board examinations: the All India Secondary School Examination for Class 10 and the All India Senior School Certificate Examination for Class 12, which is a school-leaving examination. It also prescribes the syllabi for these examinations, whose scores are necessary to gain admission in higher study institues. Many private schools through the country affiliate themselves with the CBSE. The medium for education prescribed by CBSE is either English or Hindi.

CBSE All India Senior School Certificate Examination for Class 12 is widely recognised internationally for direct admission to university undergraduate courses. CBSE also conducts the All India Engineering Entrance Examination (AIEEE) which is a common entrance examination on all-India basis for admission to engineering and architecture/ planning programmes in the country. Similarly Pre-medical and Pre-dental Tests (PMT/PDT) are conducted for medical and dental colleges after the 10+2 exams.

Central Bureau of Investigation (CBI) : The Central Bureau of Investigation (CBI), established in 1963, is the premier investigation agency of India which focuses mainly on economic crimes and corruption charges. It is analogous in structure to the FBI in the United States, and the CID in the United Kingdom. The CBI is a central subject under the Constitution of India, meaning that it reports to the Indian Government and not to the individual states. Normally, cases assigned to the CBI are sensitive and of national importance. It is a usual practice for the respective state police department, to initially register any case coming under its jurisdiction, and if necessary, through mediation by the central government, the cases may be transferred to the CBI. The CBI is the official Interpol unit for India. A director of the CBI, P.C. Sharma, was elected as Vice-President of Interpol in October 2003. The current director of CBI is Shri Vijay Shankar (since December 10, 2005).

Central India Agency : The Central India Agency was a political unit of British India, which covered the northern half of present-day Madhya Pradesh state. The Central India Agency was made up entirely of princely states, which were under native rulers. The agency was bordered by the Central Provinces and Berar to the south; the Chota Nagpur princely states to the east, which were transferred from Bengal to the Central Provinces and Berar in 1905; the United Provinces of Agra and Oudh to the north; Rajputana to the northwest; and Bombay Presidency to the west and southwest. The district of Lalitpur, part of the United Provinces, split the Central India Agency into eastern and western portions.

The agency was overseen by an agent who oversaw the affairs of the princely states on behalf of the Governor-General of India. The agency was established in 1802, when several states in the Bundelkhand and Bagelkhand regions came under British control at the conclusion of the Treaty of Bassein between the British and the Maratha Peshwa Bajirao II. British control of Bundelkhand expanded at the conclusion of the Second Anglo-Maratha War in 1805. The remaining states, including Gwalior, Indore, Bhopal, and a number of smaller states in the regions of Malwa, Nimar, and Bundelkhand, came under British control with the end of the Third Anglo-Maratha War in 1818. The state of Chanderi was ceded to the British by the Sindhia ruler of Gwalior in 1844, and became part of the United Provinces, as did the state of Jhansi, seized by the British in 1853 under the doctrine of lapse.

Central Treaty Organization : The Central Treaty Organization (also referred to as CENTO, original name was Middle East Treaty Organization or METO, also known as the Baghdad Pact) was adopted in 1955 by Iraq, Turkey, Pakistan, and Iran, as well as Britain. Although American pressure, along with promises of military and economic largesse, were key in the negotiations leading to the agreement, the United States chose not to initially participate as to avoid alienating Arab states with which it was still attempting to cultivate friendly relations. Some (particularly nationalist radicals) saw the Pact as an attempt by the British to retain influence in the Middle East as a substitute for the loss of their empire in India. In 1958 the United States finally joined the alliance. It is generally viewed as one of the least successful of the Cold War alliances. Organizations headquarters was initially located in Baghdad, Iraq.

Modeled after the North Atlantic Treaty Organisation it committed the nations to mutual cooperation and protection, as well as non-intervention in each other's affairs. Its goal was to contain the Soviet Union by having a line of strong states along the USSR's southwestern frontier. Unlike NATO, CENTO did not have a unified military command structure, nor were many U.S. or U.K. military bases established in member countries, although the U.S. had communications and electronic intelligence facilities in Iran, and operated U-2 intelligence flights over the U.S.S.R. from bases in Pakistan. The U.K. had access to facilities in Pakistan and Iraq at various times while the treaty was in effect. In addition, Turkey and the U.S. agreed to permit American access to Turkish bases, but this was done under the auspices of NATO.

On July 14, 1958, the Iraqi monarchy was overthrown in a military coup. The new government was a dictatorship led by members of the Baathist Party which aligned itself with Moscow; Iraq quit the organization shortly thereafter. The organization dropped the Baghdad Pact moniker in favor of CENTO at that time.

The Middle East and South Asia became extremely volatile areas during the 1960s with the ongoing Arab-Israeli Conflict and the Indo-Pakistani Wars. CENTO was unwilling to get deeply involved in either dispute. In 1965 and 1971, Pakistan tried unsuccessfully to get assistance in its wars with India through CENTO, but this was rejected under the idea that CENTO was aimed at containing the U.S.S.R., not India.

CENTO did little to prevent the expansion of Soviet influence to non-member states in the area. Whatever containment value the pact might have had was lost when the Soviets 'leap-frogged' the member states, establishing close military and political relationships with Arab dictarorships in Egypt, Syria, Iraq, the People's Democratic Republic of Yemen, Somalia, and Libya. Indeed, by 1970, the U.S.S.R. had deployed over 20,000 troops to Egypt, and had established naval bases in Syria, Somalia, and P.D.R. Yemen.

The Iranian revolution of 1979 spelled the end of the organization. However, in reality, it had been as good as finished after 1974, when Turkey invaded Cyprus, leading the United Kingdom to withdraw forces that had been earmarked to the alliance. With the fall of the Iranian monarchy, whatever remaining rationale for the organization was lost. Future U.S. and British defense agreements with regional countries — such as Pakistan, Egypt, and the Gulf States — were conducted bilaterally.

Centum-Satem Isogloss : The Satem languages include Indo-Iranian, Balto-Slavic (Baltic and Slavic), Albanian, Armenian and perhaps also a number of barely documented extinct languages, such as Thracian, and Dacian. Although Albanian is treated as a Satem language, there may be some evidence that the plain velars and the labiovelars were not completely merged in Proto-Albanian.

The Centum group is often thought of as being identical to "non-Satem", i.e. as including all remaining dialects. More specifically, in the sense of Brugmann's "languages with labialization", the Centum group includes Italic, Celtic, Germanic, Greek, and possibly a number of minor and little known extinct groups (such as Venetic and the ancient Macedonian language and probably the Illyrian languages).

Tocharian, on the other hand collapsed all rows into a single velar row, and is therefore typically considered "Centum", although the relative chronology of the change is unknown. And the proto-language of the Anatolian languages apparently did not undergo either the Satem or the Centum sound change. The velar rows remain separate in Luwian, while Hittite may secondarily have undergone a Centum change, but the exact phonology is unclear.

Chaat : Chaat is a word used across India and the rest of South Asia to refer to small plates of savory snacks, typically served at the side of the road from stalls or carts. Most chaat originated in North India, but they are now eaten across the country. Some believe that the chaat in Bombay (now Mumbai) is the best in the world, but other regions in India have their own styles, and would dispute that claim. Some are results of cultural syncretism—for instance, pao bhaji reflect a Portuguese influence, in the form of a bun, and bhel puri was created by a Gujarati migrant to Mumbai, whose descendants still run Vithal Bhelwala, near Victoria Terminus railway station. In each major Indian city, there are popular chaathouses or dhabas, such as Mumbai's Chowpatty Beach and Bangalore's Hot Chips, and Gangotree.

Chadak Puja : Chadak Puja a Hindu religious ceremony, observed on the last day of the Bangla month of Chaitra. It is also known as Nil Puja. It is a variation of Gambhira Puja or Shiver gajan celebrated in west bengal. Fairs lasting several days are held in the villages in connection with this Puja.

Chadak Puja is not a very old ritual. It is not mentioned in the classical texts. Lingapurana, Vrihaddharmapurana and Brahmavaivartapurana refer to dancing and singing on the occasion of Shiva Puja in Chaitra but do not mention Chadak Puja. Govindananda's Varsakriyakaumudi and raghunandan's Tithitattva of the 15th/16th centuries, which record various annual religious ceremonies, do not mention this puja.

Chador : A chador is an outer garment worn by women; it is one possible way in which a Muslim woman may follow the hijab dress code. It is a traditional Iranian garment, mostly used by practicing Muslim women in urban or rural Iran.

A chador is a full-length semi-circle of fabric open down the front. A chador has no hand openings or closures but is held shut by the hands or teeth or by wrapping the ends around the waist. Traditionally, black was eschewed for its conontations of death and funerals and white or printed fabrics were preferred. Now, except for rural elderly women, black is the universal color for a chador.

Traditionally, a chador was worn with a headscarf (rusæri), blouse (pirhan) and skirt (doman) or skirt over pants (shælvar). After the 1979 Iranian Revolution, the chador began to be worn over a headscarf (pulled over khemar mæghne or 'rusæri) and a long overcoat (jilbab or manteau) became popular for total coverage.

Chagai : Chagai district is in the north west corner of Balochistan province of Pakistan. It forms a triangular border with Afghanistan and Iran. Chagai District was created in 1896. Nushki was the only sub division of the district with two tehsils, Nushki and Dalbandin. Nokkundi sub tehsil was upgraded to tehsil in 1950. Chagai district was attached to Kalat in 1957 but was detached after two years. The Police Department is still under the Superintendent of Police, Kalat. Dalbandin Tehsil was upgraded to Sub-Division on 1st February, 1978. Taftan was created as sub tehsil in 1981. Chagai sub-tehsil was created with effect from 1st October, 1985. The Assistant Political Agent Nushki remained sub-Divisional Magistrate of Nushki Sub Division till September 1989 when an independent post of Additional Political Agent was created for the district.

Chagai Hills : The Chagai Hills are in the north of the Pakistani Province Baluchistan. The mountains and hills are carved by innumerable channels which contain water only after rains, though little water reaches the low-lying basins. On May 28, 1998, this area received international attention when used by Pakistan to test nuclear weapons.

Chai : Chai is a Hindi word which means tea. Chá is a Mandarin word with similar meaning. The word Tea originates from ancient China ('Te') and is used throughout the world in slightly different variations. Some people in India, South-East Asia and Europe interpret Chai as Masala Chai, which refers to a spiced Indian tea.

Chait Danda : It is performed in the month of Chaitra.

Chaitanya Bhagavata : Chaitanya Bhagavata of Vrindavana Dasa was the first full length hagiography in Bangla and the longest early work to document the remarkable life of the religious figure Krishna Chaitanya, ne Vishvambhara Mishra (1478-1533). Written in an earthy style, the Chaitanya Bhagavata celebrates the wondrous advent of Chaitanya, whom followers had accepted as Krishna himself. Vrindavana Dasa himself grew up in Navadvipa in the house of Chaitanya's close companion

Srivasa, who was brother-in-law to Vrindavana Dasa's mother, and so benefited from the experiences of those who knew Chaitanya well. Although Chaitanya passed many hours in Shrivasa's house, it would appear that the author was too young to have ever met him personally.

Chaitanya Charitamrita : The Chaitanya Charitamrita is the magnum-opus of the Bengali saint/author Krishna Dasa Kaviraja (1496-? CE). The book, a hybrid Bengali and Sanskrit biography, documents the life and precepts of the Vaishnava saint Chaitanya Mahaprabhu (1486 – 1533), who is considered by his followers to be an incarnation of Radha and Krishna combined. Chaitanya is a pivotal figure of the Hindu sect Gaudiya Vaishnavism. As a religious text, the Chaitanya Charitamrita is the main theological resource for Gaudiya Vaishnava Theology and is divided into three sections, Adi-lila, Madhya-lila and Antya-lila.

Chaitanya Mahaprabhu : Chaitanya Mahaprabhu (also transliterated Caitanya, IAST caitanya mahaprabhu) (Bangla) (1486 - 1534), was an ascetic Hindu monk and social reformer in 16th century Bengal, India (present-day West Bengal and Bangladesh). A great proponent of loving devotion for God bhakti yoga, Chaitanya worshiped the Lord in the form of Radha-Krishna. Gaudiya Vaishnava followers revere him as Krishna Himself descended in the mood of Radharani. He was also known as Gaura (Sanskrit for "the fair /golden one") due to his skin complexion, as well as Nimai due to being born under a Neem tree. There are numerous biographies of Chaitanya, the most popular ones being Sri Chaitanya Charitamrita of Krishnadasa Kaviraja Gosvami and the earlier Chaitanya Bhagavata of Vrindavana Dasa Thakura, both written in the Bengali language.

Chaiti Ghoda Nata : It is the most important festival of the fishermen of Orissa. Goddess basuli with a horse shaped head is worshipped from the full moon day of lunar Baishakha. According to the myth in Kaibarta Purana, the supreme god slept on the leaf of a banyan tree which was buffeted in the sea. He created a man out of the dirt of his ear to hold the rudder firmly and thus keep his leaf-bed steady. When he was dozing, the man was swallowed up by a gigantic fish. Again the leaf bed swerved and god angrily captured the fish and brought the man out.

Chakaria Sundarbans : Chakaria Sundarbans a deltaic mangrove forest of the matamuhuri river at Chakaria in Cox's Bazar district. The initial area of the Chakaria Sundarbans was about 18,200 ha. Subsequently, 7,490 ha of land was declared as Reserved Forest and the rest as Protected Forest. A selection system was followed to manage the forest. But it was modified from time to time in order to arrest the deteriorating condition of the forest. At one point restrictions were imposed on extraction of forest produce. But this could not counter the destruction of the forest. In fact, the forest has been almost completely denuded in recent years.

The entire Chakaria Sundarbans is now a barren area; stumps of trees are found all over, and only about 200 healthy trees are left. A number of factors have led to the destruction of this forest. The government policy of allowing use of the reserved forest for shrimp farms and human settlement encouraged some people to make forest clearing indiscriminately. Nevertheless studies indicate that Chakaria Sundarbans can still be rehabilitated with mangroves if biotic interference is controlled.

Chakdara : Chakdara town is located in Malakand, NWFP, Pakistan. Chakdara is an important town of Upper Dir, located on the bank of the Swat river. It is about 130 km from Peshawar and 48 km away from Saidu Sharif. The Mughals built a fort here in 1586, which was later occupied by the British in 1895, who built the present fort in 1896. The University of Malakand is located in Chakdara.

Chakdara situated in in Lower Swat Valley, has been an important center for last 3500 years and littered with remains of Aryan settlements, which represent Gandhara grave culture,Buddhists sites, and Hindu Shahi forts.

Chakiarkoothu : This form is believed to have been introduced to Kerala by the early Aryan immigrants and is performed only by the members of the Chakiar caste. A highly orthodox type of entertainment, it can be staged inside temples only and witnessed by the Hindus of the higher castes. The theatre is known as Koothambalam. The only accompaniments are the cymbals and the copper drum known as the *miazhavu*.

Chakla System : Chakla System a method of district revenue administration. The term chakla literally meaning a district or a large administrative division, gained currency in the Mughal subah (province) of Bengal since the early 18th century. The introduction of the chakla system is credited to murshid quli khan, the Diwan-Subahdar of Bengal. Its objective was the maximisation of public revenue and its punctilious remittance to the Exchequer. In order to achieve the goal, the previous division of the subah into 34 sarkars (districts) was replaced by 13 chaklas, namely, Bandar Baleswari, Hijli, Murshidabad, Burdwan, Hughli (which included Calcutta), bhusna (Faridpur) Jessore, Akbarnagar, Ghoraghat, Kuribari (Kutch Bihar and Assam), Jahangirnagar, Sylhet and Islamabad (Chittagong). Each of these chaklas was placed under a chakladar. As in the previous sarkar administration, a faujdar (military governor) was given the overall charge of the maintenance of peace and security of the chakla under his jurisdiction. The unhindered collection and remittance of the revenues to the centre also fell under his purview. A qazi and a kotwal were posted in each of the chaklas.

Chakma : The Chakma, who are also known as the Changma, is a Mongoloid tribe inhabiting the Chittagong Hill Tracts of Bangladesh. Their language is known as Changma Vaj or Changma Kodha, which uses their native script known as Ojhopath. Originally belonging to the Tibeto-Burman family, Changma Vaj had been heavily influenced by neighboring Chittagonian, an Eastern Indo-Aryan language closely related to Bangla (Bengali). Many linguists now consider Chakma Vaj part of the Southeastern Bengali branch of Eastern Indo-Aryan languages.

Although originally the rulers of Chittagong under the control of a king, the power of the King today, Devasish Roy, is no more than an association chief. Their population of 350,000 is concentrated in the Rangamati and Khagrachhari districts of Chittagong Division in Bangladesh, and in the Mizoram in India, although smaller numbers of can be found in Arunachal Pradesh, Assam, Tripura, Australia and in the USA. Their ancestors came from Arakan and settled in Cox's Bazar and Korpos Mohol, the name which was used for the Chittagong Hill Tracts until 1860. The Chakma practice Theravada Buddhism and Hinduism, although strains of Animist influence is prevalent among the Chakma.

Chakradharpur : Chakradharpur (pop 40,000 est.) is a town in the Indian state of Jharkhand located at 22.45° N 85.40° E. It is the divisional headquarters of the South Eastern Railway. It is located on the Chota Nagpur Plateau. The town serves the mineral rich areas of Jharkhand and Orissa, as well as the cement, steel and limestone industries in the region.

The first rail line on Chakradharpur Division was opened on 22nd January 1890 with laying of 72.25 miles long Purulia-Chakradharpur rail line. The rail network on the main trunk route passing through Chakradharpur Division was completed on 18th February 1891 when

Goilkera-Jharsuguda section was opened. With the opening of Goilkera-Jharsuguda section the main line route of Bengal Nagpur Railway (BNR) was completed and the official function for the opening ceremony of main line from Asansol to Nagpur, presided by the Viceroy of India, Lord Lansdowne was held at Chakradharpur station on 3rd March 1891.

Chakri Dance : Chakri dance is performed by Kanjars scattered all over the state of Rajasthan. The Chakri dancers from Hadoti areas of Kota, Bundi and Baran districts are famous. Kanjar girls mostly perform Chakri dance during weddings or at the reception of the barats although they dance on many other occasions. The dancers whirl round and round in circles in flowering skirts. As a result, the dancers appear like spinning tops. The accompanying instruments that are used are called 'Nagara'.

Chakwal District : The district of Chakwal in Pakistan was created as an independent district of the Rawalpindi Division in 1985, by combining the subdivision Chakwal of Jhelum District, the sub-division Talagang of Attock District and police station Choa Saidan Shah, carved out of subdivision Pind Dadan Khan, district Jhelum, and amalgamating it with sub-division Chakwal. Choa Saidan Shah was upgraded to the level of a sub-division in 1993.

Chaliyar River : Chaliyar River is the fourth longest river in Kerala at 169 km in length. The Chaliyar river is also known as Beypore River as it nears the sea. Nilambur, Edavanna, Areacode, Mavoor, Feroke and Beypore are some of the towns/villages situated along the Chaliyar River.

Chalukya Dynasty : The Chalukya Dynasty was an Indian royal dynasty that ruled large parts of southern and central India between 550 and 750 from Badami in Bagalkot district, Karnataka state, and again between 973 and 1190 from Manyakheta initially and later from Kalyana in Bidar district. The dynasty was established by Pulakesi I in 550. Pulakesi I took Vatapi (now the town of Badami in Bagalkot district, Karnataka) under his control and made it his capital. His sons established the frontiers of his empire to extend over most of what is now the Indian state of Karnataka.

Pulakesi II, who ascended the throne in 608, is certainly the most famous and most recognized ruler of the Chalukya dynasty. Pulakesi II started out consolidating his kingdom by conducting minor campaigns against the Alupas, Gangas and others. He clashed successfully with the Pallava empire in Tamil Nadu, and also conquered the Cheras and the Pandyas. In 609, he appointed his brother Kubja Vishnuvardhana as the Viceroy of Vengi, who subsequently declared his independence and established the Eastern Chalukya Empire. The clashes with the Pallava empire continued intermittently during his rule. Pulakesi was finally defeated by the Pallava king Narasimhavarman in 642. He died in the battle after around 36 years of rule. The Chalukya Empire was restored in 655 by Vikramaditya I; the clashes with the Pallava Empire continued until Vikramaditya II won a comprehensive victory against the Pallavas in 740. The Chalukya Empire was again overthrown in 750 by the Rashtrakutas.

Chaman : Chaman is a Pakistani town situated on the border between Balochistan and Afghanistan. Across the border in Afghanistan is the town of Spin Boldak in the province of Kandahar. The area around these two towns is a major smuggling route for many contraband items such as carpets and opium. It is also a major infiltration route for Taliban fighters attempting to destabalise the Karzai government in Afghanistan.

Chaman is home to a significant population of refugees which has helped Chaman grow considerably over the years. The refugees originally fled the civil war and the Soviet Union's intervention in 1979. The town is also home to a football (soccer) club - Afghan Football Club Chaman, which plays in the Pakistan National Football League.

Chamba : Chamba is the northwestern district of Himachal Pradesh, in India. Dalhousie and Khajjhiar are well-known towns in the district. Chamba is one of the oldest Native States in India, having been founded no later than 600 and perhaps as early as 550. It is situated in the bosom of the Himalaya Mountains, and the boundaries are as follows: On the north-west and west, Jammu and Kashmir; on the north-east and east, Ladakh, Lahul and Bara Bangahal; on the south-east and south, the districts of Kangra and Gurdaspur. River ravi flows through this district.Many hydel projects have come up here.

Chambal River : The Chambal River is a tributary of the Yamuna River in central India. The river flows north-northeast through Madhya Pradesh, running for a time through Rajasthan, then forming the boundary between Rajasthan and Madhya Pradesh before turning southeast to join the Yamuna in Uttar Pradesh state. It is a perennial river and originates at Manpura, south of Mhow town, near Indore, on the south slope of the Vindhya Range in Madhya Pradesh. The Chambal and its tributaries drain the Malwa region of northwestern Madhya Pradesh, while its tributary the Banas, which rises in the Aravalli Range, drains southeastern Rajasthan. The Chambal ends a confluence of five rivers, including the Chambal, Kwari, Yamuna, Sind, Pahuj, at Pachnada near Bhareh in Uttar Pradesh state, at the border of Bhind and Etawah districts.

Chamoli : Ten kilometres from Nandaprayag in Uttaranchal, historic Chamoli is mentioned in the Taleshwar Copper Plate Grant, one of the plates left behind by the ancient Katyuri kings, who ruled Kumaon from the time of the Gupta dynasty (3rd century A.D.) onwards, till the 14th century, when the Chand kings rose to power. The plate reveals that the ancient capital of Brahmpura had one of its administrative centres at Chamoli.

At a height of 960 metres, this pretty little town is the Headquarters of Chamoli district, which is the middle district of the three border districts. It is covered by the basin of Alaknanda, the feeding tributary of the Bhagirathi, which it joins at Deoprayag. A motor road links the two roads from Guptakashi to Chamoli via Ukhimath, Gopeshwar. On the way is the lone peak of the Tungnath temple, which is situated at 3,890 metres, higher than both Kedarnath or Badrinath. On the way to these temples are Ukhimath and Joshimath, which are also important religious spots, while others are Trijuginarayan, 5 km from Soneprayag, and Madhyamaheshwar, to the north-east of Guptakashi.

Champaner : The historical town of Champaner is a city in the Gujarat state of western India. It is located in Panchmahal District, 47 kilometres from the city of Vadodara. The city was briefly the capital of Gujarat. It was founded by Vanraj Chavda, the most prominent king of the Chavda Kingdom, in the 8th century. He named it after the name of his friend and general Champa, also known later as Champaraj. By the later 15th century, the Khichi Chauhan Rajputs held Pavagadh fort above the town of Champaner. The young Sultan of Gujarat, Mahmud Begada, captured the fort on 21 November 1484, after a siege of 20 months. He then spent 23 years rebuilding and embellishing Champaner, which he renamed Muhammadabad, after which he moved the capital there from Ahmedabad. The town finally succumbed to attacks from the Mughal Emperor Humayun in 1535.

Champaner is today the site of the Champaner-Pavagadh Archeological Park, which is on UNESCO's List of World Heritage Sites in Asia and Australasia, and is situated about 47 km from the city of Vadodara. Sultan Begada also built a magnificent Jama Masjid in Champaner, which ranks amongst the finest architectural edifices in Gujarat. It is an imposing structure on a high plinth, with a central dome, two minarets 30 meters in height, 172 pillars, seven mihrabs, and carved entrance gates with fine stone jalis.

Champaner-Pavagadh Archaeological Park : Champaner-Pavagadh Archaeological Park is a UNESCO World Heritage Site which is located in India. It was inscribed in 2004. The site contains a collection of ruins, including those of the capital of the Gujarat state from the 16th century, as well as assorted ruins from the 8th to 14th centuries. It is the only unchanged Islamic pre-Mughal city.

Champawat : Champawat is a city in the Kumaon region of Uttaranchal state in northern India. It is the administrative headquarters of Champawat District. Champwat is believed to the place where the Kurmavtar (the turtle incarnation of Lord Vishnu) took place. Champwat was formerly the capital of the Chand rulers. The Baleshwar Temple built by the Chand rulers in 16th century is an excellent monument with marvelous stone carving works. It was home to the Champawat Tiger.

Chamundi Hills : The Chamundi Hills are located in India, close to the palace city of Mysore. Its average elevation is 1,000 meters. Legend has it that that the demon Mahishasura, the king of the area that is currently Mysore, was killed by the Goddess Chamundeswari (also Chamundi) after a fierce battle. The hills hence got their name and a temple of the Goddess was built on the top. The temple has a very beautiful Idol of the Goddess wearing a garland of skulls. The temple has always been patronised by the rulers of Mysore. In earlier days, the Maharajas of Mysore would ride the ceremonial Dasara elephant during the annual Dasara festival, but after India gained independence, the Idol of Goddess Chamundi is taken on an elephant.

A panoramic view of the city is seen from the top of the hills. Among other landmarks, you can see the Race Course, the Lalitha Mahal palace, the Mysore Palace, the Karanji and Kukkarahalli lakes. At dusk, the view of the city is especially beautiful, and on Sunday evenings and during the Dasara festival, the illuminated Mysore Palace glitters like gold.

Chanakya : Chanakya (c.350—c.275 BC), also known as Kautilya or Vishnugupta, was a professor (acharya) of political science at the Takshasilâ University and the Prime Minister of the Emperor Chandragupta Maurya. He is regarded as one of the earliest known political thinkers, economists and king-makers. He was the man to envision the first Indian empire by unification of the then numerous kingdoms in the Indian sub-continent and provide the impetus for fights against the Greek conqueror Alexander. Chanakya is perhaps less well known outside India compared to other social and political philosophers of the world like Confucius and Machiavelli, but is definitely considered to be the first genuine political theorist in Indian history. His foresight and wide knowledge coupled with politics of expediency helped found the mighty Mauryan Empire in India. He compiled his political ideas into 'Arthashastra', one of the world's earliest treatises on political thought and social order. His ideas remain popular to this day in India.

In Jawaharlal Nehru's Discovery of India, Chanakya has been called the Indian Machiavelli. A south Indian group of Brahmins, Chozhiyas, claim that Chanakya was one of them. Though this may sound very improbable considering the vast distance between present day Tamilnadu in the south and Magadha in Bihar, it finds curious echos in Parishista-parvan, where Hemachandra claims that Chankya was a Dramila. Dramila, being a very common varaint of Dravida.

Chanakya was the kingmaker who actually planned the unification of India for the first time under Chandragupta. Legend has it that Chanakya was insulted by the Nanda rulers, and vowed to destroy their kingdom. Travelling through the forest, he came across a boy who had a regal bearing, and obvious leadership qualities. The way he played 'king' with his friends and conducted himself as one impressed Chankaya. He picked him up and trained him to be Chandragupta Maurya. His main philosophy was "A debt should be paid off till the last penny; An enemy should be destroyed without a trace". He seemed to have lived by his philosopy.

Chand Kings : Chand Kings were a medieval ruling clan of Kumaon region of the Uttaranchal state of India. The capital of Chand rulars was Champawat - the stronghold popularly known as Kali Kumaon, due to its vicinity to river Kali, which is now a district headquarter town. Medeival fort, Baleshwar temple, Nagnath Temple, etc., are a few remnants of once a powerful Chand reign. The Chand rule was established by Raja Som Chand in 700 AD by replacing Katyuri Kings and called their state Kurmanchal.

Chand Raat : In Pakistani Islamic culture, Chand Raat, that is, the night of the moon as it translates from Urdu, marks the end of Ramadan and the start of Eid ul-Fitr. Since the Islamic Calendar is lunar, Eid ul-Fitr is on the first of Shawwal, the tenth month of the Islamic year. Since this custom is dependent on the sighting of the moon, it can often happen on different days in different parts of the world. It is believed by many that anything wished for right after the sighting of the moon will be granted. After the moon is seen, celebrations often involve Mehndi (henna), food, and dancing begin.

Chandan Jatra : This fair is celebrated for twenty-one days in the month of 'Jaishtha' (May-June) in Orissa. When a smaller replica of Lord Jagannath is taken to the sacred tank for boating after being smeared with 'chandan' or sandal wood paste. This is aimed at providing cool comfort and relief from the summer heat. This is celebrated at places where there is a Jagannath temple and a lot of merriment goes with it when pilgrims congregate. The main centre of this fair is at Puri, the celebrated 'shrikhetra'; the original seat of Lord Jagannath.

Chandana River : Chandana river is an offshoot of the Padma, branches out at the village Dahuka of Pangsha upazila in Rajbari district. The river follows a 30 km long meander course from Pangsha to Kalukhali. Then it continues south for about 20 km through a straight course and joins the Barasia at Arkandi village between Kamarkhali and Madhukhali. From this point the river is renamed as the Chandana-Barasia or Chandana-Arkandi. The joint course of the Chandana and the Barasia flows further south through Boalmari and Kashiani upazilas and debouches into the Gorai-Madhumati north of Bhatia Bazar. The length of this part is about 50 km. In the past, the Chandana was connected with the Gorai and Kumar rivers. Actually the Kumar received part of the Gorai flow through the Chandana. But at present, the Chandana is almost disconnected from the Gorai and Kumar due to the shifting of the course of the river, construction of various flood-proofing structures, changing of landscape, etc. The river overspills during the monsoon, but its mouth remains dry in winter

Chandannagar : Chandannagar, formerly known as Chandernagore or Chandernagar, is a city in India. It lies 20 miles north of Kolkata (Calcutta) in Hooghly District of the state of West Bengal.

Chandannagar was established as a French colony in 1673, when the French obtained permission from Ibrahim

Khan, the Nawab of Bengal to establish a trading post on the right bank of the Hughli River. Bengal was then a province of the Mughal Empire. It became a permanent French settlement in 1688, and in 1730 Joseph François Dupleix was appointed governor of the city, during whose administration more than two thousand brick houses were erected in the town and a considerable maritime trade was carried on. For a time, Chandannagar was the main center for European commerce in Bengal.

In 1756 war broke out between France and Great Britain, and Colonel Robert Clive of the British East India Company and Admiral Watson of the British Navy bombarded and captured Chandannagar in March 1757. The town's fortifications and many houses were demolished thereafter, and Chandannagar's importance as a commercial center was eclipsed by that of Calcutta just downriver. Chandernagore was restored to the French in 1763, but retaken by the British in 1794 in the Napoleonic Wars. The city was returned to France in 1816, along with a 3 sq. mi. enclave of surrounding territory. It was governed as part of French India until 1950, under the political control of the governor-general in Pondicherry. By 1900 the town's former commercial importance was gone, and it was little more than a quiet suburb of Calcutta, with a population of 25,000 (1901). The European town was noted for its clean wide thoroughfares, with many elegant residences along the riverbank.

India became independent of Britain in 1947, and in June 1948 the French Government held a plebiscite which found that 97% of Chandannagar's residents wished to become part of India. In May 1950, the French allowed the Indian government to assume de facto control over Chandannagar, officially ceding the city to India on 2 February 1952. On 2 October 1955 Chandannagar was integrated into West Bengal state.

Chandela : Chandela or Chandel is a Clan found in Rajputs in India. Chandelas belong to Puru dynasty, as is proved from the inscription of Gaharwala. Chandela Rajputs are found in large numbers and are staunch Hindu in their religious faith. Chandela Rajputs ruled in Bundelkhand from the 10th to the 16th centuries. In the early 10th century they ruled from the fortress-city of Kalinjar. A dynastic struggle among the Pratiharas from 912 to 914 allowed the Chandelas to reinforce their rule. The Chandelas captured the strategic fortress of Gwalior c. 950. Dhanga (c. 950-1008) left many inscriptions, and endowed a large number of Jain and Hindu temples. Dhanga's grandson Vidyadhara (1017-29) expanded the Chandela kingdom to its greatest extent, extending the Chandela dominions to the Chambal river in the northwest and south to the Narmada River. The Afghan king Mahmud of Ghazni attacked the Chandela dominions during Vidydhara's reign, but did not retain any Chandela territory. the Chandelas built the famous temple-city of Khajuraho between the mid-10th and mid-11th centuries. In the 12th century, the Rajput Chauhan rulers of Ajmer challenged the Chandelas. The Muslim conquests of the early 13th century reduced the Chandela domains, although they survived until the 16th century as minor chieftains

Chanderi : Chanderi is a town of historical importance in Ashoknagar District of Madhya Pradesh state in India. It is situated at a distance of 127 km from Shivpuri and 37 km from Lalitpur. It is located on hill southwest of the Betwa River. Chanderi is surrounded by hills, lakes and forests and there are several monuments of the Bundela Rajputs and Malwa sultans. Chanderi finds mention in Mahabharata. Shishupal was the king of Mahabharata period. Chanderi is located strategically on the borders of Malwa and Bundelkhand. History of Chanderi goes back to the 11th century, when it was dominated by the trade routes of Central India and was proximate to the arterial route to the ancient ports of Gujarat as well as to Malwa, Mewar, Central India and the Deccan. Consequently, Chanderi became an important military outpost.

Chandigarh : Chandigarh called The City Beautiful is a city in India that serves as the capital of two states: Punjab and Haryana. However, the city does not belong to either state. Rather, the city is administered by the federal government and hence classified as a union territory. Chandigarh was due to transfer to Punjab alone in 1986, accompanied by the creation of a new capital for Haryana, but the transfer has been delayed while agreement is sought on the districts of Punjab that should be transferred to Haryana in exchange. The City Beautiful tops the list of Indian States and Union Territories with Human Development Index of 0.674.

Chandigarh Carnival : The Chandigarh Carnival is a three-day event celebrated in the second week of November shortly before or after Nehru's birth anniversary on November 14,otherwise known as Children's Day. The carnival opens with a colourful procession which everyone is encouraged to join. The carnival is a time for students to show their talent (or simply have fun) and elders too participate in a number of competitions and exhibits.

Chandio : Chandio is the name of a Sindhi tribe in Sindh, Pakistan. The region where they lived was called Chandka. The Chandka region was located in the Qambar-Shahdadkot district. The British government disabled the status of the Chandka region, however the Medical College of Larkana is called Chandka Medical College. The Chandio tribe is now spread out over all of Pakistan with a concenration in Sindh. According to a survey of Sindh Chandio Welfare Association, the Chandio tribe has a polulation of more than 5 million.

Chandni Chowk : Chandni Chowk is one of the oldest and busiest markets in central north Delhi, India.

The area is of historical importance to Delhi owing to its location between the Laal Quila (The Red Fort) and Fateh Puri Masjid. With the most famous mosque of Delhi Jama Masjid (Delhi) in the vicinity, along with Sis Ganj Gurudwara, Jain Mandir and a lot of small temples, the place witnesses a genuine cultural harmony. Chandni Chowk's speciality is the variety of its markets and their Indian-ness. From authentic Indian food, delicacies and sweets of more than 1000 kinds, to sarees with chikan, zaree work. There are lots of narrow lanes with many shops selling books, clothing, shoes and leather goods, electronic and consumer goods and what not. The area, even moreso than the rest of the city, is congested. This is also a good area for window shopping. It is the location of the original Haldiram's. A particular local delicacy are the jalebis, which are fried in pure ghee (clarified butter).

Chandra Shekhar : Chandra Shekhar was born on July 1, 1927, in a farmer's family in village Ibrahimpatti in District Ballia, Uttar Pradesh. He was President of the Janata Party from 1977 to 1988. Shri Chandra Shekhar was attracted to politics from his student days and was known as a fire-brand idealist with revolutionary fervour. After his Master's Degree in Political Science from Allahabad University (1950-51), he joined the Socialist Movement. He had the privilege of having been associated very closely with Acharya Narendra Dev. He was elected Secretary of the District Praja Socialist Party, Ballia. Within a year, he was elected Joint Secretary of the U.P. State Praja Socialist Party. In 1955-56 he took over as General Secretary of the U.P., State Praja Socialist Party.

In 1962, he was elected to the Rajya Sabha from Uttar Pradesh. He joined the Indian National Congress in January 1965. In 1967 he was elected General Secretary of the Congress Parliamentary Party. As a Member of Parliament he made a mark by taking keen interest in espousing the cause of the downtrodden and pleading for policies for rapid social change. In this context, when he attacked the disproportionate growth of monopoly houses with State patronage, he came in conflict with the centres of power.

He came to be as 'Young Turk' leader for his conviction, courage and integrity in the fight against vested interested. He founded and edited YOUNG INDIAN, a weekly published from Delhi in 1969. Its editorial had the distinction of being among the most quoted ones of the time. During the Emergency (June 1975 to March 1977) YOUNG INDIAN had to be closed down. It resumed regular publication in February 1989. He is the Chairman of its Editorial Advisory Board.

Shri Chandra Sekhar has always stood against politics of personalities and has favoured politics of ideology and social change. This propelled him more towards Shri Jayaprakash Narayan and his idealist view of life during the turbulant days of 1973-75. He soon became a focal point of dissent within the Congress Party.

When Emergency was declared on June 25, 1975, he was arrested under Maintenance of Internal Security Act inspite of the fact that he was a member of the Central Election Committee and Working Committee, top bodies of the Indian National Congress. Shri Chandra Sekhar was among the few individuals in the then ruling party who was imprisoned during the Emergency. He has always rejected the politics of power and opted for the politics of commitment to democratic values and social change.

His diary, written in Hindi while undergoing imprisonment during the Emergency period, was later published under the title 'Meri Jail Diary'. A well-known compilation of his writings is 'Dynamics of Social Change'. Shri Chandra Shekhar undertook a marathon walk (Padayatra) through the country from Kanyakumari in the deep South to Rajghat (Samadhi of Mahatma Gandhi) in

New Delhi covering a distance of nearly 4260 kms from January 6, 1983 to June 25, 1983. The Padayatra was undertaken to renew rapport with the masses and to understand their pressing problems.

He has established about fifteen Bharat Yatra Centres in various parts of the country including Kerala, Tamil Nadu, Karnataka, Maharashtra, Madhya Pradesh, Gujarat, Uttar Pradesh and Haryana to train social and political workers for mass education and grassroot work in backward pockets of the country. He has been a Member of Parliament since 1962 except for a brief period from 1984 to 1989. In 1989 he successfully contested both from his home constituency, Ballia, and the adjoining Maharajganj constituency in Bihar. He vacated the latter.

Chandra Shekhar Azad : Chandra Shekhar Azad was a revolutionary freedom fighter. He will always remain immortal in the annals of history as a man who sacrificed his life on the altar of freedom. Azad was born at a place called Jhalra in Madhya Pradesh. He ran away from home when young, reached Kashi (Benaras) and joined the freedom struggle when still young. In 1921, he received his first punishment for revolutionary activities. He was sentenced to fifteen lashes. With each stroke of the whip the young patriot shouted "Bharat Mata Ki Jai". He was undaunted and he badly scared the British with his courage and rebellion against the oppression of the Indians. He was killed in an encounter with the British forces in Allahabad.

Chandrabhaga Fair : In the month of Kartik (Oct.-Nov.) the banks of Chandrabhaga river in Rajasthan are transformed into colourful and dazzling cattle fairground. The fair held on the last day of Kartik in Rajasthan, attracts thousands of devotees who bathe in the holy water at the sacred spot of Chandrawati. On this occasion cattle from distant parts are brought for sale. Even traders from various parts of Madhya Pradesh and maharastra come here in large numbers.

Chandrabhaga Mela : The fair at Chandrabhaga begins on the seventh day of the bright fortnight in the lunar month of Magha (January-February) and continues for seven days. It is held at the mouth of sacred Chandrabhaga river near the famous temple of Konarka. This sacred site figures in the myth of shamba of the Mahabharata days who was cured of his leprosy by worshipping Lord Surya, the Sun God. The Sun Temple of Konarka and the sacred site refer to the prevalence of a strong solar cult in the coastal Orissa. It is believed that whoever takes a bath in the Chandrabhaga will be cured of leprosy and bareness. Magh Saptami mela is observed at the same time at the Join centre of Khandagiri, near Bhubaneswer, for seven days.

Chandragiri : Chandragiri is a town in the Chittoor District of Andhra Pradesh state in southern India. It is famous for the historical fort built by rulers of Vijayanagara empire in the 15th century. The site of the fort is protected and developed as a tourist location by the Andhra Pradesh Tourism Development Corporation. Tourist attractions at the fort include a sound and light show which recounts the history of the fort. This 'must see' Sound and Light show is performed every evening after sunset. Tourists can also enjoy boating in a lake right next to hill slopes.

Chandragiri is at a distance of 12 Km from Tirupati city, home of the famous temple of Lord Venkateshwara. The best way to visit Chandragiri is to take a Taxi from Tirupati, which city is connected to the rest of India by road, rail and air transport.

Chandragupta I : While his two ancestors were given the title of Maharaja, Chandra Gupta I is described in his inscriptions as Maharajadhiraj. He can therefore be considered the first Gupta emperor. According to the Puranas the Guptas ruled over territories (referred to as Janapadas) such as Prayag, Saket and Magadh. This description of the Gupta dominion precedes the reign of Samudragupta and hence must refer to the territories ruled over by Chandragupta I.

Chandragupta's rule over Magadh has been attributed to his marital alliance with the Lichchhavis. This alliance surely benefited him materially as well. In fact in one of his inscriptions, his successor Samudragupta proudly refers to himself as Lichchhavidauhitra (this refers to the fact that his mother was a Lichchhavi). It is significant that Samudragupta would refer to his maternal lineage instead of the more common reference to paternal lineage. There are also several coins issued by Samudragupta that commemorate the marriage of Chandragupta to Kumardevi, the Lichchhavi princess

Chandragupta II : The period of prominence of the Gupta dynasty is very often referred to as the Golden Age of India. It was under the rule of Samudragupta's son, Chandragupta II (very often referred to as Vikramaditya or Chandragupta Vikramaditya) spanning 375-413/15 AD, that the Gupta empire achieved its zenith. Chandragupta attained success by pursuing both a favorable marital alliance and an aggressive expansionist policy. In this his father and grandfather set the precedent. His name is Sanskrit for "protected by the moon".

Not much is known about the personal details of the great king. His mother, Datta Devi, was the chief queen of Samudragupta. The most widely accepted details have been built upon the plot of the play 'Devi-Chandraguptam' of Vishakadatta. The play is now lost but fragments have been preserved in other works (Abhinava-bharati, Sringara-prakasha, Natya-darpana, Nataka-lakshana Ratna-kosha).

There even exists an Arabic work Mujmalu-t-Tawarikh which tells a similar tale of a king whose name appears to a be corruption of 'Vikramaditya'.

The fragment from Natya-darpana mentions the king Rama Gupta, the elder brother of Chandragupta, surrendering his queen Dhruvadevi to the Saka king Rudrasimha, after a defeat at the Saka king's hands. To avoid the ignominy the Guptas decide to send Madhavasena, a courtesan and a beloved of Chandragupta, disguised as the queen. However, Chandragupta changes the plan and himself goes to the Saka King disguised as the queen. He then kills Rudrasimha and later his brother, Ramagupta. Dhruvadevi is then married to Chandra Gupta.

We do not know what liberties Vishakadatta took with the incidents, but Dhruvadevi was indeed the king's chief queen as seen in the Vaisali terracotta seal that calls her 'Mahadevi' Dhruvasvamini. The Bilsad pillar inscription of their son Kumara Gupta I also refers to her as Mahadevi Dhruvadevi. A Ramagupta too is mentioned in inscriptions on Jain figures in the District Archaeological Museum, Vidisha and some copper coins found at Vidisha. The fact that the king and Dhruvadevi are the protagonists of Vishakadatta's play indicates that marrying his widowed sister-in-law was not given any significance by the playwright. However, later Hindus did not view such a marriage with favour and some censure of the act is found in the Sanjan copperplate inscription of Amoghavarsha I and in the Sangali and Cambay plates of the Rashtrakuta king Govinda IV.

His greatest victory was his victory over the Shaka-Kshatrapa dynasty and annexation of their kingdom in Gujarat. His son-in-law Rudrasena II died fortuitously after a very short reign in 390 AD, following which Prabhavatigupta ruled as a regent on behalf of her two sons. During this twenty year period the Vakataka realm was practically a part of the Gupta empire. The geographical location of the Vakataka kingdom allowed Chandragupta to take the opportunity to defeat the Western Kshatrapas once for all. Many historians refer to this period as the Vakataka-Gupta age.

Chandragupta II controlled a vast empire, from the mouth of the Ganges to the mouth of the Indus River and from what is now North Pakistan down to the mouth of the Narmada. Pataliputra continued to be the capital of his huge empire but Ujjain too became a sort of second capital..The large number of beautiful gold coins issued by the Gupta dynasty are a testament to the imperial grandeur of that age. Chandragupta II also started producing silver coins in the Shaka tradition.

Chandragupta Maurya : Chandragupta Maurya (ruled 322–298 BC), also known as Sandrokottos to the Greeks, was the founder of the first the Mauryan Empire. The Mauryan empire, whose capital was Pataliputra (Modern day Patna)in Eastern India, is acknowledged to be the greatest empire in ancient India, and lasted until 185 BC, fifty years after the death of Chandragupta's famous grandson, Emperor Asoka. Prior to Chandragupta's consolidation of power, small regional kingdoms dominated Northern and Eastern India.

Chandragupta is acknowledged as the greatest of ancient Indian rulers, and his kingdom, which spanned from Afghanistan in the West, Bengal in the East, the Deccan plateau in the South and Kashmir in the North, was the greatest power of its day. Towards the end of his life, Chandragupta gave up his throne and became an ascetic under the Jain saint Bhadrabahu Swami, ending his days in self-starvation at Shravanabelagola, in present day Karnataka. A small temple marks the cave (called Bhadrabahu Cave) where he died

Chandraketugarh : Chandraketugarh is an archaeological site located beside the river Vidyadhari about 35 km north-east of Kolkata, India, in the district of North 24 parganas. Excavation for several years has revealed relics of several periods, though the chronological classification of the relics needs further works. Several levels of excavation shows Northern Black Polished Ware (NBPW) relics, other wares of approximately 400 BC to 100 BC, relics contemporary with the Kushanas, Maurya through the Gupta periods and late Gupta times etc. According to some historians, maybe this Chandraketugarh and the adjoining area is the place that the ancient Greek and Roman writers called 'Gangaridae.'

Chandrasekhar Azad : Chandrasekhar Azad (July 23, 1906–February 27, 1931) was a great Indian freedom fighter and revolutionary thinker. Revered for his audacious deeds and fierce patriotism, he was the mentor of Bhagat Singh, the famous Indian martyr. Chandrasekhar Azad is considered one of the greatest freedom fighters for India for he lives on in folklore, along with Bhagat Singh, Sukhdev, Rajguru, Ram Prasad Bismil, and Ashfaqulla Khan due to the famous Kakori train robbery.

Young Azad was one of the young generation of Indians when Mahatma Gandhi launched the Non-Cooperation Movement. But many were disillusioned with the suspension of the struggle in 1922 owing to the Chauri Chaura massacre of 22 policemen. Although Gandhi was appalled by the brutal violence, Azad did not feel that violence was unacceptable in the struggle, especially in view of the Amritsar Massacre of 1919, where Army units killed hundreds of unarmed civilians and wounded thousands in Amritsar. Young Azad and contemporaries like Bhagat Singh were deeply and emotionally influenced by that tragedy. As a revolutionary, he adopted the lastname Azad, which means "Free" in Hindi. Azad was also a believer in socialism as the basis for a future India, free of social and economic oppression and adversity.

Bhagat Singh joined Azad following the death of Lala Lajpat Rai, an Indian leader who was beaten to death by police officials. Azad trained Singh and others in covert activities, and the latter grew close to him after witnessing his resolve, patriotism and courage. Along with fellow patriots like Rajguru and Sukhdev, Azad and Singh formed the Hindustan Socialist Revolutionary Association, committed to complete Indian independence and socialist principles of for India's future progress. Betrayed by an informer on 27th February, 1931 Azad was encircled by British troops in the Alfred park, Allahabad. He kept on fighting till the last bullet. Finding no other alternative, except surrender, Azad shot himself in the temple.

Chandrasekhara Venkata Raman : He (November 7, 1888-November 21, 1970) was an Indian physicist, who was awarded the 1930 Nobel Prize in Physics for his work on the scattering of light and for the discovery of the effect named after him. Raman won the 1930 Nobel Prize in Physics for his work on the scattering of light and for the discovery of the Raman effect.

Raman spectroscopy, based on his effect is also named after him. It was the first time that an Indian scholar who studied wholly in India received the Nobel Prize. An interesting anecdote goes that he booked his tickets to Stockholm several months before the Nobel prizes were announced. He was knighted in 1929 and awarded the Bharat Ratna in 1954.

Chandrasekharendra Saraswati : Chandrasekharendra Saraswati- "Maha Periyaval" (1894-1994) was the sixty eighth Shankaracharya (pontiff) of Kanchi Kamakoti Peetam, according to the official account. He headed the institution for eighty-seven years. He lived the life of austerity, self-discipline and a highly spiritual life and demonstrated to the world how a renounced saint should live. His compassion is said to have touched the hearts of many devotees.

Chandravanshi : The Chandravanshi are people belonging to the Chandravansha or "dynasty of the Moon". According to legend, the Chandravanshis are descended from Chandra, the Hindu Moon God. The Chandravanshi lineage is one of the three lineages into which the Kshatriya caste of Hindus is divided, the other two races being the Suryavanshi (descended from Surya, the Hindu Sun God) and the Agnivanshi, descended from Agni, the Hindu Fire God. The Yaduvanshi lineage is the major branch of the Chandravanshi lineage. The Yaduvanshis claim descent from the Hindu God Krishna, who in turn was born into a Chandravanshi dynasty.

Chandrayaan I : Chandrayaan I which literally means "Moon Craft" is an unmanned lunar misson by the Indian Space Research Organization The mission includes a lunar orbitor as well as an impactor. The spacecraft will be launched by a modified version of the Polar Satellite Launch Vehicle. The remote sensing satellite will weigh 1304 kg (590 kg initial orbit mass and 504 kg dry mass) and carries high resolution remote sensing equipment for visible, near infrared, soft and hard X-ray frequencies. During two years, it is supposed to survey the lunar surface to produce a complete map of its chemical characteristics and 3-dimensional topography. Especially the polar regions are of interest, as they might contain water ice.

In September 2004, the Indian Space Research Organization (ISRO) announced in a press statement that planning has now made enough progress that they are confident that the mission will take place in 2007 or 2008. They estimate the cost to be only INR 3.8 billion (US$ 83 million). The mission includes six ISRO payloads and Six more payloads from other international space agencies such as NASA and ESA, and Bulgaria.

Chandubi Wildlife Sancuary : A natural lagoon and a fine picnic spot, 64 km from Guwahati. The lake is a perfect holiday resort, with ample fishing and rowing facilities.

Chang Ceremony : Side by side with the dances, is another traditional way to celebrate the harvests, or any occasion, connected or not connected, the ceremonial drinking of 'Chang' offered to the visitors by these fun loving graceful and courteous people, who know the 'joie de vivre' or the joy of life. Chang is fermented millet seeds packed into a cylindrical wooden of bamboo container with a pipe stuck in the seeds, to suck the precious liquid. A demure lass pure hot water over the seeds, explaining, at the same time, the merits of propitiating the 'evil one' by sprinkling a few drops into the air, as an offering to the 'merit-accumulating Ones.'

Other dances are 'Bara Singha Dance (the Stag dance) and Kankal Dance (the Skeleton Dance) and folk dances like, the Limbus celebrating a good harvest. There are some soft rhythm dances too in which women can participate. The Tamang (Dampu Dance) and Maruni dances (Nepali Dance) are such in which a couple wavering lighted tapers on their open palms participate. The Limbus perform the Dhol Dance after harvesting their paddy crop. Lepcha people also perform a group dance after harvests. The Lepcha folk dances are quite bristle and Gay. The Sikkimese dances find their roots in the traditional culture seasonal cycles of this fabled Himalayan state.

Changla Pass : The Changla pass in Ladakh, India is the third highest motorable mountain pass in the world at an altitude of 5270 m (17300 ft). Marsimik la is arguably the world's highest pass at 5638 m (18500 feet) however, officially Khardung la stands as the highest at 18380 feet ASL. Tanglang la is the second highest pass and is reached via the famous 21 Gata loops.

Changlang : The Changlang district is located in Arunachal Pradesh, located south of the Lohit district and north of the Tirap district. Tribal groups include the Tutsa, Tangsa, Singpho and the Lisu. Sizeable communities of the Tibetans, Hajong and Chakma refugees do exist. There are reports of Naga militants harassing the local populace and forcing them to convert to Christianity. The Namdapha Tiger reserve is located in this district.

Changuch : Changuch is the Himalayan mountain peak situated at the boundry of Pithoragarh and Bageshwar district of theUttaranchal state of India. This peak is situated above Pindari glacier The altitude of the summit is 6,322 M. This peak offers a ridge leading to Nanda Kot.This is still an unclimbed peak.On its massif Traill's pass is situated ,which connects Pindari valley to Goriganga valley

Channel [V] : Channel [V] is an international music channel chain. Owned by Star TV, it is aired in many countries around Asia and the Middle East. They play both mainstream and alternative music, with some focus on local music. Mainly English music is played, though the country-specific channels do play content of their own mother tongue.

Channel I : Channel I is a privately-owned Television network in Bangladesh. It currently broadcasts satellite transmissions using PanAm Sat, which covers most of Asia and parts of Australia and Europe. It is owned by the Impress group and started transmissions in October 1, 1999.

Chapati : Chapati or chapatti is a type of roti or Indian bread eaten in South Asia and East Africa. It is made from a dough of atta flour (whole grain durum wheat), water and salt by rolling the dough out into discs of approximately twelve centimeters in diameter and browning the discs on both sides on a very hot, dry tava or frying pan (preferably not one coated with Teflon or other nonstick material). Each disc is then held for about half a second directly into an open flame, causing it to puff up with steam like a balloon.

Often, the finished chapatis are brushed with ghee (clarified butter). Variations include replacing part of the wheat flour with millet (bajra) or maize (makka) flour. The chapatis are then referred to in Hindi as bajra roti or makke ki roti. When a mixture of millet, maize and gram flour is used, the chapati is called a missi roti. Chapatis are usually eaten with cooked dal (lentil soup) or vegetable (Indian curry) dishes, and pieces of the chapati are used to wrap around and pick up each bite of the cooked dish. The steaming (ballooning) step can also be achieved by placing the chapati in a microwave oven for five to ten seconds. However, because microwave cooking can cause the chapati to become soggy, a heated grill or open gas flame are recommended.

Chapli Kabab : The Chapli Kabab is a dish from Pakistan's North West Frontier Province. It is also popular in Eastern Afghanistan. It is made of minced beef or lamb and is lightly spiced and cooked on a large flat griddle with animal fat.

Chapora & Vagator : This is a fascinating part of the Goan coastline and more genuinely salmubrious than Anjuna. It boasts a patchwork of coconut palms and the enigmatic character of Chapora village, which is more unruly farmyard than a fishing community doubling as a beach resort. The village is on the estuary of the Chapora

River and is overshadowed by a rocky hill which supports a well-preserved Portuguese fort. There are sandy coves, pleasant beaches and rocky cliffs at nearby Vagator. Be prepared for Indian coach tourists coming to ogle sunbathing Westerners, and expect any police you encounter to regard you with some suspicion and shake you down for drugs if you mistakenly tell them you're staying at Chapora.

Char Dham : The Char Dham ('the four abodes/seats') is the most important Hindu pilgrimage circuit in the Indian Himalayas. Located in the Garwhal section of the state of Uttaranchal (formerly the northwestern section of Uttar Pradesh), the circuit consists of four sites—Yamunotri, Gangotri, Kedarnath and Badrinath. While each site in the circuit has an autonomous history and significance that predates and remains distinct from their status as a circuit, inclusion in the Char Dham has, over time, caused them be viewed together in popular imagination and actual pilgrimage practice.

The origins of the Char Dham are obscure. Originally, Char Dham was an appellation reserved for India's most famous pilgrimage circuit, four important temples—Puri, Rameshwaram, Dwarka, and Badrinath—grouped together by the great 8th century reformer and philosopher Shankaracharya (Adi Sankara), into the archetypal All-India pilgrimage circuit to the four cardinal points of the subcontinent. At some point, Badrinath, the last visited and the most important of the four sites in the original Char Dham, also became the cornerstone site of a Himalayan pilgrimage circuit dubbed the Chota (little) Char Dham. Unlike the original Char Dham, the sites of the Chota Char Dham do not share a single sectarian affiliation. Instead, the three major sectarian movements in modern devotional Hinduism all have representation, with the Vaishnava site Badrinath joined by one Shaiva site (Kedarnath) and two Devi sites (Yamunotri and Gangotri).

As late as the mid-twentieth century, the "Chota" designation was still used consistently to delineate the Himalayan version of the Char Dham. This usage probably reflects the relative importance of the circuit for most of its history. Accessible until recent times only after a two-month trek that repeatedly exceeds 4000 meters, the Chota Char Dham was long dominated by wandering ascetics and religious professionals, along with a handful of devoted retirees and wealthy patrons (who could afford an entourage). While the individual sites and the circuit as a whole were important to Hindus on the plains below, they were not a particularly visible aspect of yearly religious culture. After the 1962 war between India and China, however, accessibility to the Chota Char Dham improved drastically, as India's short-lived efforts at Himalayan expansionism required massive infrastructure investments. As pilgrim buses began to arrive, the Chota appendix seems to have dropped away, though the prefix "Himalayan" (Hindi: Himalaya ki Char Dham) is sometimes still added to avoid confusion.

With infrastructure improvements, the importance of the Char Dham as both an actual destination and an object of the national Hindu religious imagination has increased significantly. Buoyed by the development of new forms of bourgeois "religious tourism" and by the rise of a conservative Hindu population compelled by sites that speak to the existence of an all-India Hindu culture, the Char Dham has become an important destination for pilgrims from throughout South Asia and the diaspora, particularly Bengalis, Marwaris, Gujaratis, Delhites- and people from U.P, and of course citizens of Uttaranchal. Today, the Char Dham seem upwards of 250,000 unique visitors in an average pilgrimage season, which lasts from approximately April 15 until Diwali (sometime in November). The season is heaviest in the two-month period before the monsoon. Once the rains come (sometime in late July), travel is extremely dangerous: extensive road building has critically destabilized the rocks, and fatal landslides and bus/jeep accidents are a regular yearly occurrence, with mortality rates for a season often surpassing 200. Despite the danger, pilgrims do continue to visit the Char Dham in the monsoon period, as well as after the rains end.

Chari Dance : This is popular dance form in the Kishangarh region and involves dancing with a Chari, or pot, on one's head. A lighted lamp is then placed on the pot.

Charles Freer Andrews : Charles Freer Andrews (1871 - 1940) was an English priest who admired the philosophy of Mohandas Gandhi and worked with him in the Indian civil rights struggle in South Africa and in the Indian Independence Movement. He was affectionately known as Christ's Faithful Apostle; the Mahatma and his students at St. Stephen's College called him Deenabandhu, or 'Friend of the Poor'.

While working for independence for India, Charlie developed a dialogue between Christians and Hindus. He spent a lot of time at Shantiniketan in conversation with the poet and philosopher, Rabindranath Tagore. He also supported the movement to ban the 'untouchability of outcastes'. In 1925, he joined the famous Vaikkom Temple protests, and in 1933, he assisted Dr. B.R. Ambedkar in formulating Harijan demands.

About this time, Gandhi took Charlie aside and told him that it was probably best for sympathetic Britishers like himself to leave the freedom struggle to the Indians. So from 1935 onwards, Charlie began to spend more time back in Britain, teaching young people all over the country about Christ's call to radical discipleship. Over time, C.F.Andrews became affectionately known as Christ's Faithful Apostle.

Charlie Andrews died on April 5th, 1940 during a visit to Calcutta, and is buried there. He is widely commemorated and respected in India, and was a major character portrayed by British actor Ian Charleson in the 1982 film Gandhi by Richard Attenborough.

Charminar : Charminar is a monument located in the City of Hyderabad which is the capital city of the State of Andhra Pradesh in South India. Charminar is one of the most important landmarks of the city. The monument was built by Muhammad Quli Qutb Shah in 1591 to commemorate the eradication of plague, shortly after he had shifted his capital from Golconda to what now is known as Hyderabad. Legends tell that the emperor Quli Qutb Shah prayed for the end of plague and took the vow to build a mosque on that very place. He ordered the construction of the mosque which became popular as Charminar because of its four characteristic minarets. The top floor of the four-storeyed structure has a mosque which has 45 covered prayer spaces and some open space to accommodate more people in Friday prayers.

The Charminar is a beautiful and impressive square monument, with each side measuring 20 m, and each of the edges having a pointed high minaret. It derives its name from these four gracefully carved minarets which soar to a height of 48.7 m above the ground, commanding the landscape for miles around. Charminar literally means 'Four Minars'. Each minaret has four storeys, each looking like a delicately carved ring around the minaret. Every side opens into a plaza through giant arches, which overlook four major thoroughfares and dwarf other features of the building except the minarets. Each arch is 11 m wide and rises 20 m to the pinnacle from the plinth. Once upon a time each of these arches led to four royal roads. Each of the four arches has a clock which were put up in 1889.

There are two galleries within the Charminar, one over another, and above those a terrace that serves as a roof, bordered with a stone balcony. It is vaulted underneath and appears like a dome. There is a large table raised seven or eight feet from the ground with steps to go up to it. Nothing in the town seems so lovely as the outside of that building. A thriving market still lies around the Charminar attracting people and merchandise of every description. In its heyday, the Charminar market had some 14,000 shops, a unique conglomeration of a grand oriental bazaar. The whole market around the Charminar is crowded with shops which sell glass bangles in rainbow colours.

Charra Pani : Charra Pani is located about 15 km from Islamabad, Pakistan, enroute to Murree. A fairly fast water stream runs through the park. Water here is usually very cold as it originates in the hills. This place is visited by people from the twin cities (Rawalpindi and Islamabad) on a regular basis.

Charsadda : Charsadda is thought to correspond to the ancient city of Pushkalavati, the administrative center of the area of Gandhara.The history of Charsadda can be traced back to the 6th century BCE. It remained the capital of Gandhara from 6th century BCE to 2nd century CE. Many invaders ranging from the Persians, Alexander the Great's Greeks, the Mauryas, the Greco-Bactrians, the Indo-Greeks, the Indo-Scythians, the Indo-Parthians, the Kushans, the Huns, the Turks and the Hindus have ruled over this region at different times of history. It is believed Alexander the Greats army laid siege to the city in the third century BCE.

Charu Majumdar : Charu Majumdar (1918-1972) was an Indian Maoist revolutionary born in 1918 in Siliguri, West Bengal. His father was a freedom fighter. He dropped out of college in 1938. In 1946, Charu joined the

Tebhaga movement. He was imprisoned in 1962 and on July 16, 1972.

During the mid 1960's Majumdar and Kanu Sanyal organized a leftist faction in CPI(M) in northern Bengal. In 1967 a militant peasant uprising took place in Naxalbari, led by the Majumdar-Sanyal group. The same year Majumdar and Sanyal broke away and formed the All India Coordination Committee of Communist Revolutionaries. AICCCR founded Communist Party of India (Marxist-Leninist) in 1969, with Majumdar as its secretary. He died on July 28, 1972 after being tortured by police.

Charyapada : Charyapada is the oldest known Bengali written form. It is actually poems. It was written on 9th century and Harprashad Sastri discovered in the Nepal Royal Court Library in 1907.Its a palm leaf manuscript. Charyapada language is referred to as Alo-Andhari (light and shadow means twilight language). The manuscript has 47 verses, written by different 23 poets, probably lived between the 9th and 11th centuries AD. And came from the various regions of Bengal, Orissa, Assam and Bihar. Some poets were Sarhapa, shabar pa, Luipa, Dombipa, Bhusukupa, kahnapa, Kukkuripa, Minapa, Aryadev, Dhendhanpa.

Chashma Barrage : Chashma Barrage wetland site is located Indus Ganges Monsoon Forest, some 25 km southwest of Mianwali, Punjab, Pakistan. The site is comprised of a large barrage, a water storage reservoir and a series of embankments (serving as flood bounds) which divide the reservoir into five shallow lakes at low water levels. The site is comprised of a large barrage, a water storage reservoir and a series of embankments (serving as flood bounds) which divide the reservoir into five shallow lakes at low water levels.

Chattampi Swamikal : Chattampi Swamikal (b:1853 - d:1925) was one of Kerala's famed social reform activists and learned men. Chattampi Swamikal worked in parallel with his contemporary and soul mate Sree Narayana Guru to bring social equality to an otherwise heavily ritualistic and caste ridden Hindu society that prevailed around the late 19th and early 20th centuries across the present-day Kerala (erstwhile princely states of Travancore, Tirukochi and Malabar).

Chattampi Swamikal encouraged the Nair community to resist Brahmin hegemony in religion, administrative services and society. Swamikal also worked for the emancipation of Nair women from the clutches of Namboodiri Brahmin exploitation and encouraged women to come the forefront of society in respectable roles. He said that the enslavement of woman is a manifestation of male arrogance. Swamikal encouraged vegetarianism and professed non-violence (Ahimsa). He was open to learning other religions and authored several literary works on spirituality and the history of language.

Chattampi Swamikal was known by different names through his intellectually and spiritually enriched life. Swamiji's original name is said to have been Ayyappan, although he was later known as Kunjan Pilla and also as Shanmughadasan. In later life his formal name as a respected sage was Sree Vidyadhiraja Parama Bhattaraka Chattampi Swamikal.

Chattarpur Mandir : Situated in the capital of India, the Chattarpur Mandir is a fine example which presents Delhi a place that has some spectacular Hindu Temples to its credit. 4km away from Qutb Minar, stands the flamboyant and rich temples of Chattarpur. Made of shining white marble, these temples are very popular with the city's Hindus and the queues during Durga Puja have to be seen to be believed. The main temple dedicated to goddess Durga is built in south Indian style.

The temple complex is spread over a large area with beautiful lawns and gardens. Though devotees visit these temples throughout the year, the main attraction comes during the Navarathri festival, when devotees come from far and near. During this time, there are special bus services provided to the devotees.

Chau : The Chhau dance is indigenous to the eastern part of India, especially Bihar. It originated as a martial art and contains vigorous movements and leaps. During the 18th and 19th centuries, many of the princely rulers of the Orissa region took a keen interest in the development of this art. The Chhau dance is so called because the chhau or mask is an essential feature of this art. The word 'chhau' is generally traced to the Sanskrit root, chhaya, meaning shade. The techniques of Chhau dance incorporated certain basic steps, which seem to have stemmed from the pharikhanda system of exercise, which has been an important part of the training of the Sipahis, or Pharikhanda. The depiction of birds and animals is a distinctive feature of Chhau. This has given rise to several sub-forms such as Mayura Nritya or Peacock dance, Sagara Nritya or Ocean dance and Sarpa Nritya or serpent dance. There are also heroic dances using swords, bows or shields, with which the dancers demonstrate their dexterity. In such forms, the themes include the depiction of mythological heroes, such as Parashurama, Mahadev, Indrajit and others from the Mahabharata and Ramayana Epics. Over the course of time, female characters and more diverse themes got added. The drums, Nagra and Dhol and Shehnais provide the main musical accompaniment to the Chhau dance. The tunes are based mainly on the ragas of the Hindustani music. Chhau is generally performed with the onset of the month of Chaitra Parva, which comes about the middle of April every year.

There are three main recognized styles of Chhau: Seraikella, Purulia and Mayurbhanj. Mayurbhanj Chhau dancers do not wear masks. In recent times, Mayurbhanj Chhau has become popular as a medium of choreography, with its wide range of postures and movements that adapt well to modern as well as traditional treatment.

Chaudang Hussari : It is a group dance performed by boys and girls of the Ahom tribe.

Chaudhara : Chaudhara is the name of Himalayan mountain peak, situated in the Pithoragarh district of Uttaranchal state in India.The altitude of the peak is 6,510 M. This peak lies to the south of Ralam pass. The peak is so named due to the peak having four corners.The peak was climbed for the first time by an Indian team lead by A.R.Chandekar and Sherpa Ajeeba in 1973. Rajrambha is its neighbouring peak. Chaudhara is situated at the south east end of Kalabaland Glacier-Sankalp Glacier-Yangchar Glacier group.Chaudhara is the part of Himalayan massif between Ralam and Lassar valley.The most popular route to the summit is through west face.

Chaudhry Muhammad Ali : Chaudhry Muhammad Ali (July 15, 1905 - December 2, 1980) was a Pakistani statesman who served as Prime Minister of Pakistan from 1955 to 1956. Born in Jalandhar, he completed his education at Punjab University. Afterwards, he began working in the financial sector of Indian government, and was also one of the highest ranking Muslim civil servants in the British Raj.

Upon the formation of Pakistan, Ali was made the Secretary General of the new nation and was instrumental to setting up a budget for the fledgling nation. In 1951 he was promoted to Finance Minister. Four years later, Chaudhry Muhammad Ali was made Prime Minister by Governor General of Pakistan Iskander Mirza in 1955, after the removal of Muhammad Ali Bogra. While Prime Minister, Ali's greatest achievement was the formation of a new constitution for Pakistan, one that made it a republic in 1956. The constitution was extremely popular across Pakistan, and intended to mix democracy and Islam.

Despite this success, Chaudhry Muhammad Ali failed at healing rifts within his political party, the Muslim League. Splits within the party led to the formation of a new party, the Republican party. The new party claimed to hold the majority of seats in the National Assembly, while the Muslim League contested this and tried to have Ali check the Republican Party. Despite the demands of his own party, Ali would refuse claiming that as Prime Minister, the interests of the nation, and not of his party were primary to him. As the situation deteriorated, he resigned from both the position of Prime Minister, and from the Muslim League. Chaudhry Muhammad Ali died in 1980.

Chaudhry Pervez Elahi : Ch Parvez Elahi son of Ch Manzoor Elahi was born on November 1, 1945. He graduated in 1967, and obtained diploma in Industrial Management from London.

He comes of a distinguished political, social and industrial family. An industrialist, who served as Chairman, District Council Gujrat during 1983; and has continuously been serving as member of the Provincial Assembly of Punjab since 1985, having been elected for the sixth consecutive term in General Elections 2002 from two constituencies.

He functioned as Minister for Local Government and Rural Development during 1985-88, 1988-90 and 1990-93. He has served as Deputy Leader of the Opposition in the Punjab Assembly during 1993-96, and also acted as Leader of the Opposition. He has the honour to serve as Speaker of the Punjab Assembly during 1997-99. He is serving as Chief Minister Punjab appointed since November 29, 2002.

Chaudhry Shujaat Hussain : Chaudhry Shujaat Hussain was born on January 27, 1946 in Gujrat and graduated from Forman Christian College, University of Punjab in 1967. His father, Chaudhry Zahoor Elahi, was a seasoned parliamentarian who played an important role in restoring democracy and human rights in Pakistan and was duly honored as the "Prisoner of Conscience" by Amnesty International. Chaudhry Shujaat entered politics after his father was assassinated on September 25, 1981. Chaudhry Shujaat became member of the federal parliament (Majlis-e-Shoora) in 1981 and worked till 1985.

Chaudhry Shujaat for the first time contested in the general election from Gujrat on both the National and Punjab Assemblies seats in 1985 but had to vacate his Punjab Assembly seat and become a member of the then Prime Minister Muhammad Khan Junejo's cabinet as the Industries Minister. He also acted as the parliamentary party leader of the PML in the National Assembly. He was appointed the Information and Broadcasting Minister in the Junejo cabinet in 1986 and was appointed the Industries and Production Minister in 1987-88.

Chauhans : The Chauhans or Chahamana are a clan who ruled parts of northern India in the Middle Ages. The Chauhan gotra is found among the Jats, Rajputs, and Gujars. Chauhan are considered a Punjabi tribe in Pakistan. They are settled in Punjab and Sindh provinces of Pakistan. Chauhans are mentioned in the Jat history also because historians have proved that the Chauhan belong to the Takshak dynasty and some Jat gotras do belong to the Chauhan dynasty. The Chauhans were, along with the Paramara (Parmar), Pratihara (Parihara), and Solanki (Chaulukya) clans, one of the four Agni Kula or "fire born" Rajput clans. The Agni kula were said to be created by the gods in the agni-kunda or sacrificial fire on Mount Abu to fight against the Asuras or demons.

Chausath Yogini Temple : This temple is situated just above the Chausath Yogini Ghat in Uttar Pradesh. It was originally devoted to a tantric cult. Now it is devoted to Kali. The deity here is known as 'Ma' (mother).

Chavda Kingdom : The Chavda Kingdom was a Hindu Rajput dynasty which ruled northern Gujarat from 746 to 942. The Chavda clan were descendents of Indo-Scythian invaders, who settled down in Gujarat and later Saurashtra. The first king of the Chavda Kingdom was Jayshikhari Chavda, who was assassinated before his son Vanraj Chavda was born. Vanraj Chavda went on to be the most successful Chavda ruler, founding historical cities such as Anhilpur Patan and Champaner. There were five Chavda kings after Vanraj, the last of whom, Samantsinh Chavda, did not have any children. He adopted Mulraj who overthrew him in 942 and set up what came to be known as the Solanki dynasty.

Chawk Mosque : Chawk Mosque is located in the Chawkbazar area of old dhaka, the mosque has been so much altered and extended that today it is hardly possible to have an idea of its original form and design.

The northern wall of the mosque proper has been removed. Multi-storied extensions have been made on the north and east sides. The original three-domed roof has been demolished and a new one of similar nature built over the upper storey. The thickness of the walls has been reduced. The mihrabs and the doorways have been widened, and the single archway in the south is now closed. On the basis of the surviving features, combined with the accounts given by some previous authors, a short description of the original mosque and the vaulted plinth below can be attempted.

This is perhaps the earliest dated mosque in Bengal that was built on a high vaulted platform. The vaulted rooms underneath the platform must have been originally devised for providing residential accommodation for students and teachers, as in other mosques in Dhaka, eg kartalab khan's mosque (17Q0-04) and Khan Muhammad Mirdha's Mosque (1704-05). Because of this speciality the present example, like others of its kind, may be said to have been originally built as a 'Residential Madrasa Mosque'.

Chega Gadi : Chega Gadi is another important festival of the Zeliangs in Nagaland. The genesis of the this festival marks the peoples belief that on this day the Almighty showers blessings and brings good harvest and health. However the date for the celebration differs between villages and communities. The forefathers observed this festival for a duration of 4-5 days. Now it is celebrated for 3-4 days.

Cheiraoba : Cheiraoba is the new year festival of Manipur. It is celebrated on the first day of the month Sajibu (March). The festival is also related with the Chahitaba. The domestic deity, Sanamahi, is worshipped in each house. An annual festival is also arranged in the temple of Sanamahi. People wear new clothes and buy new utensils. On this day the 'Chahitaba' is also selected. The chahitaba is the man who gives his name to the year, who bears all the sins of the people for the year of the whole luck, good or ill, influences the lick of the whole community. Chahitaba is nominated by Maibas after comparing the horoscope. Many people on this day also climb the hill called 'Cheiraching' where there is a small Siva shrine. The hill is near Imphal town.

Chembai Music Festival : As part of the Ekadasi day, a 11-day Chembai music festival is held annually in Thiruvanathapuram (Trivandrum), capital of Kerala state in September in memory of Chembai Vaidyanath Bhagawathar. Organised by Sri Chembai Memorial trust this week long festival attracts more than 2000 Carnatic musicians.

A group concert mark the end of the festival on the night of Ekadasi. This includes five of Chembai's most favourite songs 'Vadapiganapatim' (Hamsadhwani), 'Rakshmam-saranagatam' (Natta)', Paavanaguru pavanapuradeeswara' (Hamsanandi)', Mamava sadaajanani' (Kanada) and' Karuna Cheivan entu thamasam Krishna' (Yadukula kamboji). The highlight of the festival is group singing of saint Thyagaraja's 'Pancharatna Krithis' on Dasami day by several leading artists.

Chembai Vaidyanatha Iyer : Chembai Vaidyanatha Iyer was one of the leading practitioners of Carnatic music in the period usually referred to as the 'Golden Era'. Old timers are enthusiastic in pointing out that he, along with Ariyakudi Ramanuja Iyengar & Maharajapuram Viswanatha Iyer formed the 'Modern Trinity of Carnatic Music', the trio who were responsible for keeping up the concert tradition in the vacuum caused by the departure of the titans in the beginning of the 20th Century before the entry of the bright young stars such as Musiri Subramania Iyer, Semmangudi Srinivasa Iyer, G.N.Balasubramanian, Madurai Mani Iyer and the female-trio comprising of M.S.Subbulakshmi, D.K.Pattammal and M.L.Vasanthakumari, who took to the stage later. But what made Chembai different from them was his voice, that booming, metallic, powerful voice which never seemed to depart from sruti.

With a knowledge of the art deeply acquired and with a voice that earned him the fame of 'Bell Metal Voiced Bhagavatar' with its power and majesty yet sweet and melodious, Vaidyanatha Bhagavatar rose to supreme heights, taking vast audiences to rapturous delights in a span of about 70 years of performance expertise. Born in a family of musicians, whose traditions ran uninterruptedly for over two centuries, and being a great grandson of 'Chakra Tanam' Subba Iyer, who was a contemporary of Saint Thyagaraja, Chembai had music in his blood. A deeply religious man, music in his family was taught and learnt as part of Vedic instruction. He had his early training under his father and equipped himself fully to give an independent performance even at the age of nine. A humble man, he attributed all his success to his favorite God—Guruvayurappan.

Chembai was the recipient of numerous honours. He received the 'Sangita Kalanidhi' title in 1951, 'Central Natak Akademi Award' and 'Padmabhushan' from President of India, and the 'Gayana Gandharva' title. Swami Sivananda conferred on him the title of Sangita Samrat. Honours were also bestowed on him by the rulers of Cochin, Mysore, Baroda, Vijayanagaram, Bobbili and Jaipur. He lived a life of a savant and passed away on October 16, 1974. Even after his demise, Chembai continues to inspire countless musicians who participate in his memorial concerts.

Chenab River : The Chenab River is formed by the confluence of the Chandra and Bagha rivers at Tandi located in the upper Himalayas, in the Lahaul district of Himachal Pradesh, India. In its upper reaches it is also known as the Chandrabagha. It flows through the Jammu region of the Indian state of Jammu and Kashmir into the plains of the Punjab, forming the boundary between the Rechna and Jech interfluves ('Doabs' in Farsi). It is joined by the Jhelum River at Trimmu, and then by the Ravi River. It then merges with the Sutlej River at Uch Sharif to form the Panjnad ('Five Rivers'), which joins the Indus at Mithankot. The total length of the Chenab is approximately 960 kilometres.

The river was known to Indians in Vedic period as Asikni or Iskmati and as Acesines to the Ancient Greeks.

In 325 BC, Alexander the Great allegedly founded the town of Alexandria (present day Uch Sharif or Mithankot) at the confluence of the Indus and the combined stream of Punjab rivers (currently known as the Panjnad River).

The Chenab has the same place in the consciousness of the people of the Punjab, as, say the Rhine holds for the Germans, or the Danube for the Austrians and the Hungarians. It is the quintessential river around which Punjabi consciousness revolves, and plays a prominent part in the tale of Heer-Ranjha, the Punjabi national epic.

Chenab River : The Chenab River is formed by the confluence of the Chandra and Bagha rivers at Tandi located in the upper Himalayas, in the Lahaul district of Himachal Pradesh, India. In its upper reaches it is also known as the Chandrabagha. It flows through the Jammu region of the Indian state of Jammu and Kashmir into the plains of the Punjab, forming the boundary between the Rechna and Jech interfluves ('Doabs' in Farsi). It is joined by the Jhelum River at Trimmu, and then by the Ravi River. It then merges with the Sutlej River at Uch Sharif to form the Panjnad ('Five Rivers'), which joins the Indus at Mithankot. The total length of the Chenab is approximately 960 kilometres.

The river was known to Indians in Vedic period as Asikni or Iskmati and as Acesines to the Ancient Greeks. In 325 BC, Alexander the Great allegedly founded the town of Alexandria (present day Uch Sharif or Mithankot) at the confluence of the Indus and the combined stream of Punjab rivers (currently known as the Panjnad River).

Chendamangalam : Chendamangalam is a small town in Ernakulam district of Kerala state, south India. It is about 42 km from Ernakulam town. It has three rivers, seven inlets, hillocks and large expanses of green plain. The Paliam Palace, residence of the Paliath Achans, hereditary Prime Ministers to the former Maharajas of Kochi, is one of the architectural splendours of Kerala. The Palace is over 450 years old and houses a collection of historic documents and relics.

The hillocks at Kottayil Kovilakom are unique as the site of a Hindu temple, a Christian church, a mosque and the remains of a Jewish synagogue, all within 1 km of each other. The synagogue was built in 1614 A.D and is in a peaceful wooded area. In the courtyard behind the synagogue, it is possible to find old Jewish graves, including one of a Jewish woman, dated 1264 A.D.

The Jews arrived in Chendamangalam after the destruction of the second temple and the final desolation of Jerusalem in (A.D. 69) and founded a colony. They moved to Fort Kochi in 1341 A.D after the Great flood. All the synagogues in Kerala—Chendamangalam, Mala, and Kochi—have similar traditional architectural features: a central bimah of brass or silver metal on a concrete or stone base, an ark on the western wall, a balcony above the eastern entry to the sanctuary that is used by the reader on certain holidays. Behind the balcony is the women's gallery, with a stairway leading up to it, usually from outside the building. Also here are remains of the Vypeenakotta Seminary built in the 16th century by the Portuguese. Adjacent to the seminary is an old Syrian Catholic Church built in 1201. It is also the site of the first printing press in India. The church was later rebuilt in Portuguese style.

Chennai : Chennai, formerly known as Madras, is the capital of the state of Tamil Nadu and is India's fourth largest metropolitan city. It is located on the Coromandel Coast of the Bay of Bengal. With an estimated population of 6.90 million (2005), the 368-year-old city is the 31st largest metropolitan area in the world.

The city is a large commercial and industrial centre, and is known for its cultural heritage and temple architecture. Chennai is the automobile capital of India, with around forty percent of the automobile industry having a base there and with a major portion of the nation's vehicles being produced there. Chennai is also referred as the Detroit of South Asia. It has also become a major center for outsourced jobs from the Western world. The 12-kilometre long Marina Beach forms the city's east coast and is one of the longest beaches in the world. The city is known for its sport venues and hosts India's only ATP tennis event, the Chennai Open.

Cheras : The Cheras were one of the three ancient Tamil dynasties who ruled the southern peninsula of India at the beginning of its recorded history. The Cheras ruled over the Malabar Coast in southwestern India, which now forms part of the modern day state of Kerala in the Indian Union. The other two major dynasties were the Cholas in the eastern Coromandel Coast and Pandyas in the south central peninsula. These dynasties held sway in the later centuries BCE, called the Sangam era, in which period the Tamil language, arts and literature flourished. The Chera capital was Vanchi, whose exact location is still a matter of conjecture. Possibilities range from Karur, near Coimbatore in Tamil Nadu, to areas closer to Kochi, the most probable of which being Thiruvanchikulam near Kodungallur. Records of the reigns of as many as twenty-five Cheran kings are available, including the dates of their reigns and the record of their accomplishments. They typically maintained large armies, warred with neighboring kingdoms and actively suppressed piracy on the high seas. In attempts to restore harmony, they sometimes inter-married with the families of their rivals. Throughout the reign of the Cheras, trade continued to bring prosperity to Kerala, with spices, ivory, timber and gems being exported to the Middle East and to southern Europe.

While Hinduism has ever been the principal way of life of this region, many other religious traditions came to this area during the period of the Chera kings. Both Buddhism and Jainism came to Kerala by the 3rd-2nd century BCE. Trade with the Middle East established early contact with Judaism; indeed, some accounts speak of King Solomon's court receiving spices, ivory and peacocks from Kerala. Fleeing the ravages of the sack of Jerusalem, Jewish settlers may have arrived as early as c.70 CE. Christianity may also have made early inroads. Malabar Christian folklore and some Eastern Christianity writings claim Thomas the Apostle visited this region in 52 CE.

Cheriyal Scroll Painting : Cheriyal scroll painting is a highly stylised from narative Nakashi art. It is one of the many forms of folk-art found in India

Cherrapunji : Cherrapunji is a town in Meghalaya, India which is credited as being one of the world's wettest places. It holds two Guinness world records: For receiving the maximum amount of rainfall in a single year: 22,987 mm (904.9973 inches) of rainfall between August 1860 and July 1861 and For receiving the maximum amount of rainfall in a single month: 9299.96 mm (366.14 in) in July 1861.

Cherrapunji receives both the Southwest and Northeast monsoon showers which give it a single monsoon season. Cherrapunji lies at an elevation of 1,370 m (4,500 feet) in the Khasi Hills. It lies in the windward side of these hills to the Bay of Bengal branch of the SW monsoons which enters India through the Ganga delta. Due to orographic rainfall, the rain-bearing clouds are forced to deposit much of their moisture and rain on these hills from June to September. In the winter months it receives the northeast monsoon showers which travel down the Brahmaputra valley. Amazingly, despite perennial rain, Cherrapunji faces acute water shortage and the inhabitants often have to trek for miles to obtain drinking water. Irrigation is also hampered due to excessive rain washing away the top soil as a result of human encroachment in the forests.

Cherumarkali : It is a harvest dance in which the dancers, both men and women move in a swift rhythm, linked in a back lock or holding arms. The costumes are in striking red and white.

Chetar Chaudas Mela : Chetar Chaudas Mela is annually held in Pehowa, in Haryana which has the holy Saraswati tank also called 'Saraswati Teertha' or 'Prithudak Teertha'. This Teertha also finds mention in the ancient Hindu texts. Here in this place the Chetar Chaudas Fair is held in the spring season. Pilgrims, both Sikhs and Hindus, flock to this place to offer 'pinds' for their ancestors. It is claimed that here in this holy spot, Yudhister had offered 'pinds' in memory of all their relatives killed in the Mahabharat war. Pilgrims take bath in the Saraswati tank during this fair.

Chettinad Cuisine : Chettinad cuisine can be found in the southernmost region of Tamil Nadu. Chettinad cuisine is one of the spiciest, oiliest and most aromatic in India. The name Chettinad cuisine comes from the fact that it is prepared by Chettiars.

Chhadakhai : In Orissa, in the sacred month of Karthika many people forego their favourite non-vegetarian dishes till Karthika Purnima as part of sacred ritual. The day after the full moon is the great day of release from this religious taboo and all indulge in non-vegetarian dishes to their heart's content.

Chhagalnaiya : Chhagalnaiya is a Upazila (Sub-district) of Feni, Bangladesh. It lies in the southern part of the district, bordering Tripura state of India and Mirsharai Upazila of Chittagong. It is rich in history and culture. The great medieval warrior Shamser Ghazi hailed from Chhagalnaiya. It is also the birthplace of many other noted historical figures including Sir A. F. Rahman, first Muslim Vice Chancellor of Dhaka University, Gaziul Haque, Advocate Kazi Fazlul Haque and Riaz Rahman

Chham Chhanak : It is the devotional Buddhist dance of the Lahul Spiti region.

Chhapar Fair : This fair is held on Anand Chaudas, the 14th day of the bright half of Bhadon in honour of Gugga Pir in Punjab. A big shrine known as 'Gugge di Marhi' has been built in his memory. The Pir was very popular in his time, and his disciples can be found all over the Punjab. He was a Chauhan Rajput and according to legend, he gently descended into the bosom of Mother Earth along with his steed, and never returned. He was believed to possess special power over all kinds of snakes. On the day this fair is held, villages scoop the earth seven times because they believe that in this way they invoke Gugga Pir to protect them against snakes. This shrine has a reputation for curing people of snake-bite. It is strongly believed that if a person is bitten by a snake, all that has to be done is to take him to the shrine and lay him beside it, he is then sure to be cured. This shrine was built in 1890. This fair provides occasion for folk songs and folk dances. Young people form themselves into groups and go about dancing and singing for hours. Some dancers don women's dress and perform Giddha for the sake of fun. The fair lasts for three days.

Chhapeli : This folk dance is performed at weddings by holding mirrors and handkerchiefs.

Chhatak : Chhatak is a town in northeastern Bangladesh, on the Surma River. It has a population of 34,498 and an area of 9.24 sq km. Chhatak expanded rapidly following the discovery of a natural gas field nearby in 1959. As well as the work generated in extracting gas, the town also has a number of industries powered by natural gas, including the largest cement plant in Bangladesh.

Chhatarpur : Chhatarpur is a city in Madhya Pradesh state of India. It is the administrative headquarters of Chhatarpur District. Chhatarpur is named after the Bundela Rajput leader Chhatar Sal, the founder of Bundelkhand independence, and contains his cenotaph. The state was ruled by his descendants until 1785. At that time the Ponwar clan of Rajputs took control of Chhatarpur. The state was guaranteed to Kunwar Suni Singh Ponwar in 1806 by the British Raj. In 1854 Chhatarpur would have lapsed to the British government for want of direct heirs under the doctrine of lapse, but was conferred on Jagat Raj as a special act of grace. The Ponwar rajas ruled a princely state with an area of 1118 square miles, and population of 156,139 in 1901, which was part of the Bundelkhand agency of Central India. In 1901 the town of Chhatarpur had a population of 10,029, manufactures of paper and coarse cutlery, and a high school. The state also contained the British cantonment of Nowgong.

After the independence of India in 1947, the rajas of Chhatarpur acceded to India, and Chhatarpur, together with the rest of Bundelkhand Agency, became part of the Indian state of Vindhya Pradesh. Vindhya Pradesh was merged into Madhya Pradesh state in 1956.

Chhath : Chhath or Dala Chhath is a Hindu festival, which is unique to Bihar state, India and Terai of Nepal. This festival is also celebrated in the north-east parts of India, Madhya Pradesh, Uttar Pradesh and some regions of Chhattisgarh. Chhath is a festival dedicated to the Sun God. It is considered to be a means to thank the Sun for bestowing the bounties of life in earth, as also for fulfilling particular wishes. Worship of the Sun has been practiced in different parts of India, and the world from time immemorial. Worship of sun has been described in the Rig Veda, the oldest Hindu scriptures, and hymns praying to the sun in the Vedas are found. In the ancient epic, the Mahabharata, references to worshipping of the sun by Draupadi, wife of the Pandavas, are found. It was believed that worshipping of the sun would help cure a variety of diseases, including leprosy, and also ensure longevity and prosperity of the family members.

Chhatrapati Shivaji Raje Bhonslé : Shivaji Bhonslé, also known as Chhatrapati Shivaji Raje Bhonslé was the founder of the Maratha empire in western India in 1674 which was instrumental in the downfall of the Mughal Empire. He is also remembered for being the only secular king in medieval India.

After his coronation, Shivaji launched a wave of conquests in southern India with a massive force of 50,000 (30,000 cavalry & 20,000 infantry). He defeated and captured the forts at Vellore and Jinji in modern day Tamilnadu. He also signed a friendship treaty with the Kutubshah of Golconda. Shivaji died in 1680 at Raigad, after running a fever for three weeks. Shivaji successfully fought the Mughals to create a powerful independent state. During his early career he was only able to defeat small Mughal contingents stationed in villages. Later on he defeated major Mughal armies in the battles of Salher and Vani-Dindori.

Shivaji established an effective civil and military administration. He also built a powerful navy and erected new forts like Sindhudurg and strengthened old ones like Vijayadurg on the west coast. The Maratha navy held its own against the British, Portuguese and Dutch till Maratha internal conflict brought their downfall in 1756.

Shivaji Maharaj was greatly inspired by the heroes of Hindu mythologies and he considered it his mission to liberate India from Islamic rulers. At a young age, he conquered the forts of Torna, Raighad, and Purandar. He used the guerrilla tactics to confront even the mightiest of the empires (that of Moghul emperor Aurangeb) India had known. He imposed a land tax called Chauth on the kingdoms he conquered and use it to build a powerful Hindu army. Chhatrapati Shivaji Maharaj was a brave and able administrator, and established a government that included such modern concepts as cabinet (Ashtapradhan mandal), foreign affairs (Dabir), and internal intelligence.

Chhatrapati Shivaji Terminus : Chhatrapati Shivaji Terminus (formerly Victoria Terminus), better known by its acronym CST, is a historic railway station of the Mumbai suburban railway. It serves as the headquarters of the Central Railways in India and is one of the busiest railway stations in India. On July 2, 2004 the station was nominated a World Heritage Site by the World Heritage Committee of UNESCO.

The station building, built in 1888, is a magnificent and ethereal building designed in the Gothic style of architecture. The building exhibits a fusion of influences from Victorian Italianate Gothic Revival architecture and traditional Indian architecture. Internally, the wood carving, tiles, ornamental iron and brass railings, grills for the ticket offices, the balustrades for the grand staircases and other ornaments were the work of students at the Bombay School of Art. The station stands as an example of 19th century railway architectural marvels for its advanced structural and technical solutions. Till 1996 the station was called "Victoria Terminus" in honour of Queen Victoria. It was renamed by the state government to Chhatrapati Shivaji, after a famed Maratha king, in keeping with the policy of renaming locations with Indian names. Since the Moniker Victoria Terminus, or VT, has been long-standing, its use among the city inhabitants is still widespread.

Chhatrasal : Budelkhand Kesri Maharaja Chhatrasal (1649-1731) along with Chatrapati Shivaji and Guru Gobind Singh formed a trinity of rebels who rose against Aurangzeb's tyranny in the 18th century. He was born in Kachar Kachnai on 4th May, 1649, to Champat Rai and Lal Kunwar. He fought under the Mughal army initially, but later took up cudgels against the Mughals in Bundelkhand and put an end to their rule in his motherland.

Chhattisgarh : Chhattisgarh, a state in central India, formed when the sixteen southeastern districts of Madhya Pradesh gained statehood on November 1, 2000. Raipur serves as its capital. It has borders on the northwest with Madhya Pradesh, on the west with Maharashtra, on the south with Andhra Pradesh, on the east with Orissa, on the northeast with Jharkhand and on the north with Uttar Pradesh. The northern part of the state lies on the edge of the great Indo-Gangetic plain: the Rihand River, a tributary of the Ganges, drains this area.

The eastern end of the Satpura Range and the western edge of the Chota Nagpur Plateau form an east-west belt of hills that divide the Mahanadi River basin from the Indo-Gangetic plain. The central part of the state lies in the fertile plain of the Mahanadi and its tributaries, with extensive rice cultivation. The southern part of the state lies on the Deccan plateau, in the watershed of the Godavari River and its tributary the Indravati. Forest covers roughly forty percent of the state. The Chhattisgarhi language, part of the East-Central group of Indo-Aryan languages, predominates language in the region. The hill districts of the state serve as a home to the Gond peoples, who speak Dravidian languages.

Chhattisgarhi : Chhattisgarhi is a language of India. It has approximately 11.5 million speakers, concentrated in the Indian state of Chhattisgarh and in adjacent areas of Madhya Pradesh, Orissa, and Bihar. Chhattisgarhi is most closely related to Bagheli and Awadhi (Avadhi), and these languages are classified in the East Central Zone of the Indo-Aryan languages, the Indian branch of the Indo-European language family. Chhattisgarhi, like Sanskrit and Hindi, is written using the Devanagari script. According to the Indian Government, Chhattisgarhi an eastern dialect of Hindi, although it is widely considered by linguists to be distinct enough from Hindi to constitute a separate language. Chhattisgarhi has several identified dialects of its own, in addition to Chhattisgarhi Proper: Baighani, Bhulia, Binjhwari, Kalanga, Kavardi, Khairagarhi, Sadri Korwa, and Surgujia.

Chhattisgarhi cultural and political movements, with origins going back the 1920's, affirmed Chhattisgarhi cultural and linguistic identity and sought greater autonomy within India, which came about in 2000 when 16 districts of the state of Madhya Pradesh became the new state of Chhattisgarh.

Chhattri Bagh : It is on the banks of the river Khan in MP. They are the tombs erected in the memory of the dead Holkar rulers and their families but the inner sanctums are locked. The largest and most impressive is that of Malhar Rao Holkar I.

Chhau Dance : Chhau dance a kind of masked dance from the Purulia-Bankura region in West Bengal. This is a martial dance with shields, swords and sticks, and is based on the ramayana and mahabharata. The characters don different masks and dresses in keeping with their roles of gods, demons or animals. The dancers are generally of strong build. Female roles are also played by men wearing women's garments and ornaments. Chhau dances used to be held with a great deal of fanfare towards the end of Chaitra or the beginning of Baishakh on the occasion of shiva puja. Nowadays Chhau dances may be performed regardless of season or occasion.

This dance is very popular among the Bagdis and Bhuiyas. In this warlike dance, the dancers jump around, kneel and suddenly rush towards their opponents. Deft movements of the head, neck, hands, upper torso and legs demonstrate different warlike stances. Leg work is very important. Whether performed individually or in a group, the dance is performed in a circular area round which the musicians sit, leaving a narrow passage for the dancers enter and exit. The main musical instruments are the drum and the shehnai. The dance opens with a hymn to ganesh and then a song of two lines to welcome the arrival of the artistes. Dance and music are more important here than singing. ashutosh bhattacharya popularised this dance form.

Chhayanat : Chhayanat is a cultural organisation in Dhaka, Bangladesh. Founded in 1961 in Dhaka, Chhayanat remains one of the most influential cultural groups in the country. As in the case of many similar organizations, it was established during the Pakistani rule in Bangladesh to promote and nurture the cultural and musical heritage of Bengal.

Chhayavaad : Chhayavaad refers to the romantic upsurge in the Hindi literature particularly poetry, which began in early 19th century. Jaishankar Prasad, Suryakant Tripathi Nirala, Sumitranandan Pant and Mahadevi Varma are considered as the four pillars of Chhayavaadi school of Hindi literature. Jaishankar Prasad's Kamayani is considered as the first magnum opus of this school.

Chheihlam : It is a tribal dance, which embodies the spirit of joy andjubilation. The dance is performed to the accompaniment of a song called 'chheihhla'.

Chhilam : Chailam is a popular dance performed on the occasion of 'Chapchar Kut' one of the most important festivals of the Mizos. In this dance, men and women stand alternatively in circles, with the women holding on to the waist of the man, and the man on the women's shoulder. In the middle of the circle are the musicians who play the drums and the mithun's horn.

The musician playing the drum choreographs the entire nuances of the dance while the one with the mithun's horn chants the lyrics of the 'chai' song. For the dance to start, the drummer beats on the drum, and upon the fourth stroke of the drum the chai song is sung with the rhythmic swaying of the dancers to the left and right, in accordance with beats of the drum.

Depending on the nuances followed, the chailam' has four versions, viz 'Chai Lamthai I, 'Chai Lamthai II, Chai Lamthai III and 'Chai Lamthai IV'. Legend has it that once a king and his men went out for hunting. Unfortunately, they faile miserably and had to be contended without a kill. The king, then seeing the utter disappointment of his men, rose to the occasion and consoles them by inviting them for a drink of rice beer at his palace. On being intoxicated by the drinks, the party then culminated by singing and dancing followed by a sumptuous feast.

Since then, every year, the community continues to enliven the memory of this occasion be celebrating it with various entertainment programs, thus giving rise to one of the most important festivals of the Mizos, the 'Chapchar Kut'. In this dance, musical instrument like drum and horns of mithun are used for making beats. The festivals continues for a week or more. In olden days, the 'Chai' dancers used to drink rice beer continuously during singing and dancing.

Chhindwara : Chhindwara is a city in Madhya Pradesh state of central India. It is the administrative headquarters of Chhindwara District. The main languages spoken in Chhindwara are Hindi and English but many other languages are also spoken here. The main tourist spots are bhartadev where a stone of 10000kg apparently stands on a pin point, and a museum which shows the culture of this state.

Chhiplakot : Chhiplakot is the High Himalayan Mountain in the Pithoragarh district of Uttaranchal, India at an altitude of 3290 m.The area is full of alpine flora and vegetation.Its slopes provides an ideal skii range. Chhiplakot is also known as 'Najurkot'.There is a big cave at Chhiplakot, where a tri yearly fair in the winters is organized. A big lake is also situated here. Local people worship God Chhipula at here. Chhiplakot is famous for its lush green alpine meadow called Bugyal.The area is a paradize for nature lovers and trekkers.

Chhokra Dance : Chhokra dance (literally, dance by young boys) featuring youths playing the roles of women, accompanies alkap songs and has been in vogue in West Bengal's Murshidabad and Maldah region for a long time. This dance is performed on a canopied stage in a mango grove or in an open field. It is directed by a sarkar who leads a fairly large team of singers, musicians, and players. A clown also forms part of the troupe. The musicians seat themselves on the sides of the stage and provide the music for the songs and dance. Others stay in the dressing room and wait their cue. Young boys dressed as girls take part in this dances as in the ghatu dance. Some parts of the alkap song and the chhokra dance can be quite vulgar and this is why performances are held late at night, for adult audiences. The story of Radha and Krishna is a popular theme.

Chholiya : It is a famous dance of the Kumaon region and is performed during marriages. As the procession proceeds to the bride's house, men dancers, armed with swords and shields, dance spiritedly.

Chhota Pandua Minar : Chhota Pandua Minar is the most important minar of all existing buildings of Chhota

Pandua in the Hughli district of West Bengal. Built both as a madhana and a tower symbolising victory and glory, it stands at the southeast side of the bari mosque (1477 AD) at a distance of 52.50m. It is round in design and consists of five storeys, each decreasing in diameter from 18m at the base to 4.50m at the top. Its total height is 37.50m. Inside there is a spiral staircase leading to the top. The staircase opens out to a terrace, which runs all round the base of each successive storey. The entrance is on the west side towards the mosque. The walls of the minar are plastered and are decorated in the three lower storeys with round flutings. Originally enamelled tiles were used in the inside walls of the tower.

The minar, because of its size and shape, has often been compared with the Qutb Minar of Delhi. But there is a difference between the two: whereas the various storeys of the Qutb Minar form a continuous tapering outline from its bottom to the top, the storeys of the present minar give a broken outline of the structure in receding shafts. The only other earlier example of its class in Indo-Muslim architecture appears to be the Chaubara of Bidar (1422-36 AD) which consists of a base and a receding storey. The fact that the plastering of the minar is in contradistinction to the sultanate style suggests Tughlaqian influence.

Chhota Sona Mosque : Chhota Sona Mosque sometimes described as a 'gem of Sultanate architecture' is situated about 3 kilometres due south of kotwali darwaza and half a kilometre to the southeast of the tahkhana complex in the Firuzpur Quarters of gaur-Lakhnauti, the capital of Sultanate Bengal. It occupies the western end of the southern bank of a large tank. A little to the west of the mosque is a modern two-storied Guest House, built several years ago by the Department of Archaeology and Museums, Government of Bangladesh. In between the Guest House and the mosque there runs north-south a modern road, which appears to have been of earlier origins, connecting the main city of Gaur-Lakhnauti with its suburb to the south through the Kotwali Darwaza.

The mosque is one of the best-preserved Sultanate monuments under the protection of the Department of Archaeology and Museums, Government of Bangladesh. The glamour of Chhota Sona Masjid has now diminished, but it still remains the most attractive monument of Gaur-Lakhnauti and the most desired spot for visitors to the area

Chhoti Bamleshwari : The temple on the plains is dedicated to the goddess bamleshwari and is popularly known as choti bamleshwari devi temple. It is in Chattisgarh. The temple was constructed on the plains for those who wished to pray to the goddess but couldn't walk all the way up to the main temple on the mountain.

Chichawatni : Chichawatni is an historic site in Pakistan. It is unique as it is a small town not very far from Saihiwal. It has all the facilities a large city in a small town, thus Chichawatni is a growing town with good economic growth. It is famous for its crops of wheat, cotton and sugar cane.

Chicken Tikka : Chicken tikka is an Indian dish made by baking chicken which has been marinaded in spices and yogurt. It is traditionally made on skewers in a tandoor (Indian clay oven) and is usually boneless. It is typically eaten with a green coriander chutney, or used in a Chicken Tikka Masala.

Chidambaram : This city is known as the 'city of the Cosmic Dancer'. It is 245 Kms away from Madras. The image of Nataraja (the dancing Shiva) represented by the bronze image known throughout the world as the most perfect synthesis in metal of art. The best time to visit the place is during April/ May and December / February.

Chika Building : Chika Building lies within the Gaur citadel to its south-east corner and is in alignment with the Gumti Gate to its east. The building is so named because of the bats that swarmed inside it prior to its repairs. It is square in plan, and was built on the same principle as the Eklakhi Mausoleum at Pandua. Hence early explorers, including Alexander cunningham, who made a thorough survey of the area, thought it to have been the tomb of Sultan Nasiruddin Mahmud Shah (1442-59 AD), the founder of the dynasty that came to occupy power after the House of Ganesha interregnum, to which the Eklakhi Mausoleum belonged. A corridor, which ran at the front of the building, however, negates this view and corroborates the traditional belief that it was built as a daftar khana (an office building). The austerity of the building is in contrast to the Eklakhi Mausoleum, and together with ruins of other structures on its sides strengthens the latter contention.

The existence of long rows of pillar bases to the west of the building suggests a stable. The Chika building, part of the administrative office of the sultan and built in alignment with the Gumti Gate of the citadel of Gaur, could very well have been built by the ruler who built the citadel and the gateway, ie Nasiruddin Mahmud Shah.

Chikan : Chikan is a traditional embroidery style from Lucknow, India. Literally translated, the word means embroidery. Believed to have been introduced by Nur Jehan, Mughal emperor Jahangir's beautiful wife, it is one of Lucknow's most famous textile decoration styles. Patterns and effects created depend on types of stitches used and the thickness of the threads used in embroidery. Some the varieties of the stitches used include back-stitch, chain stitch and hemstitch and result is an open work pattern, jali (lace) or shadow-work. Traditionally, the threads used are in the same colour as the fabric.

Chi-Khur-Chhiah : This was the share of salt given to a chief. Salt was a prized commodity in the hills. One of the commodities for which a Mizo would walk a number of days to go to a market in the plains was salt. But sometimes mineral salt would be available in the rocks. Anyone collecting such salt would pay a share to the chief from whose ram the salt was collected.

Chikmagalur : Chikmagalur is a district in the Indian state of Karnataka. It literally means City of the younger daughter in Kannada. It is sometimes called Chikmanglur.

Chilka Lake : Chilka Lake (also Chilika Lake) is a brackish water coastal lake in India's Orissa state, south of the mouth of the Mahanadi River. It is the largest coastal lake in India. It is separated from the Bay of Bengal by a narrow sandy spit. The area of the lake varies from 1165 sq km in the monsoon season to 906 sq km in the dry season, and is studded with numerous small islands. The lake was formed due to the silting action of the Mahanadi River, which drains into the northern end of the lake, and the northerly currents in the Bay of Bengal, which have formed a sandbar along the eastern shore leading to the formation of a shallow lagoon.

The lake is an important habitat and breeding ground for both resident and migratory and aquatic birds, most notably flamingoes. Migratory birds arrive in October from as far away as Siberia, Iran, Iraq, Afghanistan and the Himalaya, and generally stay until March. Part of the lake is protected by the Chilka Lake Bird Sanctuary, which harbors over 150 migratory and resident species of birds. The Nalaban Island within the lagoon is classified as a Bird Sanctuary under the wildlife protection act. The lake is also home to a diverse range of aquatic life, including 225 species of fish and the Irrawaddy Dolphin (Orcaella brevirostris). The rare limbless lizard Barkudia insularis is endemic to one of the lake's small islands.

Chimakurthi : Chimakurthi is a town in Prakasam District, Andhra Pradesh, India. This place is famous for a special type of granite which is not found anywhere else in the world. This granite is exported to all corners of the globe.

Chin Qilij Khan Asaf Jah I : Chin Qilij Khan Asaf Jah I was the founder of the Asaf Jahi dynasty that ruled Hyderabad state from 1724 to 1949. He was a general in the Mughal empire who was designated governor of the deccan, and sent to south India. Taking advantage of the decline of the mughal empire, especially their lack of control over the deccan, he asserted his independence and established the kingdom of Hyderabad, with the beautiful city of Hyderabad as its capital. This kingdom lasted till the independence of India in 1947, and was indeed the largest among the princely states of the British Raj. The Nizams (as they were later called) lived lavishly and spent fortunes on jewels and diamonds (their possession, Golconda, being rich in diamonds). The famous Koh-e-noor (Kohinoor) diamond was extracted from here, before the British pocketed it. The jewels are in display at the Salar Jung Museum in Hyderabad.

Chiniot : Chiniot is located in Punjab, Pakistan. Chiniot is subdivisional headquarter of district Jhang in Faisalabad division. It is located on baks of Chenab river. The population of Chiniot is estimated to be 1.5 million. Chiniot is on the bank of River Chenab, and is famous for its furniture industry, which it also exports. Its labor force is specially skilled in woodwork.

Chinkara : The Chinkara is a species of gazelle found in South Asia. Found in grasslands and desert areas in

India, parts of Iran and Pakistan. It is also known as the Indian Gazelle Gazella gazella bennetti.

This gazelle stands at 65 centimetres and weighs about 23 kilograms. Its summer coat a warm biscuit, or reddish-buff colour, with smooth, glossy fur. In winter the white belly and throat fur is in greater contrast. The sides of the face have dark chestnut stripes from the corner of the eye to the muzzle bordered by white stripes. The record horns reach over 39 centimetres.

It is a shy animal and avoids human habitation.They have a special characteristic which helps them survive trying times. They can go without water for long periods and can even get sufficient fluids from plants and dew drops. Although mostly seen as solitary animals, they can sometimes be spotted in small groups numbering up to 3 - 4 individuals.

Chinmaya Mission : Chinmaya Mission was founded in 1953 by the devotees of Swami Chinmayananda. It is administered by Central Chinmaya Mission Trust, Mumbai.

Chirala : Chirala is a town situated in the coastal region of Andhra Pradesh, India. It has a population of 85,455 (agglomeration 166,877) (2001) census). The town is situated at a distance of 100 km south of Vijayawada. The name has been derived from its ancient age name KsheeraPuri ("Here the sea looks as white as milk"). This town is the major hub for textile business in the district of Prakasam. Because of its wide textile business it is also called Mini-Bombay. There are some nice beaches and a few resorts.

The Indian Air Force has an air-base called Suryalanka near to Bapatla, very near to Chirala. Chirala is the major commercial centre between Tenali and Ongole and lies on the main railway line between Madras (Chennai) and Calcutta (Kolkata). This accounts for its importance.

Chiratala Bhajana : Chiratala Bhajana or Chekka Bhajana in Andhra Pradesh resembles Kolattam very closely in its movements, steps, dance and style and songs except that the players hold Chiratalu instead of sticks. All the technical terms like Jattu, Garidi, Uddi, Kopu, Ettugada, Muktayimpu, Usi are common to both Kolattam and Chiratala Bhajana. Chiratalu, a pair of wooden pieces chiseled and riveted with jingling bells and metal pieces, produces metallic and rattling sound. The two pieces can be held in a palm like a single piece by inserting the thumb and middle finger into the rings fixed in the centre on the top side of the wooden pieces. By opening and closing the palm the two pieces strike each other and produces musical sound.

In Kolattam each player hold two sticks one in each hand, in Chiratala Bhajana the players hold a pair of Chiratalu in one hand and a colourful handkerchief in another which he waves while jumping and dancing. The Kolattam Kopus are of short duration where as the Chiratala Bhajana kopus are of long duration facilitating narration of episodes from Epics and Puranas. There are nearly 100 kinds of kopus depicting variety in the steps. In modern times long narratives have been divided into small bits with different gatis and styles. In olden days lamp posts used to be erected in the middle of the circle of players. Now troupe leader stands in the middle and sings the narrative playing cymbals or Chiratalu.

A troupe consisting of 10 to 20 members forms into a circle while the leader who stands in the centre begins the bhajan, directing the troupe. All members follow him. The commencing steps are known as Adi Adugu (beginning steps). This is compulsory item. The other steps are known as Potu Adugu, Kuppadugu, Kulukula Adugu, Joku Adugu, Nemili Adugu, Gurappu Adugu, Uyyala Adugu. The players hang garlands in their necks and tie jingling bells to their ankles, they also tie colourful waist bands.

Chiring We : Chiring We is the Himalayan peak situated in eastern Kumaun of the Pithoragarh district of Uttaranchal state in India. The altitude of the peak is 6,559 M. Chiring We is the highest peak above the Kalabaland Glacier.Chiring We massif, which include peaks like Bamba Dhura 6,334 M, Suli Top 6,300 M, Trigal 5,983 M, Suitilla 6,373 m, separates Lassar Yankti valley from Kalabaland valley.The peak literally means 'Mountain of long life.

Chisti Behesti's Tomb : This tomb is situated on the eastern side of the old High Court of Dhaka and at present is known as the High Court Mazar. The square tomb structure was constructed on a high platform. Subahdar islam khan chisti died in 1613 and was at first laid to rest at Bagh-i-Badshahi (present Shishu Academy and High Court area). Tradition has it that later on his body was taken to Fathpur Sikri at the order of Emperor jahangir and interned there, and a simple structure was erected on the empty tomb at Dhaka. In course of time the tomb came to be known as 'Chisti Behestkhana' or 'Tomb of Chisti Behesti'.

Nawab Khwaja ahshanullah and Zamindar Mohini Babu repaired the almost dilapidated mausoleum. After the partition of bengal in 1905 it was decided that the tomb would be demolished in order to build the governor house. Only the intervention of Nawab khwaja salimullah saved the tomb building. The tomb gained more importance when the governor house was turned into the High Court during the Pakistani period. Later on, a modern tomb building with a massive dome was erected on the tomb. Devotees now revere it as the tomb of Khwaja Sharfuddin Chisti alias Oli-i-Bangala.

Chitau Amavasya : This is celebrated on the new moon day of the lunar month of Shravana. A special type of rice cake called 'chitau' is offered to Lord Jagannath at the temple. This cake is prepared and eaten with relish in almost every household. Gendeisuni, the goddess of snails and oysters is duly worshipped. These creatures are offered cakes and requested not to bruise the feet of farmers when they go to remove weeds from the fields.

Chitharal Jain Monuments : Chitharal Jain Monuments are located in a small village situated at a distance of 7 km from Marthandam and 55 km from Kanyakumari. Chitharal is historically known as Thirucharanathupalli – the abode of Jain monks belonging to Digambara sect.It is famous for the hillock which has a cave containing rock-cut sculptures of Thirthankaras and attendant deities carved inside and outside dating back to the 9th century A.D. Jain influence in this region was due to the Jain King Mahendra Verman-I (610-640 AD).

Chitra River : Chitra river originating from the lower part of Chuadanga and Darsana, it runs about 170 km southeast through Darsana, Kaliganj, Salikha and Kalia upazilas and joins with the Nabaganga in Gazirhat of Narail district. Afterwards the joint flow falls into the Bhairab river in Daulatpur upazila of Khulna district. In the past, the Chitra was an offshoot of the Ichamati, but it turned into a distributary of the Nabaganga due to siltation at its mouth. The river is heavily silted up and not navigable from its original point to Salikha. From Salikha to Gazirhat, it is under tidal influence and the range of the tide is about one metre. The river is navigable and a launch route from Khulna runs along its course. An Embankment along its left bank from Rathdanga to Gazirhat has been constructed under a flood control drainage and irrigation projects. The river does not show any tendency to erode or overflow its banks. It is straight in its course except for some meanders in Salikha upazila. Kaliganj, Salikha, Narail and Gazirhat are some important places situated on the banks of the Chitra

Chitra Singh : Chitra Singh is a famous India-based singer of Urdu/Hindi ghazals and wife of Jagjit Singh, also a prominent ghazal singer. They together remain one of the most popular duet teams and are considered pioneers in modern ghazal singing. Chitra Singh (maiden name Née Dutta), born in a Bengali family had no formal musical training but had strong roots of music in her family and learnt much of her music by listening to her mother's guru.

Chitra Vichitra : In the interior of Sabarkantha, at Poshina in Gujarat, the tribals get together in March and you have a fiesta of extraordinarily ethnic attires, skills, customs and dance forms.

Chitrai Festival : Chitrai is the first month of Tamils. In this month a festival is held to celebrate the advent of spring. On the full moon day, the images of gods and goddesses from the temples in and around Madurai are taken to the bed of the river Vaigai, in colourful processions accompanied by the hundreds and thousands of people and musicians. The atmosphere is one of mirth and merriment. The festival marks the marriage of Madurai's powerful presiding deity, Meenakshi with Lord Shiva. It marks the end of one financial year and the beginning of another for agriculturists in Madurai district. Payments for servants engaged in agricultural operations are made on yearly basis i.e. from one Chitrai festival to the next.

Chitrakoot : Chitrakoot is a religious town in the Bundelkhand region of central India, notable for the number of its temples and sites from Hindu mythology. It is now a separate district. It attracts huge crowds throughout the year for occasions including 'Amavasya' and Free Eye Hospital Camps. Noted 'Ayurvedic' and 'Yoga' centres like 'Arogyadham' are located in the district.

Chitral : Chitral, or Chitral, is the name of a town (35° 53' N; 71° 48' E), valley, river, district, and former princely state in the former Malakand Division of the

Northwest Frontier Province of Pakistan. Chitral Town, capital of the Chitral District, is situated on the west bank of the Chitral (or Kunar) River. The town is at the foot of Tirich Mir, the highest peak of the Hindu Kush, 7,708 m or 25,289 ft high. It has a population of about 20,000, while the District (of 14,833 sq km or 5,727 sq mi), has a population of about 300,000. The altitude of the valley is about 1,100 m or 3,700 ft.

Chitral Gol National Park : Chitral Gol National Park is situated in the beautiful valley of Chitral in Pakistan. Chitral Gol is a narrow valley, its gorge running for some 18km before broadening out into a basin surrounded by high peaks. Numerous tributaries drain into the Chitral Gol, which flows southwards into the Kunar River. Visitors and Visitor Facilities Include two hunting lodges, originally built by the Mehtars.

Chitta Ranjan Das : Chitta Ranjan Das(1870-1925) better known as CR Das and popularly known as Deshabandhu, was one of the most dynamic political leaders of twentieth century Bengal. Born in Calcutta on 5 November 1870, he belonged to an upper middle class family of vikramapura in the district of Munshiganj. His father Bhuban Mohan Das was a solicitor of the Calcutta High Court.

CR Das came to politics early in the twentieth century. He was associated with the revolutionary organisations like the anushilan samiti. As a co-worker of surendranath banerjea, bipin chandra pal and Aurovinda Ghosh, he utilised the issue of the partition of bengal (1905) for expanding revolutionary activities in Bengal. He presided over the Bengal Provincial Conference held at Bhawanipur in 1917. Responding to the call of MK Gandhi during the non-cooperation movement he left his lucrative practice at the Bar and took a leading part in the boycott of the visit of the Prince of Wales to Calcutta in 1921. The government imprisoned him on many occasions. CR Das, however, strongly criticised the announcement of the suspension of the Non-cooperation Movement by Gandhi and condemned it as a serious mistake. In his opinion, this action of Gandhi demoralised the political workers to a great extent.

Himself an ardent advocate of Hindu-Muslim unity, he succeeded in resolving the communal problem of Bengal in a memorable way. He won over the Muslims of Bengal to his side through an agreement commonly known as the bengal pact. The terms of the agreement were accepted at a meeting of the Swarajya Council Party held on 16 December 1923. Unfortunately the Pact was opposed by many of the Congress leaders of Bengal. The Muslims of the province welcomed the Pact wholeheartedly. But they were disillusioned when the Pact was rejected by the Cocanada Session of the Indian National Congress, held in December 1923.

CR Das was elected the first Mayor of the calcutta corporation following the victory of the Swarajists in the election of that organisation in 1924 and was reelected for the next term also. He presided over the All India Trade Union Congress held at Lahore and Calcutta in 1923 and 1924 respectively. He presided over the Bengal Provincial Conference held at Faridpur in 1925. He founded the weekly Forward, the organ of the Swarajya Party in 1923. He also founded the Municipal Gazette, the official organ of the Calcutta Corporation in 1924. He was against caste distinctions and untouchability. He favoured women's emancipation and encouraged female education as well as widow remarriage. His advocacy of inter-caste marriage is proved by the marriage of his own daughters with Brahmin and Kayastha families. Deshabandhu died in June 1925 when he was only fifty-five. His premature death came as a blow to the cause of communal harmony of Bengal and India as well.

Chittagong : Chittagong is the major sea-port and second largest city of Bangladesh. It is located in Chittagong District of Chittagong Division, in the south-eastern portion of the country near Myanmar (Burma). The city was built on the banks of the Karnaphuli River, which ends nearby, in the Bay of Bengal. Chittagong has a population of over 3.5 million, and is continuing to grow. One of the cleanest cities of Bangladesh, it has had an ancient reputation of great mystique and beauty.

The largest sea port of the country, a coveted post which it has held for thousands of years, Chittagong is the main route for almost all of Bangladesh's import and export, and thus generates a huge amount of revenue each year, attracting many investors, both foreign and national. Its harbour also contains extensively developed port facilities, and is particularly suitable for ocean steamers. The people of the city are diverse and multi-ethnic, and the majority has originated from the Arabs, Afghans, and Mughals, all of whom had travelled and settled in the city after arriving on its shores many hundreds of years ago. The descendents of Portuguese settlers, known as the Firingi, also continue to live in Chittagong, as Catholic Christians, in the old Portuguese enclave of Paterghatta.

The city is also Bangladesh's commercial and manufacturing centre, and home to the country's largest companies, for example M.M. Ispahani, A.K. Khan & Co. Ltd, and the P.H.P. Group. There are large factories located just outside the northern part of the city, and a large eco-park catering to ecologists and forestry-related genetic science has been opened recently in neighbouring Sitakunda. Chittagong is also home to a few of the most renowned universities of Bangladesh, Chittagong University of Engineering and Technology (CUET), the International Islamic University of Chittagong, the Chittagong University, established in 1966, the Chittagong College being notable examples. It is the hub of knowledge in the South and many madrassahs (Islamic educational centres) of excellent stature adorn its borders.

Chittagong City Corporation : Chittagong City Corporation (CCC) is a self-governing organisation which governs the municipal areas of Chittagong and some adjoining areas of south-eastern Bangladesh. CCC government is elected by popular vote every 5 years. A.B.M. Mohiuddin Chowdhury is the current mayor.

Chittagong College : Chittagong College is the topmost college in Chittagong. It is also the first college established in the greater Chittagong area. Having started out as Chittagong District school in 1836, it was upgraded to an Intermediate college in 1869. It started providing science education in intermediate section from the year 1909 and became a graduation college in 1910. Now this college is giving honors and masters degree in 16 subjects. It is also continuing its intermediate course as well. The college has five academic buildings, library with approximately 60000 books, mosque, auditoriam and other facilities. The sports ground of the college is known to all with it's famous name Parade Moidan.

Students of the college have made significant contribution in the history of Bangladesh. Also many distinguished scholars have taught here over the years. Among them were Surendranath Dasgupta, Janardan Chakravarty, Bhabatosh Dutta, Subodh Sengupta, Jogeshchandra Singha, Mansur Uddin, Motahar Hossain Chowdhury, Momotazuddin Ahmed and Dr. Muhammad Yunus.

Chittagong Collegiate School : The Chittagong Collegiate School is a notable secondary school in Chittagong, the southern port city in Bangladesh. Established in 1836, it is one of the oldest schools in the country. The school is known for its excellence in providing secondary education and attract students from all over the country. The school is located at South Nalapara, near the Chittagong Railway Station. It has a dormitory for the residential students and has a residential area for the teachers. The school campus is considered to be one of the largest campuses in the city. The school has the tradition of obtaining the best results in SSC examination.

Chittagong Collegiate School : The Chittagong Collegiate School is a notable secondary school in Chittagong, the southern port city in Bangladesh. Established in 1836, it is one of the oldest schools in the country. The school is known for its excellence in providing secondary education and attract students from all over the country. The school is located at South Nalapara, near the Chittagong Railway Station. It has a dormitory for the residential students and has a residential area for the teachers. The school campus is considered to be one of the largest campuses in the city. The school has the tradition of obtaining the best results in SSC examination.

Chittagong Division : Chittagong Division is one of the six administrative divisions of Bangladesh. It covers the most southern areas of the country and is also the second largest one.

Chittagong Divisional Stadium : Chittagong Divisional Stadium is a sports venue located in the city of Chittagong in south-eastern Bangladesh. It became a Test cricket venue on February 27, 2006, when it hosted a test match between Sri Lanka and Bangladesh.

Chittagong Hill Tracts : The Chittagong Hill Tracts comprise an area of 13,180 km^2 in south-eastern Bangladesh, and borders India and Myanmar (Burma). It is divided into three districts: Khagrachari, Rangamati and Bandarban. The Chittagong Hill Tracts were once known as Korpos Mohol, the name used until 1860. As of 2 December 1997, it is an autonumous region divided into three districts, namely, Chengmi [Hagracuri (Khagrachari) Hill District], Gongkabor (Rangamati Hill District), and Arvumi (Bandarban Hill District). During the 1970s and 80s, there were attempts by the Government to resettle the area with Bangladeshi people, a tendency prevalent in most sub-continental governments of the day including India and Pakistan. These attempts were resisted by the tribals, who formed a guerilla force called Shanti Bahini. As a result of the tribal resistance movement, successive governments turned the Hill Tracts into a militarised zone.

Chittagong Port : Chittagong Port the principal sea port of Bangladesh, is situated in the estuary of the karnafuli River, which originates in the hills north-east of the chittagong hill tracts and flows into the bay of bengal. The main significance of this port lie in the fact that it provides a deep-water anchorage a few miles inland from the sea. The steering distance is 16 kilometres from the outer bar on the Bay of Bengal to the main berths on the bank of the river Karnafuli. The location of the port and its natural harbour made it an important centre of trade and business as far back as the 9th century AD when the Arab merchants found it to be a lucrative centre for trade. By the beginning of the 15th century, the port of Chittagong was an important trading centre. Chinese Chronicler Ma Huan, who visited Chittagong in 1405 with a Chinese mission, refers to "Chit-le-gan" as a port frequented by Chinese trading vessels. The most frequent visitors to the port were the Arabs.

Chittagong Region River System : The Chittagong region consists of the 5 hilly districts of Chittagong Division - Chittagong, Cox's Bazar, Bandarban, Rangamati and Khagrachhari. It is bounded by the Bay of Bengal on the south and west, the Naf river with Myanmar on the southeast, and India on the east. The region is characterised by three distinct ecological zones: inter-tidal zone, coastal plains and extensive hill areas. The northern and eastern parts of the region constitute the hilly areas and are commonly known as the Chittagong Hill Tracts (CHT). This area is covered with a deep evergreen and deciduous forest which is a habitat of many wildlife species such as the Asian Elephant (Elephas maximus), White Duck (Cairina scutulata), Banrui (Maris crassicaudata), Banchhagal (Capricornis sumatraensis), Shajaru (Hystrix indica) and other endangered species.

Chittagong Stock Exchange : Chittagong Stock Exchange is a stock exchange located in the port city of Chittagong in South-eastern Bangladesh. This was established in 1995 as the second stock exchange of the country. The exchange is located at Agrabad commercial area.

Chittagong University of Engineering & Technology (CUET) : Chittagong University of Engineering & Technology (CUET) is a public engineering university in Chittagong, Bangladesh. It was formerly known as Bangladesh Institute of Technology, Chittagong. It was established in 1968 as Chittagong Engineering College, part of the Faculty of Engineering of the University of Chittagong. Through a government ordinance in 1986, the college was converted into an Institute of Technology. In 2003, it was upgraded into a public university. The President of Bangladesh is the Chancellor of the university.

Chittagonian : Chittagonian is an Indo-European language spoken by the people of Chittagong in Bangladesh and the much of the southeast of the country. It is closely related to Bangla, but is normally considered by linguists to be a separate language and not a dialect of Bangla, as the two are not inherently mutually intelligible. It is estimated to have 14 million speakers, in Bangladesh as well as by expatriate and second generation Chittagonian Bengalis in the United Kingdom and other countries.

Chittoor : Chittoor, also known as Chittur, is a city and district of India's Andhra Pradesh state. The city has a population of 152,966 (2001 census). Chittoor is famous for the Tirupati, Kanipakam and Sri Kalahasti temples. It lies in the Poini River valley of southernmost Andhra Pradesh, on the Bangalore-Chennai highway. It is a market center for mangos, grain, sugarcane, and peanuts. Its industries include oilseed and rice milling. It is also home to Nutrine Confectionaries, a major chocolate manufacturer in India.

Chittorgarh : Chittorgarh (also Chittor, Chittaur, or Chittaurgarh) is an ancient city in Rajasthan state of western India. It lies on the Berach River, a tributary of the Banas, and is the administrative headquarters of Chittorgharh District and a former capital of the erstwhile kingdom of Mewar. The Kingdom of Mewar was founded by Bappa Ṛawal, of the Guhilot (or Gehlot/Guhila) clan of Rajputs, who established himself as ruler of Mewar in 734, with Chittor garh (Chittor fort) as his capital. Chittorgarh was captured in 1303 by Ala ud din Khilji, Sultan of Delhi, but was recaptured in 1326 by Hammir Singh, a scion of the same Gehlot clan. The dynasty (and clan) fathered by him came to be known by the name Sisodia after the village where he was born.

By the 16th century, Mewar had become the leading Rajput state. Rana Sangha of Mewar led a combined Rajput forces against the Mughal emperor Babur in 1527, but was defeated at the Battle of Khanua. After the Mughal Emperor Akbar captured Chittorgarh in 1568, the capital was moved west to Udaipur, in the foothills of the Aravalli

Range, where Rana Udai Singh II had established a residence in 1559. Udaipur remained the capital of Mewar until it acceded unto the union of India in 1947, and Chittorgarh gradually lost its importance. However, Chittorgarh remains replete with historic associations and hold a special place in the hearts of many Rajputs, as it was a bastion of the clan at a time when every other stronghold had succumbed to invasion.

Chogolisa : Chogolisa (or Bride Peak) is a mountain in the Karakoram region of Pakistan. Chogolisa has several peaks, the highest on the SW face (Chogolisa I) rises to 7,665 metres (25,147 ft.). The second highest at 7,654 metres on the NE side (Chogolisa II) is the one named Bride Peak by Martin Conway in 1892.

Chogyal : The Chogyal were the monarchs of the former country of Sikkim. The Chogyal or divine ruler was the absolute potentate of the nation from 1642 to 1975, when the monarchy was abrogated and the people voted to make Sikkim India's 22nd state.

The reign of the Chogyal was foretold by the patron saint of Sikkim, Guru Rinpoche. The 8th century saint had predicted the rule of the kings when he arrived in the state. In 1642, Chogyal Phuntsog Namgyal was crowned as Sikkim's first ruler in Yuksom. The crowning of the king was a great event and he was crowned by three revered lamas who arrived there from three different directions, namely the north, west and south.

Chohara : This is a joyful dance of the Kinnauras, which is performed on almost all the festive occasions with the participation of both men and women. The dancing is accompanied by the tribal songs.

Cholas : The Cholas were a South Indian Tamil dynasty of unknown antiquity, antedating the early Sangam literature (c. 150 C.E.). The dynasty originated in the rich Kaveri valley, Urayur (near Thiruchirapalli) being their oldest capital. Karikalan I and Sibi were ancient legendary Chola emperors, while Rajaraja Chola and Kulothunga Chola I were the famous emperors of the Later(Great) Cholas. The Chola Empire was at its zenith during the tenth and eleventh century C.E. Under Rajaraja Chola (Rajaraja The Great) and his son Rajendra Chola, the Cholas rose as a notable military, economic and cultural power in Asia. The Chola Empire stretched from southern Maldives as far north as the Himalaya Mountains and West Bengal in North India. Rajaraja Chola conquered peninsular South India, and annexed parts of Sri Lanka by defeating the Pandyas. Rajendra Chola went beyond, occupying coastal Burma, the Andaman and Nicobar Islands, Lakshadweep, conquered the kings of Srivijaya (Sumatra, Java and Malaya in South East Asia) and Pegu islands with his fleet of ships. He defeated Mahipala, the king of Bihar and Bengal, and to commemorate his victory he built a new capital called Gangaikonda Cholapuram. Tamil Chola armies exacted tribute from Thailand and the Khmer kingdom of Cambodia. The power of the Cholas declined around the 13th century.

In the age of Cholas, considered by many scholars as the most creative period of South Indian History, the whole of South India was for the first time brought under the sway of a single government, and a serious attempt was made to face and solve the problems of public administration. In local government, in art, religion and literature, the Tamil country reached heights of excellence never reached again in succeeding ages. In all these spheres as well as in that of foreign trade and maritime activity, the Chola period marked the culmination of movements that began in an earlier age, under the Pallavas. Monumental architecture in the form of majestic temples and sculpture both in stone and bronze reached a finesse never before achieved in India.

The Chola Empire under Rajendra Chola IV was experiencing a period of continuous trouble. It coincides with an epoch of great changes in the political map of the south. The Cholas were exposed to assaults from within and without. The Pandyas in the south had risen to the rank of a great power. Hoysalas in the west threatened the existence of the Chola empire. Rajendra tried to survive by aligning with the two powers in turn. At the close of Rajendra's reign, the Pandyan empire was at the height of prosperity and had taken the place of the Chola empire in the eyes of the foreign observers. There is no evidence that Rajendra was followed immediately by another Chola prince. The Chola empire was completely absorbed by the Pandyan empire.

Choli : A choli is a midriff-baring blouse worn in India, Sri Lanka, Bangladesh, and other countries where the sari is worn. The choli is usually cut to fit tightly to the body; it will have short sleeves and a low neck. The back may be solid, or cut out. The choli may also be abbreviated, ending right below the bustline, or elongated, ending at the waist. Saris are often woven with an extra length of material meant to be cut off and fashioned into a matching choli. The choli may be sewn so that the elaborately woven borders of the sari material form the bottom edges of the choli sleeves.

Cholistan : Cholistan is a desert located in the province of Punjab, Pakistan. It continues as the Thar Desert in the eastern part of the province of Sind in Pakistan as well as in India. The dry bed of the Hakra River runs through the area, along which many settlements of the Indus Valley Civilisation have been found. The Hakra river is believed to be the remnant of ancient Sarasvati river.

Cholistan Wildlife Sanctuary : Cholistan Wildlife Sanctuary is located in Punjab, Pakistan. The Cholistan desert area in the south eastern portion of the province of Punjab contains some of the most rare and interesting wildlife in Pakistan. Some of the rare animals of this region are Desert wolf(rare), Indian fox, Red fox, Jackal, Small indian civet, Small indian moongoose, Indian grey mongoose, Indian desert cat, Jungle cat, Caracal cat, Chinkara grazelle, Blackbuck, Nilgai antelope, Houbara bustard, Peregrine falcon, Saker falcon,Black backed vulture, Indian cobra, Monitor lizard, Saw scaled viper and Russells viper.

Chorao : Chorao is an island along the river Mandovi near Panaji of Goa, in India. in 1510, this area was one of the first to be conquered by the Portuguese. Even today, one can visit this area and see the distinct churches, graveyards and buildings all with a Portuguese air. Also home to the Salim Ali Bird Sancutary which is India's only bird sancutary.

Chosker Festival : In this religious festival of Monpas in Arunachal Pradesh, the Lamas (Buddhist priests) read religious scriptures in the Gompa (Buddhist temple) for a number of days. Thereafter the villagers carry the religious books on their back in a procession under the guidance of senior Lama. The procession goes round the cultivated fields which fall within the jurisdiction of the village. The significance of this performance is to ensure better cultivation and protect the grains from the insects and wild animals and also for the prosperity of the villagers. Normally this festival is performed during the months of April-May, after the Jhum fields are prepared. The ritual involves the suspension of all outside activities for a definite period.

Chota Nagpur Dry Deciduous Forest : The Chota Nagpur dry deciduous forest is a tropical dry broadleaf forest ecoregion in eastern India. It is located in the Chota Nagpur Plateau in the states of Jharkhand, Orissa and

Chhattisgarh. Forests range from dry to wet. It is also swampy in some places. In some regions it is made up of grasslands of bamboo and bushes. Tigers, Asian elephants and bears are some of the animals found here.

Chota Nagpur Plateau : The Chota Nagpur Plateau (also Chhota Nagpur) is a plateau in eastern India, which covers much of Jharkhand state as well as adjacent parts of Orissa, Bihar, and Chhattisgarh. The Indo-Gangetic plain lies to the north and east of the plateau, and the basin of the Mahanadi River lies to the south. The plateau is made up of ancient Precambrian rocks. Deposits of Coal support the industries of the Damodar valley. Chota Nagpur is made up of three smaller plateaus, the Ranchi, Hazaribagh, and Kodarma plateaus. The Ranchi plateau is the largest of the plateaus, with an average elevation of 700 meters. The total area of Chota Nagpur is approximately 65,000 sq km.

Chottanikkara Rajarajeswari Temple : Chottanikkara Bhagavathy Temple is one of the most celebrated Hindu shrines of Kerala. The temple is located in Chottanikkara town, 17kms away from Ernakulam. Rajarajeswari (Adiparasakthi) alias Durga Bhagavathy—the mother Goddess, is the presiding deity of the temple. It is said that this deity was brought from Mookambika Temple in Kollur, Karnataka and therefore there is a presence of Mookambika (Saraswathy) Devi till 7am in the morning.

The 'Devi' in the temple is known for the healing powers, particularly relating to mental illness and disorders. The temple situated in a hilly region, is surrounded on all sides by green farms. The entry is through the west and the spiritual atmosphere in the temple gives mental peace and harmony to devotees.

In the main temple, the golden hued idol of Bhagavathy 4 to 5 ft. high, is bedecked with flowers, garlands, jewels and bathed in myriad of lights splendidly. The idol has four arms. The upper right holds the disc, the upper left bears the conch, the lower right hand is held in a boon-conferring pose and the lower left indicates the abhaya (fearlessness) pose.

The Bhagavathy is worshipped in three different forms as Saraswathy in the morning clothed in an impeccable white garment, *Lakshmi* at noon with crimson red cloth and Durga in the evening wearing a bright blue dress. Durga is a much milder form. The original idol of Bhagavathy, three or four feet high which faces east, is of laterite and is believed to be self-born (swayambhoo). This image called 'Rudraksha Sila' is irregular in shape, red in colour and is untouched by the human sculptor. This image can be seen only in the wee hours of morning at 4 am when the Nada opens for nirmalyam.

Choudhary Rahmat Ali : Choudhary Rahmat Ali (1895 - February 12, 1951) was the reactionary founder of the Pakistan National Movement, and was an early proponent of the formation of Pakistan. He is also credited with coming up with the name by which that state is now known. He completed his early studies in Lahore, and moved to the United Kingdom where he studied at Emmanuel College at the University of Cambridge and the University of Dublin, earning MA and LLB degrees.

In the early 1930s, Ali began writing about the formation of a Muslim nation in India, and voiced his ideas in the pamphlet entitled "Now or Never; Are we to live or perish forever?". He also gave birth to the term "Pakistan" to refer to the Muslim homeland that he envisioned in Northern India, as well as "Bang-i-Islam" for a Muslim homeland in the Bengal, and "Usmanistan" for a Muslim homeland in the Deccan.

Like Allama Iqbal, Ali believed that the Muslims of India had to undergo a reformation politically in order to remain a viable, and independent community there. Ali noted that Muhammad had succeeded in uniting fractured Arab tribes and that this example was to again be used by Muslims of India to pool together in order to survive in what he perceived to be an increasingly hostile India.

As such, Choudhary Rahmat Ali's writings, in addition to those of Iqbal and others were major catalysts for the formation of Pakistan. Ali dedicated a lot of time and energy to the idea of Pakistan, and after its formation in 1947, he argued on its behalf at the United Nations over the issue of Kashmir.

Interestingly, while Choudhary Rahmat Ali was a champion for the formation of Pakistan, he lived most of his adult life in the United Kingdom. The Cambridge-based pamphleteer had been voicing his dissatisfaction with the creation of Pakistan ever since his arrival in Lahore on April 6 1948. He was unhappy over a Smaller Pakistan than the one he had conceived in his 1933 pamphlet Now Or Never, and his criticisms were beginning to raise alarm while his claims of contribution to the Pakistan Movement were interpreted by his critics as boasting to be the real founder of Pakistan. Consequently, Rahmat Ali was denied a Pakistani passport, and later told to leave the country and he died in 1951, buried in Cambridge City graveyard

Chovoth or Ganesh Chaturthi : The most important and almost the national festival for Goan's is the Ganesh Chaturthi known as 'Chovoth'. The festivities run into several days, at least two and half days, when puja of Gouri and Mahadev along with Ganapati, is performed, Gouri being drawn on paper and Mahadev on a coconut. On these days married women fast.

On the Chovoth day, in the morning or evening, a clay idol of Ganapati is brought home. Before that a matov (pavilion or pandal) is prepared with bunches of betel nut, coconut, bananas and branches of mango-trees being necessary ingredients of it. The puja of Ganapati goes on until mid-day. The puja is performed with the help of the priest.

On the second day, in the evening or at night, after performing the uttara puja of the image of Ganapati, it is taken in procession and immersed into the sea, creek, river, lake or well. Before the idol is removed from its stand for immersion, it is besought for the welfare of the household and its members.

Three days of Chovoth means, days of great rejoicing for children. Girls collect different types and shapes of leaves for Gauri, Mahadev and Ganapati. There is competition in flower-making also. At least five vegetables are cooked on that day. Aartis is a special performance on the occasion of the Ganapati festival.

Chowdhary Charan Singh : Shri Charan Singh was born in 1902 at Noorpur in Meerut district of Uttar Pradesh, in a middle class peasant family. He graduated in science in 1923, and did his post-graduation from Agra University in 1925. Also trained in law, he set up practice at Ghaziabad. He shifted to Meerut in 1929 and later joined the Congress.

He was first elected to the U.P. Legislative Assembly in 1937 from Chhatrauli, and represented the constituency in 1946, 1952, 1962 and 1967. He became Parliamentary Secretary in Pandit Govind Ballabh Pant's Government in 1946 and worked in various departments such as Revenue, Medical and Public Health, Justice, Information etc. In June 1951, he was appointed Cabinet Minister in the State and given charge of the Departments of Justice and Information. Later he took over as the Minister for Revenue and Agriculture in the Cabinet of Dr. Sampurnanand in 1952. When he resigned in April 1959, he was holding charge of the Department of Revenue and Transport.

In Shri C.B. Gupta's Ministry he was Minister for Home and Agriculture (1960). Shri Charan Singh served as Minister for Agriculture and Forests (1962-63) in Smt. Sucheta Kripalani's Ministry. He gave up the Department of Agriculture in 1965 and assumed charge of the Local Self-government department in 1966. In Shri C.B. Gupta's Ministry he was Minister for Home and Agriculture (1960). Shri Charan Singh served as Minister for Agriculture and Forests (1962-63) in Smt. Sucheta Kripalani's Ministry. He gave up the Department of Agriculture in 1965 and assumed charge of the Local Self-government department in 1966.

After the Congress split, he became the Chief Minister of U.P. for the second time in February 1970 with the support of the Congress Party. However, President's Rule was imposed in the State on October 2, 1970. Shri Charan Singh served Uttar Pradesh in various capacities and won a reputation as a hard taskmaster who would not tolerate inefficiency, nepotism and corruption in administration. A gifted parliamentarian and a pragmatist, Shri Charan Singh is known for his eloquence and courage of conviction.

He was the chief architect of land reforms in U.P.; he took a leading part in formulation and finalisation of the Dept. Redemption Bill 1939, which brought great relief to rural debtors. It was also at his initiative that the salaries and other privileges enjoyed by Ministers in U.P. were drastically reduced. As Chief Minister he was instrumental in bringing about the Land Holding Act 1960 which was aimed at lowering the ceiling on land holdings to make it uniform throughout the State.

Few political leaders in the country could match Shri Charan Singh in their command of popular will at the grass-roots level. A dedicated public worker and staunch believer in social justice, Shri Charan Singh's strength stemmed essentially from the confidence he enjoyed among millions of peasants. Chaudhary Charan Singh led a simple life and spent his spare time reading and writing. He was the author of several books and pamphlets, including 'Abolition of Zamindari', 'Co-operative Farming X-rayed', 'India's Poverty and its Solution', 'Peasant Proprietorship or Land to the Workers' and 'Prevention of Division of Holdings Below a Certain Minimum'.

Chowmahalla Palace : Chowmahalla Palace was once the centre of Hyderabad, India. It was the seat of the Asaf Jahi dynasty where the Nizam entertained his official guests and royal visitors. The palace is unique for its style and elegance. Building began in the late 18th Century and over the decades a synthesis of many architectural styles and influences emerged. The palace originally covered 45 acres but only 14 acres remain. This complex today consists of two courtyards with elegant palaces, the grand Khilwat (the Durbar Hall), fountains and gardens.

Christianity : The followers of Jesus Christ are called Christians. Christianity has the largest number of followers in the world. Jerusalem, the place where Christ lived and preached is considered to be the most sacred for Christians all over the world.

Chuadanga : Chuadanga, Chuadanga district or Chuadanga Zilla is the name of a Western district (Zilla) of Bangladesh. It is a part of the Khulna administrative division that covers most districts in the south-west of the country. Records of the Greek historians and geographical formations show that this region was a part of the Kingdom of Gangaridhi and there was a city called Gangey here. During the War of Liberation in 1971 early resistance was put up in Chuadanga. During the Bangladesh Liberation War more than one hundred documented direct encounters took place between the Pakistan Army and the freedom fighters (Mukti Bahini) in Chuadanga district. According to records Chuadanga was liberated from the hands of occupying Pakistan army on 13 December 1971, three days before the invading army officially surrendered to the Mitro Bahini (allied forces of Mukti Bahini and Indian Army).

Marks of the Liberation War genocide in the district include a spot behind the Chuadanga Central Hospital, three mass graves at places on the back of the Natudaha High School, at village Dhopakhali near the Jibannagar border and on the bank of GK Canal near Alamdanga Railway Station. Two memorial monuments stand today in memory of the war. Chuadanga was separated from Kushtia and given the status of a district in 1984.

Chumb : Chumb is an area of Pakistan, near the southern tip of Kashmir. Here are people from various ethnic groups such as Gujjars, Bakerwals, Pashtuns and Mughals. The people are commonly known as Pathans by neighbouring Punjabis due to their much fairer complexions. A Baraderi system is prevailent throughout the region, and matters are taken into family leader hands. Blue, green and hazel coloured eyes are extremely common, as well as ginger, brunette, black and sandy blond hair colour. The inhabitants of this area have strong spiritual beliefs much like the rest of Pakistan and they visit dargahs regularly. Generally Pahari is spoken, but, Pushto, Gojri and Patwari are also spoken.

The people are mostly farmers. Migrants from Indian occupied Kashmir live here mostly. Many neighbouring Kashmiri regions as well as Punjabi regions reckon the origins of the Chackmerry community in Chumb are descendants of early Turkish settlers who have arrived here from Rajauri in India. They have extremely fair features and are unique in their way of life which revolves around religious contemplation. They have semitic features and can be very beautiful in appearance both males and females alike. Many of these inhabitants support the union of Kashmir state with Pakistan as they are culturally similar to Pakistan.

Chumbi Valley : Chumbi Valley is a valley in Tibet at the intersection of India (Sikkim), Bhutan and Tibet in the Himalayas. Two main passes between India and China open up here: the Nathula Pass and Jelepla Pass. The valley is at an altitude of 3,000 metres (9,500 feet) and was at the forefront of the British mission of 1904 into Tibet. The valley blooms in spring. It enjoys a temperate climate.

Churaman : Churaman (1695 – 1721) was Zamindar of Sinsini and the real founder of Jat state of Bharatpur in Rajasthan, India. He was son of Bhajja Singh and younger brother of Raja Ram. He was the first unanimously elected leader of Jats in 1695. He made Jats a political power in India.

After the untimely death of Raja Ram in the war of Bijal between Shekhawats and Chauhans on 4th July 1688, old father of Raja Ram, Bhajja Singh became the leader of Jats. Aurangzeb played a trick. He appointed Raja Bishan Singh of Amber as Faujdar of Mathura. Kachwahas were bent upon to subjugate the Jats, who were fighting for freedom from Mughal rule. Bishan Singh gave a written promise to destroy the fort of Sinsini. Mughal and Rajput armies jointly attacked Sinsini and captured it after a struggle of five months, in the month of January 1690. In this war 200 Mughals and 700 Rajputs were killed against 1500 Jats.

Church of Mae de Deus at Saligao (Bardez) : Built in 1873, is situated amidst picturesque surroundings in Goa. The shrine of the miraculous statue of Mae de Deus (Mother of God) was brought from the ruins of the convent of Mae de Deus at Old Goa. This beautiful church is the finest piece of gothic style. The Church is well illuminated at night.

Chutiya Kingdom : The Chutiya kingdom was established by Chauhan's in 1187 in northeastern Assam, with the capital at Sadiya. The Chutiya are an indigenous ethnic group that speak a alien Tibeto-Burman language. According to tradtition, Birpal at first became the chief of sixty families.

The most illustrious of the Chutiya kings was Gauri Narayan (Ratnadhwajpal), son of Birpal. He brought many other Chutiya groups into his kingdom. In 1224 Dhawal defeated Bhadrasena, the king of Swetagiri. Then he went on to subjugate Nyayapal and marched toward Kamatapur, where he formed an alliance with the Kamata ruler by marrying a princess. The he marched to Dhaka, and camped some distance away from the city. Though records exist of this expedition, there is no account of a war at Dhaka.

The hostilities with the Ahoms began in 1376 when he Ahom king, Sutupha, was killed by the Chutiya king during a friendly encounter. The simmering dispute offen flared until 1522 when the Ahoms finally took Sadiya and killed the then king Nityapal. The Ahoms established their rule by instituting the position of Sadiyakhowa Gohain, the governor in charge of Sadiya. But the Chutiya had dispersed to frontier regions, and continued raids against the Ahoms. This finally stopped in 1673 when the Chutiyas finally accepted Ahom overlordship.

Chutney : In Indian cuisine, a chutney (British spelling), chatni (Hindi transliteration) or catni (archaic transliteration) is a term for a variety of sweet and spicy condiments, originally from eastern India. In its homeland, a chutney is often made to be eaten fresh, using whatever suitable strongly flavoured ingredients are locally traditional or available at the time. It would not normally contain preserving agents, since it is intended to be consumed soon after preparation.

The Hindi word equivalent of "to make chutney" is also commonly used to signify "to crush." This is because the process of making chutney often involves the crushing together of the ingredients. In fact, the use of a stone chutney maker is often regarded as vital to create the ideal chutney. Chutney is more familiar in North America and Europe in a form that can be stored. To this end, vegetable oil, vinegar or lemon juice are used to enhance the keeping properties.

Cilappatikaram : Cilappatikaram (The Anklet) or Silappadhigaram, is one of the five great epics of ancient Tamil Literature. It was written by Prince Ilango Adigal, brother of king Cheran Chenguttuvan (in modern day Kerala), in South India. Prince Ilango Adigal wrote Cilappadhikaram as an epic. It is a record of the lives of the Tamils of second century AD. Cilappatikaram teaches three eternal truths. 1. A king failing in his duty will be punished by dharma or justice. 2. A chaste woman will be worshipped by all. 3. Fate is powerful. Ones past actions will have their repercussions in the next birth.

Cilappatikaram was written towards the end of second century AD. The story is rooted in the ordinary lives of the early Tamils. It is only one of three surviving Great Epics. No texts survive from either of the first two sangams. Coupling this extraordinary rarity with rich cultural information makes Cilappatikaram irreplaceably valuable in understanding ancient Tamil culture. The story narrates the events in three kingdoms : Chera (western), Chola (eastern), and Pandian (in the middle of South India). The story is full of information about contemporary events and personalities. From Sri Lanka, Gajabahu the

First and Ellara the just Tamil ruler of Sri Lanka are first mentioned in this Epic only.

Cis-Sutlej States : The Cis-Sutlej states were a group of Sikh states in modern Punjab and Haryana states of northwestern India, lying between the Sutlej River on the north, the Himalaya on the west, the Yamuna River and Delhi District on the south, and Sirsa District on the west.

During the Second Anglo-Maratha War of 1803-1805, some of the states in the region gave their allegiance to General Gerard Lake. At the conclusion of the war, the frontier of British India was extended to the Yamuna, and an 1809 agreement with Ranjit Singh, ruler of the Sikh Empire west of the Sutlej, brought the states under formal British protection.

The Cis-Sutlej states included Kaithal, Patiala, Jind, Thanesar, Maler Kotla, and Faridkot. Before 1846 the greater part of this territory was independent, the chiefs being subject to supervision from a political officer stationed at Umballa, and styled the agent of the Governor-General of India for the Cis-Sutlej states. A number of states were confiscated, or acquired by Britain under the Doctrine of Lapse. After the First Anglo-Sikh War the full administration of the territory became vested in this officer. In 1849 the Punjab was annexed to British India, when the Cis-Sutlej states commissionership, comprising the districts of Umballa, Ferozepore, Ludhiana, Thanesar and Simla, was incorporated with the new Punjab Province.

The name continued to be applied to this division until 1862, when, owing to Ferozepore having been transferred to Lahore Division, and a part of Thanesar to Delhi Division, it ceased to be appropriate. The remaining tract became known as the Umballa division. The princely states of Patiala, Jind, and Nabha were appointed a separate political agency in 1901. Excluding Bahawalpur, for which there was no political agent, and Chamba, the other states were grouped under the commissioners of Jullunder and Delhi, and the superintendent of the Simla hill states.

Citra Vishweswaran : Chitra Vishweswaran is famed as one of the leading Bharatnatyam dancers of India.

A competent performer, teacher and choreographer, she heads her own dance institution, 'Chidambaram Academy of Performing Arts (CAPA)', at Chennai.

City Districts of Pakistan : A City District in Pakistan is a District that consists primarily or entirely of a major city or large metropolitan area. While there are 117 Districts, there are only ten City Districts. A city district may contain subdivisions called Towns and Union Councils.

City Forest National Park : The park has an area of 9.07sq.km.and is located in the proximity of the capital city of Srinagar. The Srinagar airport is 12km from the park. The fauna found are hangul, serow etc. The birds are Chakar, monal, snow cock. April to October is the best period to visit the park.

CityCell : CityCell (Pacific Bangladesh Telecom Limited) is the first mobile communications company of Bangladesh. It is the only CDMA network operator in the country.

Clifton Beach : Clifton Beach, on the Arabian Sea, is a beach in the port city of Karachi, Pakistan. The beach has attractions for families and tourists, including beachside horse and camel rides, amusement parks, restaurants, and swimming in the Arabian Sea. Other beaches close to the city include Sandspit, Hawke's Bay, and Paradise Point—a sandstone rock promontory with a natural arch, but Clifton Beach is the most popular picnic destination in Karachi.

C N Annadurai : C. N.Annadurai (1909 to 1969), popularly called Anna (which means elder brother in Tamil language) was the first non Congress Chief Minister of Tamil Nadu, India. He was also an accomplished writer and even before his entry into politics his penmanship and the oratorial style had captivated many audiences. His mother tongue was Tamil. He belongs to a tamil community called Mudaliyars.

C Narayanareddy : Dr. Cingireddy(Singireddy But his associaation with telugu made him to keep c instead of S as initials) Narayana Reddy aka C Na Re received the prestigious Jnanpith Award in 1988 for his contribution to Telugu literature. Dr. C. Narayanareddy was born on July 29th, 1931 at Hanumajipeta, a remote village in the interior of Karimnagar district. He completed his Master's degree and Ph.D. degree in Telugu literature from Osmania University. He worked in Osmania University as a professor and attained very high positions and earned many awards. It could be surprising to learn that Dr.CNR studied in Urdu medium till his graduation. Dr.CNR is the only Telugu person who has received Jnanpith Award other than Sri Vishwanadha Sathyanarayana. He was nominated to the Rajya Sabha later. Students of Dr.CNR are often heard recollecting his grip over the language, especially his poetry reading sessions. He is also popular by virtue of being a lyricist to several famous Telugu films. The Government of India honoured him with the Padma Shri in 1977 and the second highest civilian award, the Padma Vibhushan in 1992.

Coastal Andhra : Coastal Andhra is an unofficial region of India's Andhra Pradesh state. Coastal Andhra includes the northern coastal districts of Andhra Pradesh between the Eastern Ghats and the Bay of Bengal, from the northern border with Orissa to south of the delta of the Krishna River. It generally includes the districts of

Guntur, Krishna, East Godavari, West Godavari, Visakhapatnam, Vizianagaram, and Srikakulam, and often Prakasam and Nellore. Coastal Andhra's relative prosperity is the envy of political movements seeking to form separate states for the two other major regions of Andhra Pradesh, the Telangana region in the northwest and the Rayalaseema region of the southwest.

Cochin Jews : Cochin Jews, also called Malabar Jews are the ancient Jews and their descendants of the South Indian port city of Cochin. They traditionally spoke Judeo-Malayalam, a form of the Malayalam tongue, native to the state of Kerala, in India. Several rounds of immigration of the Jewish diaspora into Kerala led to a diversity amongst the Cochin Jews.

Today most of Cochin's Jews have emigrated (principally to Israel). Large groups have settled in the town of Nevatim in the Negev (southern Israel) and in the neighborhood of Katamon in Jerusalem. In both places there are Cochin Jewish synagogues. In Kerala there are still three synagogues; the one at Mattancherry, Cochin is still functioning. Another reason why there was a reduction in Jewish population in old times was conversion to Christianity. Both during the time of St. Thomas in Kerala and later, many Jews joined the Nasrani people in Kerala. They intermingled especially with the Knanaya Christian-Jews within the Nasrani community of Kerala.

Coimbatore : Coimbatore also referred to as Kovai is one of the major industrial cities in South India and is a very small city in the state of Tamil Nadu. It is the administrative headquarters of Coimbatore district. It is well known for its textile industry and its engineering colleges. Coimbatore is known for its industrial hub, educational institutions, health care facilities, pleasant weather, friendly culture and hospitality. (Coimbatore is called City of Hospitals and Colleges) There is also a significant minority of people of North and West Indian origin in Coimbatore. People here are highly enterprising and industrious, which is one of the reasons cited for its phenomenal industrial growth. The nearest major cities are Chennai, Bangalore, Madurai which are 500 km, 335 km and 210 km from Coimbatore, respectively. Coimbatore city is well connected by rail, road and air.

Colachael : This place was the scene of the battle between the Travancore (Anglicised form of Thiruvithamkode) forces led by King Marthanda Varma (1729 - 1758) and the Dutch East India Company forces led by Admiral Eustatius De Lennoy on August 10, 1741.

The Dutch marines landed in Colachael with artillery and captured the land up to Padmanabhapuram, the then capital of Travancore. The arrival of Marthanda Varma's army from the north forced the Dutch to take up defensive positions in Colachael, where they were attacked and defeated by the Travancore forces. 28 high level Dutch officers, including Admiral D'lennoy, were captured. The defeat of the Dutch in Colachael was the turning point of the Travancore-Dutch war which had started in 1739, when Marthanda Varma annexed the domains of the native allies of the Dutch. D'lennoy went on to serve Marthanda Varma for the next two decades and was promoted to the post of the Valiya kapptithan (Senior Admiral) of the Travancore forces. He modernised the Travancore army, and built the Nedumkotta, a line of fortifications in the North of the kingdom, which held up the army of Tipu Sultan in 1791, during his ill-fated invasion of Travancore. D'lennoy is buried in the Udayagiri Fort, also known as Dillanai kotta (D'lennoy's fort) which is located 7 Km north of Padmanabhapuram.

The Indian government has built a pillar of victory in Colachael to commemorate the event. Colachael is currently in the Kanya Kumari District of the Tamil Nadu State of

India, and is an important port on the West Coast of that state.

College of Digital Sciences : College of Digital Sciences, more commonly known as CDS was established in 1988 with a vision of establishing an institution in Pakistan which could train IT professionals of international standards locally. The College offers Diploma and Degree level course in Information Technology fields with the affilications of National Computing Center (NCC) UK now known as NCC Education Ltd, and London Metropolitan University which was previously known as London Guildhall University.

Comilla Model : Comilla Model a rural development approach that originated and developed in a training-cum-research institution called the bangladesh academy for rural development (BARD) located on the outskirts of Comilla district town. The approach drew its name from that of the place of its origin. akhter hameed khan, pioneer of the Comilla Model and the first director of the Academy, conceived of the idea and developed the method of its implementation in the areas of agricultural and rural development on the principle of people's participatory role at the grassroots level and cooperatives.

Commerial Museum : Guwahati University has a commercial Museum with a collection of art and crafts, commercial products, minerals and rocks, coins etc. The museum is open daily, from 12.30am to 6.30pm. Closed on Sundays and University holidays.

Commission on Science and Technology for Sustainable Development in the South (COMSATS) : The Commission on Science and Technology for Sustainable Development in the South (COMSATS) is an international organization. It aims to reduce the ever-growing gap between the developed and developing world through useful applications of science and technology. The Third World Academy of Sciences (TWAS) initiated the proposal for the formation of COMSATS under the leadership of Nobel Laureate, Dr. Abdus Salam.The foundation-conference of COMSATS was held at Islamabad, Pakistan on 4th and 5th October 1994. Representatives from thirty-six countries attended. The participants included twenty-two Ministers, members of the diplomatic community of Islamabad and representatives of international organizations, like UNESCO, UNIDO, UNEP and the World Bank

Common Indian Toad : The Common Indian Toad Bufo melanostictus is a species of toad that is quite common in most parts of India. The species grows to almost 20 cm long. The species breeds during the monsoons and the tadpoles are black. Young toads may be seen in large numbers after the monsoons. These toads are often seen at night under street lamps especially during times when winged termites swarm.

Communist Mazdoor Kissan Party : Communist Mazdoor Kissan Party (Communist Workers Peasant Party), a political party in Pakistan formed in 1995 through the unification of Communist Party of Pakistan and Mazdoor Kissan Party. The CMKP, made up of mainly former MKP elements, later went back to calling their party MKP. In 2003 a group led by Sufi Abdul Khaliq Balooch broke away and formed a party called CMKP. This party today publishes the magazine Surkh Parcham(Red Flag).

Communist Party of India (CPI) : The Communist Party of India (CPI) is a political party in India. In the Indian communist movement, there are different views on exactly when the Indian communist party was founded. The date maintained as the foundation day by CPI is 26 December 1925. But the Communist Party of India (Marxist), which split-off from the CPI, claims that the party was founded in the USSR in 1920. During the 1920s and beginning of 1930s the party was badly organized, and in practice there were several communist groups working with limited national coordination. The British colonial authorities had banned all communist activity, which made the task of building a united party very difficult. Only in 1935 was the party ready to be accepted as the Indian section of the Communist Third International.

In connection with the change of policy of the Comintern toward Popular Front politics, the Indian communists changed their relation to the Indian National Congress. The communists joined the Congress Socialist Party (CSP), the left wing of Congress. In Kerala communists won control over CSP, and for a brief period controlled Congress there. During the Second World War, there were drastic changes for the Indian communists. After that the USSR had sided with Britain in the war, the Communist Party of India was legalized for the first time. Communists strengthened their control over the All India Trade Union Congress. At the same time, communists were politically cornered for their opposition to the Quit India Movement. In 1946 the party launched the Tebhaga movement in Bengal, a militant campaign against feudalism.

During the period around and directly following Independence in 1947, the internal situation in the party was chaotic. The party shifted rapidly between left-wing and right-wing positions. In 1948, at the 4th Party Congress in Palghat, B.T. Ranadive (BTR) was elected General Secretary of the party. In several areas the party led armed struggles against a series of local monarchs that were reluctant to give up their power. Such insurgencies took place in Tripura, Telangana and Kerala. The most important rebellion took place in Telangana, against the Nizam of Hyderabad. The communists built up a people's army and militia and controlled an area with a population of three million. The rebellion was brutally crushed and the party abandoned the policy of armed struggle. BTR was deposed and denounced as a 'left adventurist'. In the general elections in 1957, the CPI emerged as the largest opposition party. The internal split was sealed in 1964 when two different party conferences were held, one of CPI and one of the Communist Party of India (Marxist), and thus the party was split.

•

Communist Party of India (Marxist) or CPI(M), : The Communist Party of India (Marxist), or CPI(M), is a political party in India. It is strongest in the states of Kerala, West Bengal and Tripura. In West Bengal and Tripura states, as of 2004, it currently holds the government. It split from the Communist Party of India in 1964 because of what it describes as the latter's revisionism and sectarianism. CPI(M) got 5.66% of votes polled in last parliamentary election (May 2004) and it has 43 MPs. It won 42.31% on an average in the 69 seats it contested. It supports the new Indian National Congress-led United Progressive Alliance government, but without becoming a part of it. In West Bengal and Tripura it participates in the Left Front. In Kerala the party is part of the Left Democratic Front. In Tamil Nadu it is part of the Progressive Democratic Alliance. The current general secretary of CPI(M) is Prakash Karat. The CPI(M) MP Somnath Chatterjee is the speaker of the Lok Sabha (2004). The 18th party congress of CPI(M), held in Delhi April 6-11 2005 elected a Central Committee with 85 members.

Communist Party of Pakistan : Communist Party of Pakistan, a communist political party in Pakistan. CPP was founded in Calcutta (India) on March 6, 1948. A decision was taken at the Second All India Conference of Communist Party of India, which was held in Calcutta at that time, that a separate communist party ought to be created in the new state Pakistan. The thesis was that Pakistan, being a small (in comparison to India) and unstable country was ripe for revolution. The delegate from Pakistan separated themselves and held a separate session were they constituted the CPP. Sajjad Zaheer (founder, All India Progressive Writers Association), from West Pakistan, was elected General Secretary. The delegates from East Pakistan elected an East Pakistan Provincial Committee. Many muslim leaders of CPI were sent to Pakistan to help the build-up of the party there. In 1995 the CPP merged with the MKP to form Communist Mazdoor Kisan Party. The CPP accepted the criticism that they had been too uncritical towards the Soviet Union. In 1999 a group broke away and reconstituted the CPP. In 2002, the CPP split, leading to the existence of two separate CPPs, one led by Maula Bux Khaskheli and the splinter-group led by Khadim Thaheem.

Company Bagan : Company Bagan was built by the nawabs of Dhaka on the western side of dilkusha and bangabhaban. The garden spread over the area of the present day Motiur Shishu Park, the Stadium, Baitul Mukarram, GPO and adjacent areas. In these areas, Paltan was a cantonment of east india company. In 1840, the cantonment was shifted and the area came under the control of Dhaka Municipality. In 1874 khwaja ahsanullah, nawab of Dhaka, got permission from the governor of Bengal to establish a garden at Paltan.

After the shifting of the cantonment, the Purana Paltan area became desolate and soon the outskirt of the Company Garden became a jungle. On 14 July 1888, Nawab Ahsanullah got approval from the Municipality to develop the adjacent areas of the garden. The area was soon transformed into a wide terrain by cleaning the copses and filling low-lying areas. Consequently, the environment of the Company Garden improved. One piece of land of this area was used as a playground.

In 1905, when Dhaka became the capital of East Bengal and Assam, the government took permanent lease of the southern side of Company Garden and Dilkusha Garden of the Nawabs in order to build Government Offices and Courts. During the fall of the Nawabs, Company Garden lost its lustre due to lack of maintenance. Parts of the garden were sold off in course of time. Later, various institutions were set up in almost all areas of the Company Garden, during 1960s a part was named 'Ayub Children Park'. Now it is known as 'Matiur Children Park'.

Connaught Place : Connaught Place (officially called Rajiv Chowk, but referred to as C.P. by Delhiites) is a central business district of New Delhi, India. It is instantly recognisable on any map of Delhi, being the big circle in the middle with radial roads spreading out in all directions, like spokes on a wheel. Although Connaught Place appears to be a logically planned area, specific shops have become frustratingly hard to find due to the various one way streets and heavy traffic. The centre circle (there are three) and Palika Bazaar are undergoing a lot of construction due to the introduction of the New Delhi Metro system. Connaught Place's obvious Victorian architecture is modeled after the Royal Crescent in Bath, England.

Constituent Assembly of India : The Constituent Assembly of India was elected to write the Constitution of India, and served as its first Parliament as an independent nation. It was elected by millions of Indian adults and by universal suffrage. It first met on December 9, 1946 in Delhi, while India was still under British rule. It originally included the provinces that now compose Pakistan, and the representation of the princely states of India. In June 1947, the delegations from the provinces of Sindh, East Bengal, Baluchistan, West Punjab and the North West Frontier Province formed the Constituent

Assembly of Pakistan in Karachi. On August 15, 1947, India became an independent nation, and the Constituent Assembly became Indîa's Parliament. Dr. Rajendra Prasad was the President of the Constituent Assembly, and would later became the first President of India.

The Assembly, much like the modern Parliament system, was divided into committees and sub-committees to deal with specific branches of government. Dr. B.R. Ambedkar served as the Chairman of the Drafting Committee, responsible for writing the Constitution. India's political leaders such as Jawaharlal Nehru, Sardar Patel, Purushottam Das Tandon and others were all members of this Assembly.

Members of the Constituent Assembly also varied across the political spectrum - Communists, Socialists, former Raj loyalists and Indian conservatives. The Assembly approved the Constitution on January 26, 1949, making it official. On January 26, 1950, the Constitution took effect - a day now commemorated as Republic Day nationwide. At this point, the Constituent Assembly became the Provisional Parliament of India, until the first elections under the new Constitution took place in 1952.

Constituent Assembly of Pakistan : The Constituent Assembly of Pakistan was formed to write Pakistan's constitution, and serve as its first parliament. It first convened on 11 August 1947, just days before the end of British rule on August 14, 1947. It had mostly completed the process of writing the constitution when it was dissolved on October 24, 1954. After fresh elections were held, it was reconstituted on May 28, 1955 lasting until March 23, 1956 when the new constitution came into place and Pakistan became a Republic.

Constitution of Bangladesh : The constitution of Bangladesh is the supreme law in Bangladesh. Following the Bangladesh Liberation War of 1971, Bangladesh became independent on December 16, 1971. After the independence, the first constituent assembly was formed by the lawmakers from Awami League who were previously elected in East Pakistan provincial assembly in the Pakistani election of 1970. The constitution of Bangladesh was adopted by the Constituent Assembly on 4 November 1972. It came into effect from 16 December 1972, on the first anniversary of the victory day. The constitution of Bangladesh is divided into 11 parts, which are further subdivided into 153 articles. In addition, there are 4 schedules.

Constitution of India : The Constitution of India is the constitution of the Republic of India. It was passed by the Constituent Assembly on November 26, 1949, and came into effect on January 26, 1950. India celebrates January 26 each year as Republic Day. It is the longest written constitution of any independent nation in the world, containing 395 articles and 12 schedules for a total of 117,369 words in its English language version.

The Constitution lays down the basic structure of government under which the people are to be ruled. It establishes the main organs of government - the executive, the legislature and the judiciary. The Constitution not only defines the powers of each organ, but also demarcates their responsibilities. It regulates the relationship between the different organs and between the government and the people. The Constitution is superior to all other laws of the country. Every law enacted by the government has to be in conformity with the Constitution. The Constitution lays down the national goals of India - Democracy, Socialism, Secularism and National Integration. It also spells out the rights and duties of citizens

Constitution of Pakistan : There have been several documents known as the Constitution of Pakistan. These will be dealt with here in chronological order. The 1973 Constitution provided for a parliamentary system with a President as head of state and popularly elected Prime Minister as head of government. However, in 1988 the Eighth Amendment made Pakistan's government a Semi-presidential system. Pakistan has a bicameral legislature that consists of the Senate (upper house) and the National Assembly (lower house). Together with the President, the Senate and National Assembly make up a body called the Majlis-i-Shoora (Council of Advisors) or Parliament.

The first major step in framing a constitution was the passage by the Constituent Assembly of the Objectives Resolution of March 1949, which defined the basic principles of the new state. Seven years of debate, however, failed to produce agreement on fundamental issues such as regional representation or the structure of a constitution. This impasse prompted Governor General Ghulam Mohammad to dismiss the Constituent Assembly in 1954. The Supreme Court of Pakistan upheld the action of the Governor General, arguing that he had the power to disband the Constituent Assembly and veto legislation it passed. This preeminence of the Governor General over the legislature has been referred to as the viceregal tradition in Pakistan's politics.

The revived Constituent Assembly promulgated Pakistan's first indigenous constitution in 1956 and reconstituted itself as the national legislature—the Legislative Assembly—under the constitution it adopted. Pakistan became an Islamic republic. The Governor General was replaced by a President.

Zulfiqar Ali Bhutto, Prime minister from 1971 to 1977, lifted martial law within several months after his election, and after an "interim constitution" granting him broad powers as President, a new constitution was promulgated in April 1973 and came into effect on August 14 of that year, the twenty-sixth anniversary of the country's independence. With reagard to provincial rights the 1973 constitution was in fact the most centralised of Pakistan's various constitutions. The Government of India Act 1935; that Pakistan adopted as its first working constitution gave the federation 96 items of powers. The 1956 constitution reduced it to 49. This number was retained in the 1962 constitution but in 1973 it was enlarged to a massive 114. In 2003 an amendment to the Constitution of Pakistan (The Constitution (Seventeenth Amendment) Act, 2003) was passed, after over a year of political wrangling between supporters and opponents of Pakistani President Pervez Musharraf. This amendment made many changes to Pakistan's constitution. Many of these changes dealt with the office of the President and the reversal of the effects of the Thirteenth Amendment.

Cooch Behar : Cooch Behar is a district of the state of West Bengal, India, as well as the name of the town which gives its name to the district. During the British Raj, the town of Cooch Behar was the seat of a princely state of the same name, ruled by the Narayan dynasty. In course of time, Cooch Behar has been transformed from a kingdom to a State and from a State to the present status of a district. Before 28 August 1949, Cooch Behar was a Princely State ruled by the king of Cooch Behar, who had been a feudatory ruler under British Government. By an agreement dated 28th August, 1949 the king of Cooch Behar ceded full and extensive authority, jurisdiction and power of the state to the Dominion Government of India. The transfer of administration of the state to the Govt. of India came into force on 12 September 1949. Eventually, Cooch Behar was transferred and merged with the province of West Bengal on 19 January 1950 and from that date Cooch Behar emerged as a new District in the administrative map of West Bengal.

Cool Drink : Cool drink is a term used to refer to soft drinks or sodas in South India. In the north, they are referred to as 'Cold drinks.' Popular examples of such drinks include Limca, Mirinda and Thums Up, as well as the sodas, sold by multinational corporations, which those drinks were intended to replace, like RC Cola, Fanta, Coca-Cola and Pepsi. Other popular drinks in India include the fruit drinks Maaza and Frooti, as well as lassis of various flavors, falooda, sugarcane juice, and various fruit juices.

Coonoor : Coonoor is a small quiet hill town in the Nilgiri hills in Southern India. It has a reputation for being a reality-defying idyllic Shangri-La of sorts. However, the growing networked economy, and the rampant influx of tourists to the region in the past few decades have eroded this image of Coonoor to some degree.

Coonoor's economy relies primarily on the seasonal tourist traffic during the summer months, and on the tea industry year round. The town is the second largest in the Nilgiri hills after Ooty, the district head quarters. The local populace almost entirely depends on the tea trade.Floriculture and STRAWBERRY cultivation are taking root oflate .The massive private tea plantations that surround the hills produce fresh green tea leaves which are picked, processed and packaged in bulk in local factories, for sale at auction houses in Coonoor, Coimbatore and Cochin.

Coonoor's dominant demographic is a healthy mix of religions, languages and cultures—caused by the tourists who decide to retire here, the Indian Army's regimental headquarters and Staff College (DSSC) in neighboring Wellington, and the local boarding schools. Christianity is a dominant minority religion, with many locals practicing Christianity along with Hinduism or Islam. The photograph of the Coonoor bazaar is a testament to the economic divide that is as much a part of Coonoor, as it is of India. The market, composed mostly of small traders in the foreground is an unplanned mess, the distant hills in the background are home to many of the affluent elite.

Corbett National Park : Previously known as the Hailey National park, this park is situated in Kalagarh and Ramnagar Forest Divisions in Garhwal and Nainital districts. It spread over an area of 521sq.km. and has the distinction of being the first National park of the country. It was set up in 1931. The nearest town and the railhead is Ramnagar, 19km away from the park. The nearest airport is Pholbagh (District Nainital) at a distance of 80km.

The legendary land of Jim Corbett is a paradise for nature lovers. It covers the majestic ranges of the Himalayas. Patlidoon bordering the river Ramganga and undulating Shivaliks with flat plains known as "Chaurs". Here is a dynamic ecosystem with a variety of cover and trees of Sal, Khair, Kisson, etc. capable of sustaining diverse fauna.

Coringa Wild Life Sanctuary : Coringa Wild Life Sanctuary in Andhra pradesh is situated 20 Kms from Kakinada and 70 Kms from Rajahmundry, this sanctuary is a part of river Godavari and has a rich growth of Mangrove plantation.

Coromandel Coast : The Coromandel Coast is the name given to the southeastern coast of the Indian peninsula. It is generally thought to be derived from the Tamil phrase Chola Mandal, or the region (mandalam) of the Chola, an ancient dynasty of southern India. Historically the Coromandel Coast generally referred to the stretch of coast between Point Calimere (Kodikkarai), near the delta of the Kaveri River, north to the mouths of the Krishna River. Presently the Coromandel Coast is shared by the states of Tamil Nadu, Andhra Pradesh and the union territory of Pondicherry

Cotigao Wildlife Sanctuary : Cotigao Wildlife Sanctuary is located in the Canacona takula (or district) of Goa, in India. Founded in 1969, this is the second largest sanctuary in Goa. I Is noted for it's array of not just animal but it's plant biodiversity as well. The ancient Jeevottam Partagal Math, known for their vedic studies make their home in the forests. Also the Kunbi and Velip tribal communities still live in the forests.

Council for the Indian School Certificate Examinations (CISCE) : The Council for the Indian School Certificate Examinations is a board of school education in India, like the CBSE. It conducts two examinations in India: for the Indian Certificate of Secondary Education and for the Indian School Certificate. The CISCE was set up in 1956 at the meeting of the Inter-State Board for Anglo-Indian Education a proposal was adopted for the setting up of an Indian Council to administer the University of Cambridge Local Examinations Syndicate's Examinations in India. It is an all-India, but not a government affiliated board (unlike the CBSE). Both CBSE and the CISCE more of less follow a similar pattern of education, though there might be significant differences in some areas. It is based in New Delhi.

Council of Scientific & Industrial Research (CSIR) : CSIR is a national Research & Development organisation in India. It is funded mainly by the Science Ministry of India. The R & D activities of CSIR covers various fields such as aerospace engineering, ocean sciences, molecular biology, metallurgy, chemicals, mining, food, petroleum, leather, and environment. The current Director General of CSIR is Dr. Raghunath A. Mashelkar. CSIR celebrates its Foundation Day on 26th September.

Covert Operations : There were a couple of covert operations launched by the Pakistan Army to infiltrate Indian airbases and sabotage them. The SSG (Special Services Group) commandos were parachuted into enemy territory and, according to the then Chief of Army Staff General Musa Khan, more than 180 commandos penetrated the enemy territory for this purpose. Indian sources however claim as many as 800-900 commandos were airdropped, though the figure is for the whole war. Given that most of the Indian targets (Halwara, Pathankot and Adampur) were deep into enemy territory only 11-15 commandos made it back alive and the stealth operation proved ineffective. Of those remaining, 136 were taken prisoner, and 22 were killed in encounters with the army, police or the civilians. The daring attempt proved to be a disaster with the Commander of the operations, Major Khalid Butt too being arrested.

There have been only a few neutral assessments of the damages of the war. According to Global Security Organization, "The losses were relatively heavy—on the Pakistani side, twenty aircraft, 200 tanks, and 3,800 troops. Pakistan's army had been able to withstand Indian pressure, but a continuation of the fighting would only have led to further losses and ultimate defeat for Pakistan."

Cox's Bazar : Cox's Bazar in Bangladesh is the world's longest natural beach (120 km). It is located 152 km south of Chittagong. Cox's Bazar is also known by the name "Panowa", the literal translation of which means "yellow flower". Its other old name was "Palongkee". The modern Cox's Bazar derives its name from Lieutenant Cox (died 1798), an army officer serving in British India. It is also one of the fishing ports of Bangladesh.

Cripps' Mission : The 'Cripps' mission was an attempt in late March of 1942 by the British government to secure Indian cooperation and support for their efforts in World War II. The mission was headed by Sir Stafford Cripps, a senior Labour Party politician and government minister in the War Cabinet of Prime Minister Winston Churchill.

C Rajagopalachari : Chakravarthi Rajagopalachari (December 1878 - December 25, 1972), known as or Rajaji or C.R., was an Indian lawyer, writer, statesman and a Hindu spiritualist. He was the second Governor-General of independent India. Later he became the Chief Minister of Madras State.

At one time considered Mahatma Gandhi's heir, this brilliant lawyer from Salem, Tamil Nadu was regarded in pre-independence years as one of the top five leaders of the Congress 'along with Jawaharlal Nehru, Rajendra Prasad, Sardar Vallabhbhai Patel, and Maulana Abul Kalam Azad. Rajaji was also related to Mahatma Gandhi - Rajmohan Gandhi is the grandson of both of them. Of the five, Rajaji, Nehru and Patel were christened the "head, heart and hands" of Gandhi, in whose shadows they remained till his death.

Rajaji was perhaps the earliest Congress leader in the 1940s to admit to the likelihood of the Partition. After serving time in British prisons for his work in the independence movement, he became a member of the Governor's Council in 1946. In 1948, after Indian independence was attained, he replaced Mountbatten to become the only Indian Governor-General of India, in which post he continued till the Republic was declared on January 26, 1950. The office was replaced by that of President, first held by Rajendra Prasad.

Rajaji became a member of Jawaharlal Nehru's cabinet, first without portfolio, then, after Patel's death, as Home Minister. He was chief minister of Madras from 1952 to

1954. On leaving government, he was among the first recipients of the Bharat Ratna, the Indian government's highest civilian award. After his retirement from active Congress politics, C.R. became a strident critic of Nehru and the Congress. As a founder of the Swatantra party in the 1950s, he attacked the license-permit Raj fearing its potential for corruption and stagnation, even while the tide was in favour of Nehru's socialistic pattern.

As a writer, besides his own material, he published English translations of many important Indian and Hindu works: His translations of the Ramayana, Mahabharata, Bhagavad Gita, Upanishads and Bhaja Govindam remain the standard versions. He also translated the Ramayana into Tamil. The nonagenarian's public life, spanning nearly eighty years are perhaps best recognized by Mahatma Gandhi's rich tribute to him praising him as: "the keeper of my conscience".Rajaji died in December, 1972 after a short illness.

Crochet Lace : Introduced in the middle of the 19th Century in Andhra Pradesh to provide employment to the poverty-striken women of the area, lace work was, to start with, sent to friends and relatives abroad as gifts which were highly appreciated. Starting with a mere dozen designs, the local skills were used to evolve as many as 300 designs over the years which speaks of the high artistic sense of the artisans. The raw materials and implements required for this industry are simple, consisting of only a hooked needle and cotton thread. The thread used is twisted mercerised cotton yarn made out of superior grade cotton. The craft is carried on by thousands of women working part time at their homes in Narsapur and Palakol areas of West Godavari District and Razole Taluka of East Godavri District. Articles produced include those that are wholly lace, as well as those in which lace work is used as decorative insertions in cloth.

C Subramaniam : Chidambaram Subramaniam (commonly known as CS) (January 30, 1910—November 7, 2000), held ministerial positions at the State and the Centre. He was conferred the Bharat Ratna in 1998. He was elected to the Lok Sabha in 1962 and was the Minister for Steel and Mines. Subsequently, he handled important portfolios like agriculture in 1965 when he spearheaded the Green Revolution, and later the portfolios of Finance and Defence. He was a minister in Tamil Nadu before moving to the Centre. He was the finance minister during the emergency. He also worked as the deputy chairperson of the planning commission of India.

He was appointed the Governor of Maharashtra in 1992 and had to resign after a newspaper reporter overheard and published an informal remark of his criticising the style of functioning of the then Indian Prime Minister, Mr P.V. Narasimha Rao. Even after his resignation, he continued to be active in public life, associating himself with various institutions. During various periods, he headed the Bharatiya Vidya Bhavan and the Ramakrishna Mission.

Cubbon Park : Cubbon park was planned by Sir. Richard Sankey, the then chief Engineer of Mysore and named after Sir Mark Cubbon, Bangalore's longest serving commissioner. With in the sprawling cubbon park are situated the Attara Kacheri, the central library, the aquarium, the Jawahar bal bhavan with its mini theatre and toy train, the museum, VITM and KSLTA tennis court.

Cuddalore : Cuddalore is a large industrial city in the Tamil Nadu state of southern India. It is the headquarters of Cuddalore District. Located south of Pondicherry on the Bay of Bengal, Cuddalore has a large number of industries which employ a great deal of the city's population. However, one industrial pocket -SIPCOT—has also secured it a place in the dubious club of Global Toxic Hotspots owing to the area's high levels of popllution.

Cuddalore is well-known for its temples. The most famous of these is the temple of Shiva, one of the three prime deities of Hinduism. The incarnation of Shiva at Cuddalore is called Padaleeshwarar. The temple itself is located in Thiruppadirippuliyur. Chidambaram, a city which is known for dance and temples also, is only 43 km away from Cuddalore. Cuddalore's magnificent beaches are becoming a tourist attraction, especially the well-known Silver Beach. The boat house near the beach is known for its beauty.

Curzon Hall : Curzon Hall is part of the school of science of the University of Dhaka. Curzon Hall meant to be a town hall, was named after Lord Curzon, the Viceroy of India, who laid its foundation in 1904.

A year later Bengal was partitioned and Dhaka or Dacca as it was known then, became the capital of the newly created province of East Bengal and Assam. Following the annulment of partition in 1911 it was used as a premise of Dhaka College, and after the establishment of the University of Dhaka in 1921, became part of the university's science section and continues as such. Curzon Hall has attained great significance in the history of the Language Movement. It was here, in 1948, that students of Dhaka University uttered their first refusal to accept Mohammad Ali Jinnah's declaration that Urdu alone would be the state language of the whole of Pakistan.

Cuttack : Cuttack is one of the oldest cities in India and the Business Capital of Orissa. It is situated in a tongue of land formed by the river Mahanadi and its main branch the Kathajodi at their points of bifurcation in 20.29° N 85.52° E. It's actual pronunciation is 'Katak'. Cuttack is also the headquarters of Cuttack District. It lies near

Bhubaneswar, Puri and Konark. It is more than a thousand years old, and was the capital of Orissa for almost nine centuries, before Bhubaneswar was made the capital city. With its world famous unique filigree works in silver, ivory and brass works and textiles of woven silk and cotton, Cuttack is perhaps the grandest showroom of Orissa.

D

Dachigam National Park : Dachigam National Park, a place with abundant natural beauty is located 22km north east from Srinagar in the state of Jammu and Kashmir. It covers an area of 141 square kilometers with altitude ranging from 5500 ft to 14000 ft above mean sea level. Due to this variation, the park is differentiated as upper and lower Dachigam. The park has been a protected area since 1910, first under the care of the Maharaja of Jammu & Kashmir and later under the observation of the concerned government authorities. It was upgraded and declared a National Park in the year 1951.

Dadabhai Naoroji : Dadabhai Naoroji (4 September 1825–30 June 1917) was a Parsi intellectual and educator, and an early Indian political leader. He was a Member of Parliament in the Parliament of the United Kingdom between 1892 and 1895, and the first Asian to be a British MP. The son of Maneckbai and Naoroji Palanji Dordi, a poor Athornan Parsi family, Naoroji was educated at Elphinstone College and later became a teacher. By 1855 he was Professor of Mathematics and Natural philosophy. He moved to England in 1855, first working in business, later becoming professor of Gujarati at University College London.

In 1867 Naoroji helped establish the East India Association. In 1874 he became Prime Minister of Baroda and was also a member of the Legislative Council of Bombay (1885-88). He also founded the Indian National Association from Calcutta a few years before the founding of the Indian National Congress in Bombay, with the same objectives and practices. The two groups later merged into the INC, and Naoroji was elected President of the Congress in 1886.

Naoroji moved to Britain once again and continued his political involvement. Elected for the Liberal Party in Central Finsbury in July 1892, he was the first British Indian MP. He refused to take the oath on the Bible as he was not a Christian, but was allowed to take the oath of office in the name of God on his small book of Avesta. In Parliament he spoke on Irish Home Rule and the condition of the Indian people. In his political campaign and duties as an MP, he was assisted by Muhammed Ali Jinnah, the future Muslim nationalist and founder of Pakistan. In 1906, Naoroji was again elected president of the Indian National Congress. Naoroji was a staunch moderate within the Congress, during the phase when opinion in the party was split between the moderates and extremists. By the time of his death in 1917, Naoroji was known as the 'Grand Old Man of India', a mentor to Mahatma Gandhi. He was married to Gulbai from the age of eleven.

Dadasaheb Phalke Award : The Dadasaheb Phalke Award is an annual award given by the Indian government for lifetime contribution to Indian cinema. It was instituted in 1969, the birth centenary year of Dadasaheb Phalke, considered the father of Indian cinema. The award for a particular year is given during the end of the following year along with the National Film Awards.

Dadra and Nagar Haveli : Dadra and Nagar Haveli is a Union Territory in western India. Nagar Haveli is wedged between Maharashtra and Gujarat, whereas Dadra is an enclave lying a few km north of Nagar Haveli in Gujarat. Its capital is Silvassa. Dadra and Nagar Haveli are in the watershed of the Daman Ganga River, which flows through the territory.

The towns of Dadra and Silvassa both lie on the north bank of the river. The Western Ghats range rises to the east, and the foothills of the range occupy the eastern portion of the district. The territory is landlocked, although the Arabian Sea coast lies just to the west in Gujarat. It was a Portuguese colony, dependent of Daman, from 1779 until 1954 when it was occupied by India. It became a Union territory in 1961. The major spoken language in the territory is Gujarati. Manufacturing is the main economy in Dadra and Nagar Haveli as the taxes are low — no excise. The territory is run by a Lieutenant Governor.

Dahi : Dahi (Hindi and Urdu), doi (Bengali), or thayir (Tamil) is naturally cultured plain yoghurt widely consumed all over South Asia. It is consumed in a variety of ways—just plain, as a shake (lassi), a kind of dip (raita), a dessert (mishti doi), with rice (bagala bhath — thayir-sadam — mosroo-anna), and so on. It is also a very common ingredient in many recipes, as a souring agent (especially in Marwari cuisine), or as a base for marinades.

Dahi Vada : Dahi Vada is an Indian fast food, or chaat, prepared by soaking Vadas in thick yogurt. The hot deep fried vadas are first put in water and then transferred to thick beaten yogurt. For best results the vadas have to soak for at least a couple of hours before serving. To add more flavor it can be topped with mint leaves, crushed black pepper, curry powder, chaat masala, shredded coconuts, green chilli or boondi.

Dahipuri : Dahipuri, or Dahi puri, is a sort of of chaat that is based on the mini-puri shell used for its relatively more popular cousin, the pani puri, with which it is often offered in the same chaat stand.

The round, hard, puffy puri shell is first broken on top and partially filled with the main stuffing of mashed potatoes or chickpeas. A little haldi powder and/or chilli powder may be added for taste, as well as a pinch of salt. Sweet tamarind chutney and spicy green chutney are poured into the shell on top of the stuffing. Finally, sweetened beaten yoghurt is generously poured over the shell, and the finished product is garnished with sprinklings of crushed sev and finely chopped coriander leaves.

Dahi puri typically comes in a plate-sized order, consisting of 5 or 6 dahi puris per plate. Unlike pani puri, a plate of dahi puri is not served one morsel at a time, but all at once. A spoon is provided with each plate, and each dahi puri is intended to be eaten whole, like the pani puri, so that the spectrum of flavors and textures within may hit the mouth together for full effect.

Dahod : Dahod is a town in the Gujarat state of India. It is 200 km away from Ahmedabad and 150 km away from Vadodara. The famous Aurangzeb fort is here. It is located in Dahod District. Previously coming under the panchmahal district, now it is a proper district. The expansion of this small town into a bustling mini-city is commendable. The far flung area of Godi road, Godhra Road has been considerably developed, making the overall habitation and commercial area very expansive. Quite recently the foundation stone for dental college has been laid by the trust of the very esteemed philanthropist Shri Girdharlal Sheth, known as the Dahod Anaj Mahajan.

Dak Dance : Dak dance is a battle dance, popular in Manikganj. Its object is to call fellow warriors to battle. The team leader calls out that the enemy has launched an attack. At the call, a number of dancers come running onto the stage. This part of the dance is known as dak or call.

The second part is devoted to exhibiting martial skills with the help of sticks. The drum is the main musical instrument.

Dakatia River : Dakatia River is one of the trans-boundary rivers of Bangladesh. It enters the country from India's Tripura state at Bagsara of Comilla district. It is a tributary of the Meghna. The main source of flow of this river was the Kakrai, but the Little Feni cuts back and captured its upper portion. The Dakatia now has its source in Chauddagram Khal, which connects it with the Little Feni. The Dakatia sends out a channel southward, which forms the Noakhali Khal. The main channel meanders westward to Shekherhat, from where the old course goes south to join the Meghna at Raipur, and the new and stronger channel passes through Chandpur Khal to join the Meghna west of Chandpur town. Total length of the Dakatia is about 207 km. Tidal currents feed the Dakatia through the Meghna for three-fourths of the year.

Dakshina Kannada : Dakshina Kannada, also called South Kannada, South Kanara, or South Canara, is a coastal district of India's Karnataka state. It is bordered by the districts of Udupi to the north, Chikkamagaluru to the northeast, Hassan District to the east, Kodagu to the southeast, and Kasaragod in Kerala to the south. The Arabian Sea bounds it on the west. Mangalore is the capital and chief city of the district.

The population of the district is 1,896,403 (2001 census). The population of the district increased 14.51% from 1991 to 2001, and 15.98% in the 1981-1991 period. The district is divided into five talukas, Mangalore, Bantwal, Puttur, Sullia, and Belthangady.It used to include three northern talukas, Udupi, Kundapur and Karkal, but these were separated in August 1997 to form Udupi district. Dakshina Kannada and Udupi districts are often called Tulu Nadu, as Tulu is the majority language in the region.

Dakshineswar : Dakshineswar, a small place situated alongside the Vivekananda Setu, in the Hooghly district, north of Calcutta, on the East bank of Hoogli River, is famous for its temples. In 1847, Rani (Queen) Rasmani of Bengal wanted to go upon a pilgrimage to the sacred city of Banaras to express her devotions to the Divine Mother Kali. The Goddess appeared in her dream and asked her to erect her temple in Bengal itself. Rani immediately looked for and purchased land there and immediately arranged for the construction of the temple.

The 12-spired temple, built between 1847 and 1855, with its enormous courtyard has a shrine of the goddess Kali and is surrounded by 12 other temples dedicated to Lord Shiva and Radha-Krishna. A scholarly and elderly sage was chosen as the head priest and the temple was consecrated in 1855. Within the year this priest died and his responsibility passed to his younger brother, Sri Ramakrishna, who over the next thirty years would bring great fame to the Dakshineswar temple. Ramakrishna did not serve for long as temple's head priest however. One of the famous visitors to this temple includes Keshab Chandra Sen.

Dakshineswar Kali Temple : It is situated alongside the Vivekananda Bridge north of Calcutta, about20 km. from BBD Bagh. It is famous for its association—with Ramkrishna who achieved spiritual vision here. This temple was built by Rani Rashmoni in 1847. The 12- spired temple with its enormous courtyard is surrounded by 12 other temples dedicated to Lord Shiva. It is a world famous place of pilgrimage. It was here the famous religious thinker Rama Krishna Paramahamsa achieved his spiritual vision and preached the unity of all religions.

Dakshinpatha : The ancient Buddhist and Brahmanical texts use the expression Dakshinpatha as a name for both the southern high road and for the region lying south of

Majjhimdesa or Mid India. The first reference to Dakshinapatha occurs in the Rig-Veda where it refers to the region where the exile goes on being turned out. In the opinion of several scholars, this means the South beyond the limits of the Saptasindhu— the then recognised Aryan world.

Dakshinapatha is found in Panini (IV.2.98). Baudhyana mentions Dakshinapatha or Dakshinatya in association with Saurashtra. Jataka and Vinaya Pitaka attest name Dakshinapatha coupled with Avanti as in Avantidakshinapatha where it seems to refer to Janapada of Avanti and implies its location in Dakshinapatha. In Mahabharata, Dakshinapatha is placed beyond Avanti and Vindhyas and to south of the kingdom of Vidarbhas and southern Kosalas, the latter being located on the banks of Wardha and Mahanadi.

The epic hero Rama who had set out from Ayodhya into voluntary exile had taken a route which extended from Ayodhya into Dakshinapatha or the southern direction. The Sutta Nipata Commentary seems to explain Dakshinapatha as the road leading to the Dakshinajanapada, the latter name referring to a Janapada located to south of Ganges. In the same Sutta Nipata, the name Dakshinapatha also refers to a remote Aryan settlement located on the banks of the upper Godavari. A Kossalan Brahmin named Bavari had left Savathi (capital of Kosala) to set up his hermitage at the junction of river Mula and Godavari, midway between the kingdoms of Assaka and Mulaka, which place has been noted as lying in Dakshinapatha.

Dakyang : It is usually performed in the gompas during festivals. Stories relating to the lamas are told through this dance.

Dal : Dal is a Sanskrit term common to many South Asian languages referring to pulses which have been stripped of their outer hulls and split, as well as to the thick, spicy stew prepared therefrom, a mainstay of Indian cuisine. The latter can be seen as a milder cousin of the South Indian sambar. The hulling of a pulse is intended to improve digestibility and palatability, but carries some cost in nutrition by reducing fiber content, not unlike that suffered in the milling of whole grains into refined grains.

Dal Lake : The Dal Lake lies on the suburbs of Srinagar in the east. It is at the foot of the mountain range. The lake is 4 miles long and 11 miles broad. Against the mountain background which is reflected in its calm expanse and enclosed by trees the lake looks superb. In summer, it is a paradise for visitors who glide over its waters in shikaras and houseboats. The Manasbal lake is the deepest lake in the country. Its greenish-blue waters are wondrous and beautiful.

Besides these lakes, which are fed by the melting snows from the mountains, there are hosts of mountain tarns form-glared by the glacial action and other phenomenal activities of range nature. There are several glaciers on Haramoukh. On the South side they only descend to about 13,500 ft., but alter the North 1,500 ft lower. They are fed by the large snow fields on the summit, which are of great thickness. The snow cliffs on the middle peak show a vertical thickness of nearly 200 feet. In there seen all the surrounding valleys. There are lakelets varying in size from mere ponds to sheets of water a mile or so in length and quarter a mile broad., most of these occur at a height of 11,500 feet. There can be no doubt that they are all due in some way to glacial action, and that they are not of very remote age. Tydall points out that a glacier 900 feet deep would produce a vertical pressure of 486, 000 lbs. upon every square inch of its bed. But the small glacier on the shoulders gone, of such mountains as Haramoukh or Tutakuthi would not exceed

200 feet in thickness, and would not be capable of excavating hard rocks beneath.

So the numerous tarns and lakes may be own regarded as due chiefly to the formation of embankments across line of drainage. Sometimes such embankments may have been caused by the deposit of avalanche debris from a slide slope or by the advance of a side glacier with its lateral moraines. The lakes and lakelets found in upper valleys around Haramukh mountain are Gangabal, Lool Gool and Sarbal. They are at an elevation of nearly 12,000 feet above sea level. The shimmering waters lend glory to the Gangabal Lake, which stands at an elevation of 11,800 feet. To the South cast of the Pir Panchal range lies the lake Konsar Nag (12,800 feet) surrounded by three peaks. Its is fed by glaciers. It is said to be a source of the Jhelum. In the spring and summer, the water is some 40-ft higher than in winter. In the spring, its surface is said to be covered with icebergs, which are driven about by the wind.

Dalai Lamas : In Tibetan Buddhism, the successive Dalai Lamas (taa-la'i bla-ma) form a tulku lineage of Gelugpa leaders which trace back to 1391. Tibetan Buddhists believe the Dalai Lama to be the present incarnation of Avalokitesvara ("Chenrezig" [spyan ras gzigs] in Tibetan), the bodhisattva of compassion. Between the 17th century and 1959, the Dalai Lama was the head of the Tibetan government, controlling a large portion of the country from the capital Lhasa. The Dalai Lamas never had authority over every region of Tibet nor over the other sects of Tibetan Buddhism. The current Dalai Lama (the 14th) is a respected Tibetan Buddhist religious leader and figurehead of the International Tibet Independence Movement; in English, he is often granted the style "His Holiness" (or HH) before his title.

The Dalai Lama is often thought to be the head of the Gelug school, but this position officially belongs to the

Ganden Tripa (dga' ldan khri pa) (Holder of the Throne of Ganden [dga' ldan], the first monastery established by Tsongkhapa [btsong-ka-pa], founder of the Gelug).

Dalalpur Bridge : Dalalpur Bridge a Mughal structure, spans the Pankhiraj Khal (canal) on the northern side of Panamnagar in sonargaon and connects Adampur and Dalalpur. It has three arches. The middle arch was made wider and higher for the safe passage of boats. The pathway is made of bricks set in circular rows. The bridge slopes down steeply on either side.

Dalbandin : Dalbandin is located in Balochistan, Pakistan. Dalbandin is famous for fruit orchards. Hilly terrains, arid plains and inhospitable weather are the distinct features of Balochistan. As Balochistan lies between 20-33 N and 61-70 E it has got all types of climate, i.e tropical, sub-tropical, and temperate. Thus suitable for growing variety of fruits viz: almond, apple, apricot, grapes, peach, plum, pear, pomegranate, cherry, pistachio, dates, mango, citrus, banana, guava, loquat, papaya, chiko, coconut, fig, etc. However, among fruit crops, date-palm holds the largest acreage, i.e. 42,607 hectares of which 41,928 are bearing and 679 non-bearing areas.

In spite of the fact that Balochistan is the largest date-palm growing province, no adequate attention has been paid to the problems of date-palm growers at any level. For example, a drought-like situation for the last couple of years has led to outbreak of field rats in the date-palm grove in Maskhel, Gualstop and Dalbandin in district Kharan causing widespread damage to both bearing and non-bearing date-palm trees.

Dalhousie : Dalhousie is a beautiful hill station in Himachal Pradesh. Established in 1854 by the British Empire in India as a summer retreat for its troops and bureaucrats, the town was named after Lord Dalhousie who was the British Viceroy in India at that time.

Dalit : In South Asia's caste system, a Dalit — formerly called untouchable — is a person outside the four castes, and considered below them. Included are leather-workers, scavengers, street handicrafters, poor farmers and laborers.

The origin of the Dalit community, and of the caste system itself, is unclear. Some intepretations of the Indo-Aryan migration hypothesis theorize that the caste system was a product of an invasion, with the Aryans reserving the higher castes for themselves and relegating the darker-skinned, native inhabitants that they conquered to lower castes and untouchable status. A more modern theory, however accepts a more peaceful mingling of the Aryans and natives, and holds that Dalit existed before the Aryan migration as an oppressed class among the native Dravidian peoples of South Asia. In this latter theory, the Dalit status was simply preserved and expanded by the Aryans as part of the integration of Aryan and Dravidian societies. In the context of traditional Hindu beliefs, Dalit status has often been historically associated with occupations regarded as ritually impure: any occupation involving killing or handling dead bodies, or anything involving disposing of refuse or human waste. Engaging in these activities was considered to be polluting to the individual who performed them, and this pollution was considered to be 'contagious'. As a result, Dalits were commonly banned from fully participating in Hindu religious life, and elaborate precautions were sometimes observed to prevent incidental contact between Dalits and higher-caste Hindus.

In modern India the word 'Dalit' has been applied to all people who do not belong to any of the four castes of Hinduism. Defined in this way, 'Dalit' includes not only low-caste or outcaste Hindus, but also aboriginal followers of animist religions, and possibly may have included immigrant communities that subscribed to beliefs that were seen as incompatible with orthodox brahmanist and Hindu traditions.

Many Dalits who have converted to other religions in the past few centuries continue to retain their Dalit identity. In the 1991 census, Dalits constituted more than 16% of India's population, with the greatest numbers living in Uttar Pradesh, West Bengal, and Bihar. They are also found in Nepal. In Pakistan, more than 60% of all Hindus are Dalits, keeping in mind that Pakistan is predominantly Muslim.

Dalkhai : This vigorous dance is performed by women of some of the tribes in Sambalpur, Barghar and Sonepur districts in Orissa at the time of seasonal festivals. It is mostly performed in the Oriya month of aswina during the Durga Puja festival. A dummy horse version is the Chaiti Ghorha, danced by a community of fishermen.

Dalshone and Cholamba Dances : These dances belong to the Ropa valley in Himachal and in these the patterns formed by the dancers look like coiled serpents. The Cholamba dance is performed when a tiger is killed. The skin of the dead animal is stuffed and a gold ornament is put in his nose. The carcass is then rotated and the people dance around it. The *Nagas Kayang* is a dance which copies the movement of a snake. The *Herki Kayang* is faster in tempo and is danced to a romantic song. This dance is performed by young men and women. The *Shuna Kayang* dance is danced in most villages in the area and it combines both slow and fast movements. This depicts scenes from the life in the village as also the forest.

Daltonganj : Daltonganj is the headquarters of Palamu district in the state of Jharkhand in India. Situated on the banks of the river North Koel, the town is named after the British commissioner of Chota nagpur, Col Dalton. It is 825 km south east of New Delhi and is accessible by train from Patna, Ranchi, Calcutta and Delhi. The nearest airport is at Ranchi (180 km) and Daltongunj is well connected with Ranchi by road.

The famous Palamau National Park known for its wild life is located nearby. The park is spread over a core area of 250 square kilometers. The area is rich in flora and fauna but also prone to severe droughts. The Palamau National Park was brought under Project Tiger in the year 1973 and is among the original Tiger Reserves of India. Sal and Bamboo are the main vegetation.

World's first tiger-census was done in the Palamau forests in the year 1932. Counting was based on pugmarks. There were around 44 tigers when the last census was done. There are several other wildlife found in the sanctuary—Chital, Chinkara, Common Langur, Dhole (wild dogs), Elephants, Gaur, Hares, Indian porcupine, Nilgai, Monkey, Mouse Deer, Leopard, Pangolin, Panther, Sambar, Sloth Bear, Wild Boar and Wolves. Peafowl, Red Jungle Fowl and Partridges are the common birds found here.

Damaan : Damaan is located in Punjab, Pakistan. Damaan is the floodplains region in the western central Pakistan. Gigantic hill-torrents occasionally pouring down from its western Sulaiman Mountain Range and finally joining the mighty Indus River in the east played vital role in making its diverse geographies and determining its histories and cultures. Damaan was once considered to be the gateway to South Asia owing to its traversable numerous mountain passes connecting Afghanistan and the Central Asia to Pakistan. Invaders and traders continued to pass through Damaan for centuries before the advent of new transportation and communication technologies. Owing to its geo-political significance and strategic location, Damaan turned to be a multi-ethnic and multi-cultural region. Though Damaan is still predominantly Siraiki speaking region but other major ethno-cultural groups include Punjabis, Balochs and Pakhtuns. Chashma is a major city in Damaan area.

Daman : Daman, also known as Damão, is an enclave on the western coast of India, surrounded by Valsad district of Gujarat on the north, east and south and the Arabian Sea to the west. The district has an area of 72 km^2, and a population of 113,949 (2001 census), which increased 83% between 1991 and 2001. Daman lies at the mouth of the Daman Ganga River. Major industries have factories here. The closest railway station is Vapi (7 km). It is also famous for its beach, Portuguese architecture, and church, and for the scenic beauty in the twin cities of Nani-Daman and Moti-Daman, which lie opposite each other across the Daman Ganga. The chief occupation has been fishing. The city of Surat lies to the north, and Mumbai lies approximately 160 km (100 mi) south of Daman on the Arabian Sea coast in Maharashtra state. Daman was occupied by the Portuguese in 1531, and was formally ceded to Portugal in 1539 by the Sultan of Gujarat. It remained a Portuguese possession until it was occupied by Indian forces on 19 December 1961.

Daman and Diu : Daman and Diu is a union territory in India. For over 450 years these coastal enclaves on the Arabian Sea coast were part of Portuguese India, along with Goa and Dadra and Nagar Haveli. Goa, Daman, and Diu were occupied by the Republic of India on December 19, 1961; Portugal did not recognize Indian rule in these territories until 1974. Goa, Daman, and Diu were administered as part of a single union territory until 1987, when Goa was granted statehood, leaving Daman and Diu as a separate union territory; each enclave constitutes one of the union territory's two districts. Gujarati is the main language; use of Portuguese is declining because it is not official or taught at school (but still spoken by 10% in

Daman). There are Portuguese-based creole languages in Daman (known as Língua da Casa, "Home Language") and Diu (Língua dos Velhos, "Elder's Language"). The Creole of Diu is rapidly becoming extinct by the pressure of Gujarati.

Daman Ganga : The Daman Ganga is a river in western India. The river's headwaters are on the western slope of the Western Ghats range, and it flows west into the Arabian Sea. The river flows through Maharashtra and Gujarat states, as well as the Union territories of Daman and Diu and Dadra and Nagar Haveli. The industrial towns of Vapi, Dadra and Silvassa lie on the north bank of the river, and the town of Daman occupies both banks of the river's estuary.

The Government of India's National Water Development Authority (NWDA) has proposed the Daman Ganga-Pinjal River Linking Project, which would build a new aqueduct linking the Daman Ganga river to the Pinjal River to the south, allowing water from the Daman Ganga to be diverted south to Mumbai via the Pinjal. In April 2003 the state government of Gujarat raised objections to the proposal.

Damdama Sahib : Damdama Sahib is located in Talwandi Sabo (village near Bhatinda). One of the five most sacred places in Sikhism. This is where Guru Gobind Singh Ji stayed for almost a year and compiled the final edition of the Guru Granth Sahib in 1706.

Damodar River : The Damodar River is a river in India. It rises from the Chhota Nagpur plateau of the Jharkhand state, India. The river originates near Chandwa village, Palamu district, and flows eastward about 592 kilometres through the states of Jharkhand and West Bengal to join the Hoogli River, southward of Kolkata. The Damodar River has a number of tributaries. The Valley of

Damodar River includes India's large reserves of coal and mica, and the area is a highly developed industrial belt of India. The dams on the Damodar River have several hydroelectric power plants. Of late, the Damodar has become one of the most polluted rivers of India, polluted with chemical, and other pollutants like minerals, mine rejects, and toxic effluents, and the river banks are infested by coal dust and wastes from several big and small industries which are located in its basin.

Damodar Valley : The Damodar Valley lies in the Chota Nagpur plateau of the state of Jharkhand, India. It also extends to some parts of the state of West Bengal. The valley derives its name from the Damodar river, which arises from the plateau of Chota Nagpur. The Damodar Valley is one of the most industrialised parts of India. Damodar Valley contains a variety of mineral deposits, including very large deposits of iron ore and coal. The valley is called "the Ruhr of India". The valley also generates 60% of India's medium grade coal. Several dams have been constructed in the valley, for the generation of hydroelectric power.

Damoh : Damoh District is a district of Madhya Pradesh state in central India. The town of Damoh is the district headquarters. The district is part of Sagar Division. The district has many places oh historical importance. Nohata is one such town of historical importance situated at a distance of 21 km from Damoh. Nohata is situated on the banks of River Gauraya and was a capital of the Chandela Rajputs. A number of temples are there in Nohata.

The ancient fort at Rajnagar village, 6 km from Damoh, was founded by the Mughals. Singhorgarh fort is another place of historical importance. It was built by Raja Vain Bason. Gond Rajas stayed in it for a long time. It was with Gond Raja Dalpat Shah and his Rani Durgawati at the end of 15th century. After the death of Raja Dalpat Shah, the Senapati of the army of Mughal emperor Akbar had a battle with Rani Durgawati at village Singrampur.

Danda Shah Bilawal : Danda shah bilawal is a village in Punjab, Pakistan in the road between Peshawar and Islamabad. It is between Islamabad and Mianwali Chashma, D.I.Khan. 40 persons took part in world war one and two give there lives. Papulation 7000, Farmar depend on Rain. Syed cost is in mejority.

Dandi : Dandi is a small village in the district of Surat, Gujarat, India. It is located on the coast of the Arabian Sea near the city of Surat. It shot into worldwide prominence in 1930 when Mahatma Gandhi selected it to be the place for the Salt Satyagraha. He marched from Ahmedabad to Dandi with some of his followers to protest against the imposition of a tax on salt. It could be said that in this village the beginning of the fall of British rule in India started.

Dandiya : Dandiya and Garba are the featured dances of Navratri evenings in North India, originating in Gujarat. Navaratri is the longest Hindu festival celebrated all over India for nine consecutive nights in praise of Lord Rama (Hero of the Epic Ramayana) and Goddess Durga from the end of September to early October.

Originated as devotional Garba dances, which were performed in Durga's honor, this dance form is actually the staging of a mock-fight between the Goddess and Mahishasura, the mighty demon-king, and is nicknamed "The Sword Dance". The sticks of the dance represent the sword of Durga. The women wear traditional dresses such as colorful embroidered choli, ghagra and bandhani dupattas (traditional attire) dazzling with mirror work and heavy jewellery. The Men wear special turbans and kedias, but can range from area to area. The dancers whirl and move their feet and arms in a choreographed manner to the tune of the music with lots of drum beats. The dhol is used as well as complimentary percussion instruments such as the dholak, tabla and others.

Dandiya Raas : The Dandiya variety of the Raas Nritya of Gujarat is generally performed by a group of youthful persons, both males and females, who move in circles to measured steps, beating time with small sticks (called Dandia) singing to the accompaniment of Dhol, Cymbals, Zanz, flute or Shehnai. When the time beat is given by the clapping of palms and performed only by males, it is called Garbi. The Gof variety of the Raas is an intricate performance wherein the performers holding coloured strings attached to a top, move in circles weaving and unweaving different patterns.

Danes : The Danes were the last of the colonial powers to set foot in India. Their only trading outpost was in Tranquebar, Tamil Nadu, established in 1620. Their outpost was never too important and was sold to the British in 1845. Other colonial nations such as Belgium, Italy and Germany did not set foot in India. Spain did not have territorial rights to India due to the Line of Demarcation drawn by Pope Alexander VI in 1493 with the Bull Inter caetera, ceding the eastern hemisphere to Portugal. Japan briefly occupied the Andaman and Nicobar Islands during World War 2.

Dangi Nrita : The Gangis are unique tribals, a blend of Gujarati and Maharashrian culture mixed harmoniously with original Dravidians. The dance performed by Dangis is called Dangi Nritya. Men and women join hands forming a chain or shrinkala making serpentine movements with one of them leading. The movements is very fast, swift and create various choreographic patterns in a fraction of a second. Each variety of step is called 'Chala' and there are about 27 varieties of these Chalas. One of the most amazing sights of this dance is the creation of a human pyramid

Dangs Darbar : The 10-day festival in Gujarat, held at Ahwa in March every year, is a wonderful spectacle of tribal dance, music and lifestyle.

Danish East India Company : The Danish East India Company (Danish, Dansk Ostindisk Kompagni) was founded in 1616, following a privilege of Danish King Christian IV. It was focused on trade with India and had its base in Tranquebar. After a short blossoming, it lost importance quickly and was dissolved in 1729. In 1732, it was refounded as Asiatische Compagnie ("Asiatic Company"), yet in 1772 it lost its monopoly. During its heyday, the Danish and Swedish East India Company imported more tea than the British East India Company - and smuggled 90% of it into Britain, where it could be sold at a huge profit. During the Napoleonic Wars, in 1801 and again in 1807, the British navy attacked Copenhagen in the Battle of Copenhagen (1807). As a consequence of the last attack, Denmark lost its entire fleet and the island of Helgoland. British control of the seas spelled the end of the Danish East India Company

Dankara : Dankara or the gaatka dance is a dance of celebration and forms part of wedding festivities. Two men, each holding colourful staves, dance round each other and tap their sticks together in rhythm with the drums.

Dantewada District : Dantewada District, also known as Dantewara District or South Bastar District, is a district in the Indian state of Chhattisgarh. Dantewada is the district headquarters. The district is part of Bastar Division. Until 1998, the Dantewada District was a tehsil of the larger Bastar District. Dantewada District has an area of 10,238.99 km^2. It is bounded on the north and northeast by Bastar District, on the east by Malkangiri District of Orissa state, on the south and southwest by Khammam District of Andhra Pradesh state, and on the east by the Indravati River, which forms the boundary with Karimnagar District of Andhra Pradesh and Gadchiroli District of Maharashtra.

Before Indian Independence, the district was part of the princely state of Bastar. After Indian Independence in 1947, Bastar's ruler acceded to the government of India, and the erstwhile state became part of Bastar District of Madhya Pradesh state. Bastar District was divided into the districts of Bastar, Dantewada, and Kanker in 1999. In 2000, Dantewada was one of the 16 Madhya Pradesh districts that constituted the new state of Chhattisgarh. Encompassing with hilly tracks, dales and valleys, numerous brooks and rivers, and many forests, Dantewada is home to many species of wildlife such as the tiger, leopard, deer, bison, etc. Two species characteristic to the area are the pahadi maina and the wild buffalo.

Dappu Dance : Dappu is a percussion instrument. It is a counterpart of Dandora of North India. It is also called Tappeta in coastal Andhra. It is made out of calf hide fixed to the margosa wooden structure in a circular shape. It is beaten with two sticks one thin and the other thicker. The form belongs exclusively to Harijans. Dappu dance is a vigorous type of dance as the Dappu is a powerful percussion instrument.

A troupe consisting of ten to twenty artistes presents Dappu dance during marriage processions, car festivals of deities and village fairs and festivals. Tiger steps, bird steps, horse steps are some of the styles of dance movements presented in the Dappu dance. Sometimes the songs sung verge on obscenity as in Lella Patalu to settle old scores.

The beat of the Dappu and the foot work of the dancers synchronise with each other so perfectly that from a slow moving, low-beating rhythm, it reaches its climax with the frantic drums keeping pace with the dazzling foot work by the dancers. They play several kinds of rhythms like Trisra, Chaturasa, Mirsa, Khandagati, Sankeerna, Jatis, comprising seven type of beats. They follow different kinds of dance, leaping from one side to another with complicated foot work. They tie jingling bells to their ankles. Spectators throw coins on a Dappu placed on the ground. When the players around that Dappu beat their drums vigorously, the Dappu placed on the ground responds to the sound vibrations and the coins over it dance and slide down to be picked up as a reward by the artistes.

Darasbari Madrasa : Darasbari Madrasa is situated about a kilometre to the southwest of kotwali darwaza, and about half a kilometre from the Chhota Sona—Kotwali Road in Ghoshpur mauza of the Bangladesh side of Gaur-Lakhnawti. It has been erected between two tanks, one on its east and the other on its west; the latter is longer and separates the madrasa from the darasbari mosque. The madrasa, according to the inscription, was erected in 909 AH (1504 AD) by Alauddin husain shah. However, its existence was revealed only in the seventies of the 20th century when the site was excavated and the plan fully exposed. Its discovery has removed the confusion between the location of the madrasa and that of the belbari madrasa, erected two years earlier. The discovery of the madrasa is significant. It is the lone example of this architectural form from medieval Bengal and demonstrates the development of the present dormitory style through the earlier Buddhist Viharas discovered in mainamati, paharpur, and elsewhere.

Darasbari Mosque: Darasbari Mosque is the largest mosque in the Bangladesh part of Gaur-Lakhnauti, now in ruins. It is situated in the Darasbari quarter of the mediaeval city on the west side of the Chhota Sona-Kotwali Darwaza Road, at present a desolated area near the Indian border. The name Darasbari is derived from its being located within a darsbari (place of lesson or learning), pointing to the madrasa to the east of the mosque, separated by a large tank, forming a typical Muslim educational complex. According to its inscription, which is now preserved in the Indian Museum at Calcutta, the mosque was built in 1479 AD by Shamsuddin Abul Muzaffar Yusuf Shah. The Darasbari Mosque at one time must have been one of the most beautiful examples of Sultanate mosques in Gaur-Lakhnauti.

Built in the early years of the city, this mosque together with other contemporary examples initiated the 'Gauriya' style which spread to other parts of Bangala and came to be known as the independent Bengal style of the mediaeval period.

Dargah Sharief : Situated at the foot of barren Taragarh hill in the old part of the town of Ajmer in Central Rajasthan, is the tomb of the Sufi saint Khwaja Moin-ud-din-Chisti (1140-1235), popularly known as Dargah Sharief, the most famous Muslim pilgrimage center in India.

This grand marble shrine begun by Iltutmish and completed by Humayun, contains the relics of the great Sufi saint. It is considered the second holiest pilgrim site after Mecca. It is believed that seven pilgrimages to Ajmer equal one to Mecca.

Khwaja Moin-ud-din-Chisti was a Persian orphaned at the age of 16 who later turned to spiritual life. Believed to be a direct descendant of Ali, the son in law of Prophet Mohammed, the saint arrived in Ajmer in 1192 at the age of 52 during Prithwiraj Chauhan's rule. It was the time when Islam was on the verge of spreading to India. The saint who came in peace devoted his life to the poor people of Ajmer and its region. He never owned a house or even proper clothing cause he believed that private property was a hindrance to spirituality. The force of his spiritual presence won over, even the Hindu Rajputs at that time.

Not only the Muslims but people of other religions also throng the holy dargah and pray for the fulfillment of their desires. The shrine is considered to be a place of wish fulfillment for those who pray with devout and pure hearts. The devotees also offer flowers, velvet cloth, perfume and sandalwood at the shrine.

Dariyaon Fort : Dariyaon Fort a mud-fort of Nilambar, the Khen king of kamarupa to secure his southern frontier against possible Muslim attack. After the Muslim conquest of north Bengal in the early 13th century, the frontier of the Muslim kingdom in the north gradually extended as far as the karatoya which then was a considerably larger stream. Beyond that lay the Hindu kingdoms of northeast Bengal and Assam. To arrest Muslim penetration deeper into the northeastern territories, the Ahom and Khen kings of Kamarupa built a chain of bulwarks and mud forts along the trans-Karatoya basin. Derelict remains of some of these can still be traced in Rangpur, Dinajpur, Jalpaiguri districts and adjacent Kuch Bihar state. They include Dariyaon fort near Kantaduar, Devipur, Batason in Rangpur, Mainamatirgarh and Dharmapalagarh near Domar, Baro-Paikergarh near Belwa in Dinajpur, bhitargarh in Panchagarh, Ghoraghat Fort in Dinajpur, etc.

Darjeeling : Darjeeling is a town in the Indian state of West Bengal and headquarters of Darjeeling district, situated in the foothills of the Himalaya at elevations of between 2,000 and 3,000 metres above sea level. With India attaining independence on 15 August 1947, the district of Darjeeling remained in the partitioned section of Bengal (West Bengal) and therefore in the Indian union. With the district's sub-Himalayan and geographical condition, it occupied a unique status in the state. The only remaining industry, tea, continued to play a major role in the economy of the area and the country as well. Its other natural wealth, forests, have been adversely affected by the ever-growing population, now estimated to be around 1,200,000. In the years since independence, much has been done for the area's education, communication, attention to cash crops like orange, potato, cardamom, ginger, etc. The region is best known for its tea.

Darjeeling has a modest tourism industry, with attractions including the 'Tiger Hill' sunrise, the zoo, the monastery and of course the tea gardens. The town is also sometimes used as a base by trekkers in the Himalayas, and served as the starting point for many attempts on Indian and Nepali peaks in the 20th century. Tenzing Norgay, one of the two men to first climb Mt. Everest, grew up in the Sherpa community in Darjeeling. His Everest ascent provided the impetus to establish the Himalayan Mountaineering Institute in Darjeeling in 1954.

Darjeeling Himalayan Railway : The Darjeeling Himalayan Railway, nicknamed the "Toy Train", is a 60 cm narrow-gauge railway from Siliguri to Darjeeling in the state of West Bengal in India, run by the Indian Railways. It was built between 1879 and 1881 and is about 86 km long. The elevation level is from about 100 m in Siliguri to about 2200 m in Darjeeling. It is still to this day powered by a steam engine. A modern diesel engine is used for Darjeeling's mail. Since 1999 the train has been a World Heritage Site as listed by UNESCO.

Darra Adam Khel : Darra Adam Khel is a town in the Northwest Frontier Province of Pakistan, located between Peshawar and Kohat, very close to the Federally

Administered Tribal Areas. It is inhabited by Pashtuns of the Afridi khel (clan). The town consists of one main street lined with shops, with some alleys and sidestreets containing workshops. Darra Adam Khel is devoted entirely to the production of ordnance. A wide variety of firearms are produced in the town, from anti-aircraft guns to pen-guns. Weapons are handmade by individual craftsmen using traditional manufacturing techniques, usually handed down father-to-son. The quality of the guns are generally high and craftsman are able to produce replicas of almost any gun. Guns are regularly tested by test-firing into the air.

Daryaganj : Daryaganj (lit. "River Trading Post/ Warehouse") - a well known residential locality within the walled street of (Old) Delhi. The "Darya" (lit. "River") refers to the river Yamuna which was just outside the walled city. The current President of Pakistan, Pervez Musharraf was born and used to live in Daryaganji before migrating to Pakistan after the Partition of India in 1947. Daryagang continues to be a major commercial hub of modern Old Delhi.

Dasa Sahitya : Dasa Sahitya is the devotional literature composed by devotees in honor of Lord Vishnu or one of his avatars. Dasa is literally servant in kannada and sahitya is literature. Haridasas ("servants of God") were preachers of devotion to Lord Vishnu or one of his avatars. The devotional literature of these Haridasas is collectively referred to as Dasa Sahitya. It is in the kannada language.

Dasam Granth : The Dasam Granth is a holy book of Sikhism composed by 10th Sikh Guru, Guru Gobind Singh. From 1892 to 1897, scholars assembled at the Akal Takht, Amritsar, to study the various printed Dasam Granths and prepare the authoritative version. They concluded that the Dasam Granth was entirely the work of Guru Gobind Singh. Further re-examinations and reviews took place in 1931, under the ageis of the Darbar Sahib Committee of the Shiromani Gurdwara Prabhandak Committee they too vindicated the earlier conclusion and its findings have since been published.

On 20 February 2000, at Gobind Sadan, Virsa Singh released the first complete Punjabi translation of the writings of Guru Gobind Singh, plus other scholarly works about the life and teachings of Guru Gobind Singh. Gurbani such as 'Chandi Di Var' were recited from the Dasam Granth before major battles to bolster the Sikh warriors with inspired courage.

Dashashvamedh Ghat : The best time to visit the Ghat is early dawn. There are a lot of Ghats on the Western bank of the Ganges. Most of them are used for bathing. Some are used for cremating bodies. Dashashvamedh Ghat is one of the most important Ghats in Uttar Pradesh. You can see the Pandas (Brahmin Priests) sitting under huge umbrellas offering prayers for their clients, exercises of young wrestlers, devotees praying and drinking water from the holy river.

Daskathia : 'Daskathia', once a popular performance of Ganjam, has spread to all other districts of Orissa. 'Dasa' means a devotee. 'Katha' means two wooden pieces played in tune with the prayer of the devotee. The party consists of two persons. One is the chief singer, the other is the 'Palia' who helps him in all respects in singing and acting. The two persons stage a whole drama, act all the parts, change their tone hour after hour. They introduce humorous stories to break the monotony.

Data Durbar : Data Durbar is the tomb of Hazrat Syed Abul Hassan Bin Usman Bin Ali Al-Hajweri, the famous Sufi saint of South Asia, where hundreds of thousands of people come each year to pay their respects and to say their prayers. It is located in Lahore, Punjab, Pakistan. The large complex also includes Jamia Hajveria, or Hajveri Mosque.

Data Ganj Bakhsh : Syed Abul Hassan Bin Usman Bin Ali Al-Hajweri, also known as Shaikh Ali Hajweri, Data Ganj Bakhsh, or Data Sahib, was a scholar of Islam and a Sufi saint, and writer of the 11th century. His contribution in spreading of Islam in Indian subcontinent is huge. He was born in Ghazna (in present day Afghanistan) and died in Lahore (in present day Pakistan) in 1073CE. His most famous work is Kashf al Mahjub ("Unveiling the Veiled"), which was the first Persian language treatise on Sufism. His mausoleum, popularly known as Data Durbar, is located in Lahore, Pakistan

Datia : The town of Datia is the administrative center of Datia District in the Indian state of Madhya Pradesh. It was formerly the seat of the eponymous princely state in the British Raj. Datia is situated near Gwalior and on the border with Uttar Pradesh (U.P); the town of Jhansi in U.P. is only about 25 km away. The old town is surrounded by a stone wall, enclosing handsome palaces and gardens; the 17th century palace of Bir Singh Deo is one of the finest examples of Hindu domestic architecture available in north India.

Datia had formerly been a vassal state of the Maratha empire and came under the sway of the British by the provisions of the Treaty of Bassein (1802), made between the Peshwa and the HEIC. The ruling family were Rajputs of the Bundela clan; they descended from a younger son of a former raja of Orchha. The state was administered as part of the Bundelkhand agency of Central India. It lay in the extreme north-west of Bundelkhand, near Gwalior, and was surrounded on all sides by other princely states of Central India, except on the east where it bordered upon the United Provinces. The land area of the state was

911 mi^2 its population in 1901 was 173,759. It enjoyed an estimated revenue of £70,000/- and paid a tribute to the Sindhia of Gwalior, through the British. The state suffered from famine in 1896-97, and again to a lesser extent in 1899-1900.

After India's independence in 1947, the Maharaja of Datia acceded unto the dominion of India; it later merged with the union of India. Datia, together with the rest of the Bundelkhand agency, became part of the new state of Vindhya Pradesh in 1950. In 1956, Vindhya Pradesh state was merged with certain other areas to form the state of Madhya Pradesh within the Union of India.

Dauki River : Dauki River is a small hilly river that originates in the southwestern region of the Shillong Massif in Lower Assam. It enters Bangladesh at Jaflong in Jaintiapur upazila of Sylhet district. The river is named according to the Dauki Fault System that borders the country and separates Meghalaya all along the northern border of greater Sylhet. The fault also defines the southern margin of Shillong Plateau. The Dauki is generally a hilly river with a rather strong current. In Bangladesh it shows a somewhat meandering pattern.

The river flows southwest to Sunamganj district. In the monsoon the heavy rainfall in the upper catchment intensifies the discharge of the river to such an extent that it can carry large boulders from the hills of the Shillong Plateau. These boulders are then collected for use in construction. The water of the river is very clear as it receives a continuous flow from the upper catchment. From the aesthetic point of view this river and the adjoining area is an attractive site for people to visit. Every year thousands of people come here for picnic and enjoy the beauty of nature, particularly in winter

Daulat Quazi : Daulat Quazi (Also Quazi Daulat, Daulat Kazi) was a medieval Bengali poet. He lived sometime in the 17th century. He lived in Arakan though he wrote in Bangla. Quazi is believed to the first Bengali poet to write under the patronage of the Arakan court. His patron Ashraf Khan was a commanding officer of king Shrisudharma who ruled between 1622 and 1638. There is evidence that both Khan and Quazi were Sufis. Ashraf Khan asked Daulat to render the west Indian stories of Lor, Chandrani and Mayana into Bangla. Daulat Quazi died before he could finish his poem. It was completed years later by Alaol.

Daulatbad : 13 Km between Aurangabad and the Ellora caves is the magnificent hilltop fortress of Daulatbad in Maharashtra. The fort built by Bhilam Raja of the Yadava dynasty in 1187 was earlier called Deogiri. This fort is considered as one of the oldest existing and impregnable forts of India. One of its attractions is the tower, Chand Minar.

Davanagere : Davanagere, also known as Davangere, is one of the major cities in the Indian state of Karnataka. It is the administrative headquarters of Davanagere District. Previously known for its cotton mills, it is fast developing into one of the major cities of Karnataka. Davanagere was famous for textiles. It is also famous for its educational institutes. It has two medical colleges, three engineering colleges and a number of other colleges offering courses in arts, commerce and science. The student population is made up of the people from different cities and states in India. There are a limited number of foreign students studying at Davanagere. Davanagere has Chigeteri Mills.

Dawn : Dawn is a leading English daily newspaper of Pakistan. Founded by Jinnah on October 26, 1941, as a mouthpiece for the Muslim League, it was originally a weekly publication, produced in the Indian capital Delhi. Jinnah summed up the paper's purpose when he stated

"The Dawn will mirror faithfully the views of Muslim India and the All India Muslim League in all its activities : economic, educational and social and more particularly political, throughout the country fearlessly and independently and while its policy will be, no doubt mainly to advocate and champion the cause of the Musalmans and the policy and programme of the All India Muslim League, it will not neglect the cause and welfare of the peoples of this Sub-continent generally". Dawn became a daily newspaper on October 1942. It won India-wide fame under its first editor, Pothan Joseph. After the creation of Pakistan, the newspaper moved to Karachi, the capital of the newly formed nation state.

Dawood College of Engineering and Technology : Dawood College of Engineering and Technology is located in Karachi, Sindh, Pakistan. Dawood College of Engineering and Technology is affiliated with Mehran University of Engineering and Technology, Jamshoro. Dawood college offers degree program in affiliation with Mehran University in Electronics Engineering, Chemical Engineering, Industrial Engineering, Metallurgical Engineering and Architecture.

Daya Mata : Sri Daya Mata is the current president and sanghamata (Mother of the Society) of Self-Realization Fellowship (SRF Headquarters in Los Angeles, CA) and the YSS (Yogoda Satsanga Society in India).

Born Faye Wright on January 31, 1914, in Utah, her interest in spirituality was apparent since childhood. It reached a point of craving when she first met Paramahansa Yogananda in 1931. Braving reluctance from her family, she joined Yogananda's ashram a few weeks later. After the passing away of Yogananda and his successor Rajarsi Janakananda, Daya Mata became the third president of YSS/SRF in 1955. She is the first woman to lead a religious organization in the world.

Dayananda Saraswati : Swami Dayananda Saraswati was born in Tamil Nadu. He became a swami as a young man and was the assistant to Swami Chinmayananda when he took the initiative to establish Vishwa Hindu Parishad.

In 1986, Swami Dayananda Saraswati founded the Arsha Vidya Gurukulam, a Gurukula that has branches in India and the United States. Arsha Vidya Gurukulam is an institute for the traditional study of Advaita Vedanta, Yoga, Ayurveda, Jyotish, Sanskrit and other classical Hindu studies. The word Arsha means that which is from the Rishis—the great seers of ancient India. The word Vidya means knowledge. Thus, Arsha Vidya means the knowledge flowing from the Rishis. The word Gurukulam, means "family of the teacher", referring to a residential center for learning with the Teacher. Arsha Vidya Gurukulam offers Indians and non-Indians, Hindus and non-Hindus alike an opportunity to study the profound spiritual knowledge of the Upanishads, Bhagavad Gita, Brahma-sutras, and other classical Vedanta texts. Swami Dayananda also founded AIM for Seva for social work in India.

Debendranath Tagore : Debendranath Tagore (May 15, 1817—January 19, 1905) was a Bengali philosopher from current-day West Bengal, in India. He was born in Calcutta, India. His father, Dwarkanath Tagore was a rich and famous Bengali landlord.

Debendranath believed in religious reform and was opposed to societal Hindu practices like sati. He advocated universal education to free Bengal from such baseless beliefs. He was an active Brahmo, and was against sati, idol worship and the concept of multiple gods. He was asked by the leader of Brahmo Samaj Raja Ram Mohan Roy to continue his work in his absence. He came to be known as Maharishi Debendranath Tagore. Rabindranath Tagore was his son.

Debsa Pass : Debsa Pass lies in the Himalaya mountains at an elevation of 5340 metres (17520 feet) between the Kullu and Spiti Districts of Himachal Pradesh, India. Discovered in 1993 and crossed in 1995 for the first time by a small team led by Joydeep Sircar, this pass crosses from the Upper Parbati valley to the till-then unexplored Debsa Glacier whose outflow stream falls into the Parahio which in turn flows into the Spiti River. It provides an alternative and shorter route than the traditional Pin-Parbati pass route between Kullu and Spiti and has thus become popular.

Debu Bhattacherjee: Debu Bhattacherjee (1930-1994) was a Bengali composer, music director. Born in Brahmanbaria district in 1930 in a family that hailed from Fakirhat under Bagerhat district, Debu Bhattacherjee obtained his graduation in painting from Calcutta Art School in 1950. His childhood name was Prankumar Bhattacherjee but later his name in school was registered as Devdas Bhattacherjee. Shilpacharya zainul abedin was his teacher and while a student of art, he became close to celebrated painters like Quamrul Hassan and SM Sultan.

The masterpieces of this great composer include some Bengali patriotic songs written by leading poets of the country. He was honoured with the National Flim Award—1976 as the best background music composer for the film Charitrahin, directed by Baby Islam. In 1997, he was posthumously awarded the Ekushey Padak in appreciation of his contributions to music.

Deccan Chronicle : Deccan Chronicle is a regional english daily in India. It is circulated in Andhra Pradesh and Chennai city. It has a more tabloid perspective of news. Its online version can be accessed on its website www.deccan.com. The group which publishes this newspaper also publishes the Asian Age newspaper. It has a ABC certified circulation of 4.30 lakhs in Andhra

Pradesh. The circulation figures for Chennai are not yet out.

Deccan Festival : Deccan Festival is celebrated in Hyderabad every year on 25th February. This five-day long festival reflects the culture of the Deccan and highlights Hyderabad's arts, crafts, culture and the famous Nawabi cusine. Cultural programs organised include Ghazals, Qawalis and Mushairas, Poetry etc., typical of the city. Various renowned singers and dancers are invited for performances and this is a not to miss for every person who visits. This exclusive festival is conducted by the Department of Tourism. This festival also includes Pearls and Bangles fair, displaying creations in lustrous pearls and multi-hued bangles that are local specialties, and a Food Fair, with items covering both Andhra and Hyderabadi cuisine. Cultural programs, food stalls, arts and craft shops etc. are well organized.

Deccan Herald : The Deccan Herald is the largest English-language daily newspaper in the state of Karnataka in India. It is published by the Printers (Mysore) Private Limited and has a number of editions in Bangalore, Hubli, Mysore, Mangalore and Gulbarga. Deccan Herald was started in 1948. Its sister publications are the Prajavani daily newspaper in Kannada, the weekly magazine Sudha, and the monthly magazine Mayura all in Kannada. The head office of Deccan Herald is on MG Road, Bangalore

Deccan Plateau : The Deccan Plateau is a vast plateau in India, encompassing most of Central and Southern India. It comprises the whole of peninsular India south of the Vindhya range and has an elevation which ranges from 1,500 to 2,500 feet (450 to 750 m). It is bounded in the west by the Western Ghats and in the east by the Eastern Ghats. These two formations form one of the vertex of a triangle which encompasses the plateau with the Vindhya range forming the third side. This region is one of the most stable land masses of the world.

The Deccan is home to many languages and people. Bhil and Gond people live in the hills along the northern and northeastern edges of the plateau, and speak various languages that belong to both the Indo-European and Dravidian families of languages. Marathi, an Indo-Aryan language, is the main language of the north-western portion of the Deccan plateau. Urdu, Telugu, and Kannada, are the predominant languages of Andhra Pradesh and Karnataka respectively, they occupy the plateau. Tamil is the main language of the country to the south of the plateau, and Malayalam that of the hills and coast to the south-west. Moreover, the city of Hyderabad is an important centre of Urdu language in the Deccan; its surrounding areas also host a notable population of Urdu speakers.

Deccan Sultanates : The Deccan sultanates were five Muslim-ruled kingdoms—Bijapur, Golconda, Ahmednagar, Bidar, and Berar of south-central India. The Deccan sultanates were located on the Deccan plateau, between the Krishna River and the Vindhya Range. They became independent states during the breakup of the Bahmani Sultanate: Bijapur, Ahmednagar and Berar in 1490, Bidar in 1492, and Golconda in 1512. In 1510, Bijapur repulsed an invasion by the Portuguese against the city of Goa, but lost it later that year.

Although generally rivals, they did ally against the Vijayanagara empire in 1565, permanently weakening Vijayanagar in the battle of Talikota. In 1572, after a coup in Berar, Ahmednagar invaded and conquered it. In 1609 Bidar was annexed by Bijapur. The sultanates were later conquered by the Mughal Empire; Berar was stripped from Ahmednagar in 1596, Ahmednagar was completely taken between 1616 and 1633, and Golconda and Bijapur conquered by Aurangzeb's 1686-7 campaign.

Deccan Thorn Scrub Forests : The Deccan thorn scrub forests is a xeric shrubland ecoregion of India and northernmost Sri Lanka. It covers the arid portions of the Deccan Plateau, extending across the Indian states of Maharashtra, Karnataka, Andhra Pradesh, and Tamil Nadu to the Northern Province of Sri Lanka.

Deccan Traps : The Deccan Traps is a large igneous province located in west-central India and is one of the largest volcanic features on Earth. It consists of multiple layers of solidified flood basalt that together are more than 2,000 m thick and cover an area of 500,000 km^2. The name is derived from the Swedish word for steps which refer to the step like hills forming the landscape of the region.

The Deccan Traps formed between 60 and 68 million years ago, at the end of the Cretaceous period. The gases released in the process may have played a role in the extinction of the dinosaurs. Before it was reduced to its current size by erosion and continental drift, it is estimated that the original area covered by the lava flows was as large as 1.5 million km^2. The volume of basalt is estimated to have been 512,000 km^3 (VEI-10).

It is postulated that the Deccan Traps eruption is associated with a deep mantle plume or hotspot. The plume or hotspot, known as the Réunion hotspot, is suspected of causing both the Deccan Traps eruption and opening the rift that once separated the Seychelles plateau from India. Seafloor spreading at the boundary between the Indian and African Plates subsequently pushed India north over the hotspot, which now lies under Réunion island in the Indian Ocean, southwest of India. The mantle plume model has, however, been challenged.

Deeg : Deeg is a town in Bharatpur district of Rajasthan state in India. It is situated in the north of Bharatpur at a distance of 32 km. It is an ancient town.

It finds mention in Skanda Purana as "Dirgha" or "Dirghapura". Deeg was the first capital of the newly carved out Jat state of Bharatpur, when Badan Singh was proclaimed its ruler in 1722. In 1730, the Maharaja Suraj Mal erected the strong fortress of Deeg. After Suraj Mal moved the capital to Bharatpur, Deeg became the second capital of the rulers of Bharatpur princely state. It is known for its number of forts, palaces, gardens and fountains.

Now a days Deeg is famous for the three day fair held in the month of september.When the forts of Deeg are brought to liveliness.Deeg has various kinds of palaces, the most famous among them is "SAWAN-BHADON", the palace has a hollow ceiling with rolling iron spheres in it.when water is made to flow into the celing, these spheres collides with each other and produce a sound like raining clouds.

Deeksha Bhoomi : Deeksha Bhoomi is a holy monument for Buddhists where Buddhists receive Deeksha every year on 'Ashok Vijaya Dashmi Day' in Maharashtra. Every year a mass congregation of all the followers of Lord Buddha and Dr. Babasaheb Ambedkar assemble here from all parts of the country.

Deepak Chopra : Indian born Deepak Chopra has earned fame as a great physician in the field of alternative medicine in the US. Dr. Chopra serves as the Director of Education at the Chopra Center, which offers training programs in mind body medicine. He has established a new life giving pattern which has a crucial connection between mind, body, spirit and healing.

Born in Delhi, India in the year 1947, Chopra was raised in a family infused with both Western Medicine and Traditional Hindu beliefs and practices. His father, Krishnan Chopra was a prominent cardiologist who served as the dean of a local hospital and a lieutenant in the

British army and his grandfather was an Ayurveda practitioner. His vision to establish a medical system based upon the premise that health is a lively state of balance and integration of body, mind, and spirit led him to open the Chopra Centre for well being in California in 1995. Through this Center, Chopra is trying to expand his healing approach using the integration of the best of western medicine with natural healing traditions.

Deepak Chopra's popularity as an international presenter and keynote speaker is exemplified in an impressive list of honorariums. Esquire Magazine designated him as one of the top ten motivational speakers in the country; and in 1995, he received the Toastmasters International Top Five Outstanding Speakers award, earlier received by President Nelson Mandela, Congresswoman Barbara Jordan, Tom Peters and Garrison Keillor. He is the recipient of the Einstein Award through Albert Einstein College of Medicine in collaboration with the American Journal of Psychotherapy.

Deepavali : Deepavali is the festival of lights. The chief feature in the celebration of this festival, is that all bathe early in the morning rubbing their head and body with oil, though an oil bath is prohibited on the new-moon day on which the festival generally, falls. After bath they take sweets and enjoy themselves. The children fire off crackers. All this is done as a thanks offering for ridding the world of the oppression of the Naraka by the god Krishna.

Deepika : Deepika, a Malayalam newspaper, is one of the oldest newspapers published from India. It is also the first Malayalam daily. Deepika has now its editions in Kottayam, Kochi, Kannur, Thrissur, Thiruvananthapuram and Kozhikode. It has a circulation base of over 180,000 copies.Deepika has a history of over a century. It was first published by a Roman Catholic priest, Nidhirikkal

Manikkathanar, under the masthead Nasrani Deepika, in 1888.

The word Deepika in Malayalam means oil candle. It was then printed on a crude handmade wooden press. As its first name denotes Deepika is more popular among Nasranis or Syrian Catholics in Kerala. For many years Deepika was run by Carmelites of Mary Immaculate(CMI), a religious order within the Roman Catholic Church. In the mid 90s the daily was taken over by a Public Limited Company, Rashtra Deepika, which consists mostly bishops and priests as board of directors.

Defence Intelligence Agency (DIA) : This agency was established on 5 March 2002 with the appointment of Lt. General Kamal Davar as the first Director General (DG). The DG reports to the Chief Of Defence Staffs (CDS). It is supposed to be the nodal agency for all defence related intelligence, thus distinguishing it from the RAW. This agency also controls the Directorate of Signals Intelligence and the Defence Image Processing and Analysis Centre (DIPAC).

Dehradun : Dehradun, previously called Dehra Doon, is the capital city of Uttaranchal state of India and is also the headquarter of Dehradun District. It is located in the Doon valley, 230 kilometers north of Indian captial New Delhi and the Delhi metro. It is surrounded by the Himalayas mountains on the north, Shivalik Hills on the south, and the river Ganges east and the river Yamuna on the west. The water divide of Ganga and Yamuna passes through the city. It is also located on the northern side of the fertile Gangetic plains of India.

Before the creation of Uttaranchal on November 9th 2000, Dehradun was a part of the historic state Uttar Pradesh. Neighbouring cities and towns include Haridwar, Rishikesh, Roorkee, Mussoorie and Saharanpur. A popular item that has made Dehradun known across the world is "Dehradooni basmati rice", which is grown in the fields surrounding the neighbouring Saharanpur.

Deknni or Dakhnni : It is a form of song-cum-dance in the Christian repertoire of song among the people of Goa. It is a song composed by Christian artistes perhaps an expression of the Goan Christian nostalgia for their lost Hindu past, where the Devadasi or Kolvont in Konkani was an alluring symbol. The term Dakhnni in Sanskrit means devil of a female. It is danced in a manner that verges on the voluptuous, with gyrations and significant gestures which are so suggestive in character. The main danseuse is joined by other females, enticing in their appearance, who announce themselves to the audience. Then begins the pleading and coaxing by the women, including finally the boatman with offerings of anklets, bracelets, nose-ringlets, by turns and finally clinching the deal with the offer of a kiss, which latter the boatman accepts in the surrender to their wiles, to ferry them across to the other side of the river to a place belonging to a man called Damu, where they have to perform at the wedding.

Delhi : Delhi is a metropolis in India. The name Delhi also refers to the National Capital Territory of Delhi (NCT), which is a special union territory jointly administered by the Central government, NCT's elected government and three municipal corporations: Delhi, Delhi Cantonment and New Delhi. New Delhi, an urban area within the metropolis of Delhi, is the seat of the Government of India.

Delhi's metropolitan area, known as the National Capital Region (NCR) encompasses the entire NCT as well as the neighbouring satellite towns of Faridabad and Gurgaon in Haryana, and Noida and Ghaziabad in Uttar

Pradesh making it the 5th most populous megalopolis in the world, with 19.5 million people.

Delhi has the most vibrant history among prominent cities or towns of India. It was the "capital of seven empires" in Indian history and has over 60,000 recognized monuments built over several millennia, as per the Archaeological Survey of India. It is believed to be the site of Indraprastha, founded by the Pandavas of the Mahabharata around 5000 BC.

The name Delhi may originate from the Persian word Dahleez (English: threshold, or frontier) or from the name of a Mauryan king, Raja Dhillu. Another possible etymology is the the city's original name, Dhillika. The people of Delhi are known as Delhi-ites. The latter is a historical and cultural term describing people of the old city and the associated diaspora. The Persianized surname Dahelvi is also related to residents of Delhi.

Delhi derives its historic importance from its position in Northern India between the Aravalli Hills to the southwest and the Yamuna river on whose western banks it stands. This enabled it to dominate the old trade routes from northwest India to the plains of the Ganges. As a result, it has always been an important cultural and intellectual centre. With a steadily-increasing quality of life, a booming economy and consumer market, and being the nation's capital, Delhi's cultural and intellectual life too are burgeoning. Delhi also has hosts many of India's major educational institutions, and many quality schools. It is home to a number of think tanks, museums, art galleries, parks and theatres.

Delhi Sultanate : The Delhi Sultanate, or Sulthanath-e-Hind/Sulthanath-e-Dilli refers to the various Afghan dynasties that ruled in India from 1210 to 1526. Several Turko-Afghan dynasties ruled from Delhi: the Slave dynasty (1206-90), the Khilji dynasty (1290-1320), the Tughlaq dynasty (1320-1413), the Sayyid dynasty (1414-51), and the Lodi (1451-1526).

During the last quarter of the twelfth century, Muhammad of Ghor invaded the Indo-Gangetic plain, conquering in succession Ghazni, Multan, Sindh, Lahore, and Delhi. Qutb-ud-din Aybak, one of his generals, proclaimed himself Sultan of Delhi and established the first dynasty of the Delhi Sultanate, the Slave or Mamluk dynasty (mamluk means "slave") after Muhammad's death in 1206. The territory under control of the sultans expanded rapidly. By mid-century, northern India from the Khyber Pass to Bengal was under control of the sultanate, although the northwest was contested with the Mongols. Iltutmish (1210-35), and Balban (1266-87) were among the dynasty's most well-known rulers. Faced with revolts by conquered territories and rival families, the Mamluk dynasty came to an end in 1290.

The Khilji or Khalji dynasty, who had established themselves as rulers of Bengal in the time of Muhammad Ghori, took control of the empire in a coup which eliminated the last of the Mamluks. The Khiljis conquered Gujarat and Malwa, and sent the first expeditions south of the Narmada River, collecting tribute and sacking temples as far south as Tamil Nadu. Muslim rule continued to extend into southern India, first by the Delhi sultans, then by the breakaway Bahmani Sultanate of Gulbarga, and, after the breakup of the Bahmani state in 1518, by the five independent Deccan sultanates. The Hindu kingdom of Vijayanagar united southern India and arrested Muslim expansion for a time, but it fell to the Deccan sultanates in 1565.

In the first half of the 14th century the Sultanate introduced a monetary economy in the provinces (sarkars) and districts (parganas) that had been established and founded a network of market centers through which the traditional village economies were both exploited and stimulated and drawn into the wider culture. State revenues remained based on successful agriculture, which induced sultan Muhammad bin Tughluq (1325-51) to have village wells dug, offer seed to the peasants and to encourage cash crops like sugar cane (Braudel 1984, pp 96f, 512ff).

The Delhi Sultanate is the only sultanate to stake a claim to possessing one of, if not the only female ruler in India, Razia Sultan (1236-1240). While her reign was unfortunately short she is regarded well in the eyes of historians.

The sultans of Delhi enjoyed cordial, if superficial, relations with Muslim rulers in the Near East but owed them no allegiance. The sultans based their laws on the Qur'an and the sharia and permitted non-Muslim subjects to practice their religion only if they paid jizya or head tax. The sultans ruled from urban centers—while military camps and trading posts provided the nuclei for towns that sprang up in the countryside. Perhaps the greatest contribution of the sultanate was its temporary success in insulating the subcontinent from the potential devastation of the Mongol invasion from Central Asia in the thirteenth century. The sultanate ushered in a period of Indian cultural renaissance resulting from the stimulation of Islam by Hinduism. The resulting "Indo-Muslim" fusion left lasting monuments in architecture, music, literature, and religion. The sultanate suffered from the sacking of Delhi in 1398 by Timur (Tamerlane), and independent Muslim sultantates were established in Awadh, Bengal, Jaunpur, Gujarat and Malwa. The Delhi Sultanate revived briefly under the Lodhis before it was conquered by the Mughal emperor Babur in 1526.

Delwar Hossain Sayeedi : Delwar Hossain Sayeedi (often commonly referred to as Allama Saydi), is a Bangladeshi politician, a M.P. of the Bangladeshi Parliament, and one of the most important leaders of the Jamaat-e-Islami Bangladesh, a primary member of the ruling coalition Bangladesh Nationalist Party-led government.

Sayeedi is one of the most famous religious telepreachers in Bangladesh. His many critics have alleged that he does not represent Islam, only uses its name to suit the many financial and business enterprises of his political organisation Jamaat , and they, along with several historians, have alleged that Sayeedi participated in war crimes through assisting and financing the Pakistani military , with whom Jamaat's political branch in Pakistan had a link with, in their suppression of the liberation movement which later granted Bangladesh its independence. The latter of these charges have been denied by Sayeedi, though there has never been a full-scale investigation of his involvement in the war.

Democratic Students Federation (DSF) : Democratic Students Federation (DSF) is a Left-wing student organization in Pakistan. It emerged as a splinter group of National Students Federation(NSF) in the early Seventies when a pro-China faction of NSF parted from its pro-Moscow parent party Communist Party of Pakistan. DSF was active on various colleges and universities of Pakistan but its influence started to decline after the collapse of Communism in the early Nineties.

Denzongpa : Tshering Phintso "Danny" Denzongpa (born February 25, 1948) is an Indian actor. Denzongpa was born in the state of Sikkim, at that time an independent monarchy. He has acted in numerous Hindi films such as Ashoka and 16 December. He has also starred in an international films, the most famous being

Seven Years in Tibet where he acted alongside Hollywood actor Brad Pitt.

In 2003, Denzongpa was awarded the Padma Shree, India's fourth highest civilian honour. Denzongpa is noted for his roles as a villain. He is also the only actor to have come from Sikkim.

Deolali Camp : Deolali Camp is an important Indian military center. Deolali camp which is one of the oldest in India, is located 16 km away from Nasik. The center was set up by the British in 1861. An officer of the rank of Major General holds the position of the head of the Artillery school here. In the days of the British Raj, soldiers who cracked up under the stresses and strains of life in British India were invariably packed off to a military psychiatric hospital here to recover. Its name became synonymous with nervous breakdown; hence the English idiom "to go doolally", meaning to become insane or eccentric. Deolali market is famous for shopping. In the Temple Hill nearby, there is a famous temple of Lord Khandoba.

Deolo Hill : Deolo Hill is one of the two hills that the town of Kalimpong stands. Kalimpong is situated on a ridge connecting the hills of Durpin and Deolo. The hill is 1,704 metres (5,590 feet) above msl and is the highest point of Kalimpong town. The hill is located north east of the town. The two water reservoirs which serve as the primary drinking water source to the town are present atop this hill. The topwn of Kalimpong, the surrounding villages of Relli valley, Teesta River and its valleys all can be viewed from this point.

Deosai National Park : Deosai National Park is located above the tree line and at an average height of 13,500 feet above sea level, the Deosai Plains are among the highest plateaus in the world. The Deosai Plains cover an area of almost 3,000 square kilometers. For just over half the year - between November and May - Deosai is snow-bound. In the summer months when the snow clears up, Deosai is accessible from Skardu in the north and the Astore Valley in the west.

Dera Bugti : Dera Bugti district is in the south west of Balochistan province of Pakistan. Dera Bugti is named after its headquarter town 'Dera Bugti'. Dera (a Balochi word) means `abode' or `habitat', while `Bugti' is the name of the major Baloch tribe. Thus Dera Bugti means the abode of the Bugtis, the dominant tribe of this district. Dera Bugti district has three sub-districts : Dera Bugti, Sui and Phailawagh. Natural gas is the major mineral wealth of Dera Bugti district. There are four major gas fields : Sui Gas field, Pir Koh Gas field, Loti Gas field and Uch Gas field. Natural Gas was discovered at Sui in 1963 for use all over the country.

Dera Ghazi Khan : Dera Ghazi Khan is a district in Punjab, Pakistan. The district of Dera Ghazi Khan contains an area of 5306 sq. m. The district is a long narrow strip of country, 198 m. in length, sloping gradually from the hills which form its western boundary to the river Indus on the east. Below the hills the country is high and arid, generally level, but sometimes rolling in sandy undulations, and much intersected by hill torrents, 201 in number. With the exceptions of two, these streams dry up after the rains, and their influence is only felt for a few miles below the hills.

Dera Ismail Khan : Dera Ismail Khan is city in North West Frontier Province, Pakistan. The town is situated on the right bank i.e. the west bank of the Indus River.

Derajat : Derajat is an area of Pakistan, located in the region associated with the Baloch tribes. Derajat consists of two districts, Dera Ghazi Khan, which was founded by

Ghazi Khan Nawab, and Dera Ismail Khan, founded by Ismail Khan Mirani. A smaller district, Rajanpur, has recently been separated from Dera Ghazi Khan. The language of Derajat is Derawali (also known as Siraiki), but Balochi and Urdu are also spoken there.

Derawali : Derawali is an Indo-European language spoken in western parts of Punjab, Pakistan; it is a dialect of Saraiki (western Punjabi) language. Derawali speaking Hindus (Derawal) migrated to India in 1947 and have dispersed all over north India.

Derawar Fort : Derawar Fort is an ancient fort located in Cholistan Desert in Pakistan. The Fort was built by Deoraj, a prince of Jaisalmer. It was in possession of royal family of Jaisalmer when it was captured by Abbasis in 1735. In 1747 the Fort slipped from the hands of Abbasis in the reign of Nawab Bahawal Khan due to his pre-occupations at Shikarpur. Nawab Mubarak Khan took the stronghold back in 1804.

Desabhimani : Desabhimani is a Malayalam newspaper run by Communist Party of India (Marxist). Originally started as a weekly in 1942 and later converted to a daily in 1946. It has different editions published from Kozhikode, Kochi, Thiruvananthapuram, Kannur, Kottayam and Trichur.

Desert Festival : For three days Jaisalmer gets a chance to parade its charms to the world. Some chosen and cherised moments of its glorious past and rich culture are on display. The traditional dances accompained by high pitched music on instruments take the folk dancers one step back into time. The famous Gair dancers and the fire-dancers steal the show whenever they perform. There is further excitement afoot with the turban-tying competition and Mr. Desert contest. The grand finale is a trip to the sand dunes at Sam where one can enjoy and have the pleasure of a camel ride and at times also view the musicians and dancers performing on the dunes.

Desert National Park : The Desert National Park is situated in the west Indian state of Rajasthan near the town of Jaisalmer. This is one of the largest national parks, covering an area of 3162 km^2. The Desert National Park is an excellent example of the ecosystem of the Thar Desert. Sand dunes form around 20% of the Park. The major landform consists of craggy rocks and compact salt lake bottoms, intermedial areas and fixed dunes. Despite a fragile ecosystem there exists an abundance of birdlife. The endangered Great Indian Bustard is one magnificent bird found in relatively fair numbers. It migrates locally in different seasons. The region is a haven for migratory and resident birds of the desert. One can see many eagles, harriers, falcons, buzzards, kestrel and vultures. Short-toed Eagles, Tawny Eagles, Spotted Eagles, Laggar Falcons and kestrels are the commonest of these. Sand grouse are spotted near small ponds or lakes. The most suitable time to visit the area is between November and January.

Desh : Desh is a region of Maharashtra state in central India. Desh is bounded on the west by the Western Ghats or Sahyadri range, on the north by the Kandesh and on the east by the Marathwada regions of Maharashtra, and on the south by the state of Karnataka. The region is hilly and slopes towards the east, and is drained by the upper reaches of the Godavari and Krishna rivers and their tributaries.

The Desh region was the birthplace and core of the Maratha Empire, founded by Shivaji in the 17th century, and is home to a number of cities, like Satara and Pune, associated with Maratha history. The region came under British rule in 1818, at the conclusion of the Third Anglo-Maratha War. Most of the region was ruled directly by the British as part of the Bombay Presidency, but several princely states, including Satara and Kolhapur, remained under Maratha rulers in subsidiary alliance with the British. Satara was annexed by the British in 1848. After Indian Independence in 1947, Bombay Presidency became the Indian state of Bombay. Bombay state was divided into the states of Maharashtra and Gujarat in 1960.

Deshiwals : The Deshiwals are a tribe of the Swati origin residing on the eastern slopes of the Black Mountain of Hazara, had a fighting strength of over 1000 armed men at the end of the 19th century, who saw action against the British. Deshi or Deeshan is the name given to the country to north of Agror, and lying to the west of Nandhiar. It comprises a portion of the eastern slopes of the Black Mountain, a beautiful part of the Swati country, wooded spurs with intervening watercourses, on the banks of which are the villages. They are a united tribe, equally among themselves and when external danger threatens.

Devajyoti Ray : Devajyoti Ray is an up-and-coming Indian artist, who has been described by The Tribune of Delhi as "one of the most promising among the new generation" of Indian artists. He was born in 1974 and studied economics in Presidency College, Kolkata, and later at Jawahar Lal Nehru University. Ray, who presently alternates between living in Bangalore and Calcutta, is also credited with the beginning of pseudorealism, a new style of art in India. Ray is also a writer and an officer for the Government of India.

Devaki Nandan Khatri : Devaki Nandan Khatri was the first author of mystery novels in Hindi. He wrote Chandrakanta, Chandrakanta Santati, Kajar ki Kothari, Bhootnath, etc. He was born at Muzaffarpur, Bihar. After his earlier education he moved to Tekari Estate in Gaya. He became an employee of the Raja of Benares. He started a printing press called "Lahari" and started a Hindi monthly, "Sudarshan", in 1898.

Devanagari : Devanagari, in English pronounced is an abugida writing system used to write, either along with other scripts, or exclusively, several North Indian languages, including Sanskrit, Hindi, Marathi, Sindhi, Bihari, Bhili, Konkani, Bhojpuri, Nepali from Nepal and sometimes Kashmiri and Romani. It is written and read from left to right. Devanagari emerged around 1200 AD out of the Siddham script, gradually replacing the earlier, closely related Sharada script. Both are immediate descendants of the Gupta script, ultimately deriving from the Brahmi script attested from the 3rd century BC; Nagari appeared in approx. the 8th century as an eastern variant of the Gupta script, contemporary to Sharada, its western variant. The descendants of Brahmi form the Brahmic family, including the alphabets employed for many other South and South-East Asian languages.

Devaparvata : Devaparvata meaning 'the mountain of gods' is the name of an ancient city in samatata. It is situated on the isolated mainamati ridge near comilla. Recent archaeological excavations and explorations in the Mainamati area have revealed its extraordinary historical importance and archaeological wealth. They provide a large variety of epigraphic records, over 400 ancient gold and silver coins, innumerable seals and sealings, an exceptionally rich collection of stone, bronze and terracotta sculptures, an extraordinary variety of architectural treasures and various other objects of art and everyday use—original, authentic and contemporary source materials for reconstructing the long-forgotten history and civilisation of this region. Devaparvata is indeed more than a mere city; it is a prominent landmark in the history of the region.

Devdas : Devdas is the eponymous male protagonist of a tragic Bengali novel, written by Sarat Chandra Chattopadhyay in 1917. The novel has been made into a movie in multiple Indian languages including Bengali, Hindi (thrice), Telugu (twice) and Tamil. A number of famous actors have played the role of Devdas, actors such as K.L. Saigal, Dilip Kumar, Shahrukh Khan and Akkineni Nageswara Rao. All the Devdas movies have been box-office hits.

Devprayag : Devprayag is a city in the state of Uttaranchal in northern India. It is significant because it is the point where the Bhagirathi and the Alaknanda join to form the Ganga. It is one of the five sacred confluences in the hills and is a great place of pilgrimage for devout Hindus. Devaprayag stands at an elevation of 2265 ft. on the side of a hill which rises above it 800 ft. On a terrace in the upper part of the village is the temple of Raghunath, built of huge uncemented stones, pyramidical in form and capped by a white cupola. Bishnupur (Bankura, West Bengal) is famous for its terracotta temples and the balucheri sarees. The land is also called Mallabhum after the Malla rulers of this place. The Malla rulers were Vaishnavites and built the famous terracotta temples during the 17th and 18th century at this place. The terracotta temples here are the best specimen of the classical style of Bengal architecture.

Dewas : Dewas is a city in the Indian state of Madhya Pradesh. It is the administrative center of the Dewas District, and was formerly the seat of two princely states during the British Raj. Today, Dewas is an industrial town, with companies like Ranbaxy and Tata International being prominent players. Dewas lies northeast of Indore, southeast of Ujjain, and southwest of Shajapur. The town is located on the level plains of the Malwa plateau; to the south, the land rises gently to the Vindhya Range, which is the source of the Chambal and Kali Sindh rivers that flow north through the district on their way to the Ganges. Dewas lies at the foot of the conical Chamunda

Hill, on the summit of which is the Devi Vindhyavasini temple. Nagara, which is home to Jain and Hindu temple ruins, lies just south of the city of Dewas.

Dhaka : Dhaka, population 12,560,000 (2005), is the capital of Bangladesh. The city is situated on the Buriganga River, a channel of the Dhaleshwari River, in the heart of the world's largest jute-growing region. It is the industrial, commercial, and administrative center of Bangladesh, with trade in jute, rice, oilseeds, sugar, and tea. Manufactures include textiles and jute products. Dhaka is famous for its handicrafts. Geographically, Dhaka is located at 23°42' North, 90°22'30" East (23.7, 90.375).

Dhaka is known to be in existence since the 7th century A.D. It grew as an urban center, when it became the provincial capital of Mughal Bengal in 1608. The origin of the name of Dhaka is shrouded in mystery. Some believe that it is derived from the Dhakeshwari Temple, which was originally built around 12th century by a Sena King. Legend says that the King found a statue of the Hindu Goddess Durga covered under the bushes near the Buriganga river. He decided to clean up the jungle and established a temple for the Goddess, which he called Dhakeshwari (Concealed Goddess). Others believe that the name is derived from the Dhak (drum), which was beaten during the inauguration of the capital by the Mughal Subahdar Islam Khan.

Dhaka was also known as Jahangir Nagar for some time during the Mughal period in honor of the Mughal Emperor Jahangir. The city passed to British rule in 1765. It became the capital of East Pakistan in 1947. In 1971, the city became capital of the newly independent country Bangladesh. It was formerly known under the spelling Dacca. Modern Dhaka has vastly outgrown the so-called Old Dhaka. Statistically, its population has grown to around 13 million during recent decades, due to a population shift from rural areas. Old Dhaka with its important port and various historical sites can still be found at the southern end of the sprawling and disorganised modern city.

Dhaka Central Jail : Dhaka Central Jail is the historic jail located in the old section of Dhaka, Bangladesh.

Dhaka City Corporation (DCC) : Dhaka City Corporation (DCC) is a self-governing corporation that is associated with the task of running the affairs of the city. The incorporated area is divided into several wards. Each ward has an elected ward commissioner. The mayor of the city is elected by popular vote every five years.

Dhaka City Corporation was established as the Dacca Municipality on August 1, 1864. Prior to that, a Committee for the improvement of Dacca was established in 1823. The act of 1884 added the provision of elected representives called commissioners. In 1978, it gained corporation status. In 1982, two adjoining municipalities — Mirpur and Gulshan—were merged with Dhaka Municipality. In 1983, it was renamed as Dhaka Municipal Corporation. Finally, in 1990, it was renamed as Dhaka City Corporation. Until 1994, mayors were added by the Government. The first mayor elected by popular vote took office in 1994. As of 2006, Sadeque Hossain Khoka is the incumbent mayor.

Dhaka College : Dhaka College, located in Dhaka, is one of Bangladesh's most important and earliest higher educational institutions. It offers HSC, three years bachelor's and four years honour's course in various majors. The college is affiliated with the University of Dhaka. Several thousand students study here, it has a number of student halls and many students participate in politics.

Dhaka College was established by Dr. James Taylor (Civil Surgeon at Dhaka) in 1835 as an English School. Dr.

James organized a local Committee of Public Instruction with the help of district magistrate Mr. Grant. The school building was built partly out of public donations on the grounds of an English factory. The school rose to college status in 1941 and buildings were completed in 1946, with the aid of the Bishop of Calcutta. In the first graduating class there were both Muslim and Hindu students, as well as a number of foreign students, mainly from Armenia and Portugal. The college was relocated in 1873 to a large building to the east of Victoria Park in order to accommodate the physics and chemistry laboratories. Later it shifted in 1908 to Curzon Hall while the science departments were housed in the present chemistry building of the University of Dhaka. In 1921 the college shifted again to the present High Court Building. During the Second World War it moved to Siddique Bazar. At present, it has its own campus near Dhaka New Market.

Dhaka Division : Dhaka Division is an administrative division within Bangladesh. The capital and largest city is Dhaka. The division covers an area of 31,119.97 km^2, and has a population of 38,678,000 in 2000. Dhaka Division bounds the Indian state of Meghalaya to the north, Barisal and Chittagong Divisions on the south, Sylhet and Chittagong Divisions to the east, Rajshahi and Khulna Divisions to the west. Dhaka division consists of one city corporation, 17 districts, 58 municipalities, 21 Thanas, 119 upazilas, 1239 union parishads, 12765 mouzas, 549 wards, 1623 mahallas and 25244 villages. The districts are Dhaka, Gazipur, Narsingdi, Manikganj, Munshiganj, Narayanganj, Mymensingh, Sherpur, Jamalpur, Netrokona, Kishoreganj, Tangail, Faridpur, Madaripur, Shariatpur, Rajbari and Gopalganj.

Dhaka International Buddhist Monastery : Dhaka International Buddhist Monastery founded in 1981 by the theravada Buddhist community. It was initially set up in a rented house near the Malibag rail crossing in dhaka. Sundarananda Bhikkhu (Sukomal Barua) was its first principal. From the beginning it played an important role in propagating buddhism and preserving its culture and tradition in Bangladesh. The monastery moved to its permanent building at Merul Badda in 1989. At the beginning, its activities were conducted by the Dhaka International Buddhist Monastery Committee. Later, this responsibility was taken over by the Bangladesh Buddhist Federation.

The monastery has a women's sub-committee to conduct devotional rites. Many dignitaries visit the monastery. Buddhist diplomats posted in Dhaka regularly visit it with their families and take part in religious and cultural ceremonies. Among the archaeological relics preserved at the monastery are two statues of the Buddha from Thailand. One of the statues, which is 4' 6" high, is made of bronze and weighs about 260 kg. The other, which is made of astadhatu, eight metals, is about 7' high and weighs 777 kg.

Dhaka Medical College and Hospital (DMCH) : Dhaka Medical College and Hospital (DMCH), established in 1946 during the British colonial rule, is the top medical school in Bangladesh. Situated at the heart of the city near the Bangladesh University of Engineering and Technology, Dhaka Medical College is an educational institution with a rich heritage. Established in 1946, it took about 10 years for the Dhaka Medical College and Hospital to start operations because of bureucratic entanglements. The Dhaka Medical College and its affiliate, Dhaka Medical College Hospital, were accommodated in a building constructed in 1904 as the Secretariat Building for the province of East Bengal and Assam. The building was transferred to the University of Dhaka in 1921. One part of it was converted into the university's medical centre, one part into a student dormitory, while the residual part was allotted for use as the academic wing of the Faculty of Arts.

Dhaka News: The Dhaka News is a weekly periodical, first published on 18 April 1856. It appeared every Saturday and cost two annas per copy. Annual subscription was two and a half rupees. Though its focus was mainly indigo, with its title at one time including the words 'Planters' Journal, it also included regional news and published letters. It was edited by Alexander Forbes, who subsequently edited the Harkara.

The periodical initially consisted of one page only, but then expanded to four pages and finally to eight. Supplements were also published on current market rates. The magazine was printed at Dhaka Press. Its management changed on 30 October 1858 and publication stopped in 1869.

Dhaka Prakash : Dhaka Prakash was the first Bangla newspaper published from Dhaka. Its first issue was published on 7 March 1861 from Bangala Jantra in Babu Bazar. The epigraph, siddhih sadhye samamastu (success can be gained by ability), was inscribed under the title of the newspaper. It used to come out every Thursday. The yearly charge, including postage, was Rs 5. Initially, advertisements were placed on the left side of the first page.

Initially, Dhaka Prakash was published as a mouthpiece of the Brahmos; but with a change in ownership the outlook of the paper also changed. As a result, the paper sometimes supported the Brahmos and sometimes orthodox Hindus. On political issues the paper followed the middle course and tried to establish peace between the ruler and the ruled. As a result it had to face numerous problems during the anti-partition movement and the swadeshi movement. Nevertheless, it was an influential paper whose opinion had considerable impact on public opinion. During the 19th century the Report on Native Papers used to quote news mainly from Dhaka Prakash. The paper began with a circulation of 250. In the nineties, circulation increased to 5000, indicating the paper's popularity. It survived for nearly a century, exceeding in longevity all other newspapers of East Bengal. Indeed, it is not possible to understand the political, economic, social and cultural history of Dhaka or of East Bengal without the help of Dhaka Prakash.

Dhaka Stock Exchange : Dhaka Stock Exchange is the main stock exchange of Bangladesh. It is located in Motijheel at the heart of the Dhaka city. It was incorporated in 1954.

Dhaka Viswavidyalay Patrika : Dhaka Viswavidyalay Patrika research journal of the university of dhaka, was first published in December 1973. Professor Serajul Islam Choudhury, who edited it up to October 1988, was its founder editor. During its first four years (1973-1976), the journal was published annually. every December. From 1977 to 1983 it was published on a half-yearly basis, in June and December. In 1984 it was published in June and October. Since 1985 it is being published thrice a year, in February, June, and October.

Research essays written in Bangla on a variety of subjects such as literature, history, religion, philosophy, fine arts, music, trade and commerce, law, science, sociology, economics, politics, etc. are published in the journal. Up to 1997 only teachers and researchers of Dhaka University and its affiliated colleges could contribute to the journal. At present there is no such restriction.

Dhakeshwari : Dhakeshwari is a famous Hindu temple in Dhaka, Bangladesh. The meaning of the name is "Temple of the Goddess of Dhaka". Legend has it that the city of Dhaka was named after this temple. The origin of the Dhakeshwari temple is obscure. According to the popular legends, the original temple was built in 12th century by a Sena King and the name of the city was coined after this temple. But the researchers found that the style of architecture of the temple cannot be a resemblance of that period.

The temple complex has undergone repairs, renovation and rebuilding in its long years of existence and its present condition does not clearly show any of its original architectural characteristics. Therefore, it is necessary to do a careful research to find its origin and retain back to its original condition. Nevertheless, it is certainly an essential part of the cultural heritage of Dhaka city. The temple is located in the old town near the Dhaka University area.

Dhakeshwari River : Dhakeshwari River, about 160 Km long, a distributary of the Jamuna River in central Bangladesh. It starts off the Jamuna near the Northwestern tip of Tangail District. After that it divides into two branches. The north branch retains the name Dhaleshwari andmerges with the other branch, the Kaliganga River at the southern part of Manikganj District. Finally the merged flow meets the Shitalakshya River near Narayanganj District. The combined flow go southwards to merge into the Meghna River.

Dhala River : Dhala river originated from the eastern hills of Tripura (India). Flowing north from its source the river enters Bangladesh through Kulaura upazila of Maulvi Bazar district and meets with the Manu river southwest of Rajnagar upazila of the same district. The joint course of the Manu and Dhala flows towards Maulvi Bazar and turning north debouches into the Kushiyara at Manumukh

Dhali Dance : Dhali dance enacts a duel between two men whose weapons are thickly woven cane shields and bamboo sticks. Drums and brass cymbals provide the musical accompaniment. The main objective of this dance is to display the dancers' physical prowess and martial skills. To start with, the two warriors face each other threateningly, in tune with the music, and then launch their attacks and counterattacks either standing or kneeling. This mock war goes on until a climax is reached. Dhali dance is usually arranged at folk fairs in Jessore and khulna regions.

Dhamal (Dhamyal) : It is the leading dance of Haryana, often also known as the Duph, practised during the sowing season. It is notable for the sounds of pounding feet and beating daffs. This dance is especially popular in the Ahir areas of Gurgaon.

Dhammapada : The Dhammapada (Pali, translates as Path of the Dharma. Also Prakrit Dhamapada, Sanskrit Dharmapada) is a Buddhist religious scripture, containing 423 verses in 26 categories. According to tradition, these are answers to questions put to the Buddha on various occasions, most of which deal with ethics. A fifth century commentary by Buddhaghosa includes 305 stories which give context to the verses. The Dhammapada is a popular section of the Pali Tipitaka and is considered one of the most important pieces of Theravada literature. Although the Pali edition is the most well known, a Gandhari edition written in Kharosthi and a seemingly related text in Sanskrit known as the Udanavarga have also been discovered.

Dhamtari : Dhamtari is a district in the Indian state of Chhattisgarh. It was officially formed on July 6, 1998, from an amalgamation of Dhamma and Tarai (hence the name). Dhamtari district is officially formed on 6th July 1998 dividing the Raipur district currently the capital of Chhattisgarh along with Mahasamund. As a result the boundaries of the Raipur district is converted into the districts e.g Raipur, Mahasamund and Dhamtari. Dhamtari, Kurud and Nagari are included in Dhamtari district as tehsils, and Dhamtari, Kurud, Nagari and Magarlod are included as blocks. The district headquarter is itself Dhamtari. Mahanadi is the principal river of this district and Mahanadi is so far named as Kankannadi, Chitrotpala, Neelotpala, Mandvahini, Jairath etc.

Dhamu Samkranti : This festival is celebrated on the first day of Solar pousha month in Orissa. The month of pousha is considered the month of plenty. After collecting the harvest there is a festival of general rejoicing with special sweets of 'Maun'.

Dhanbad : Dhanbad is the headquarter of Dhanbad District of Jharkhand state, India. Dhanbad is famous for its coal mines and industrial establishments. Dhanbad is also called the Coal Capital of India. The Indian School of Mines located here draws students from all over the world. Central Mining Research Institute, and Central Fuel Research Institute are located here. Agencies like DGMS, CMPDIL, CMPF are there and play wide variety of roles in their respective disciplines to serve the coal industry. Bharat Coking Coal Limited (BCCL) is also situated here. Dhanbad is the second highest revenue generator for railways in India.

Dhangari Gaja : Dhangari Gaja is performed by Dhangars (Shepherds) of Sholapur District of Maharastra. The Dhangars rear sheep and goats to make their living. The surrounding green pastures and evergreen trees inspire them to compose poetry. The poetry is in a form called 'Ovi' which is made up of couplets. Sometimes fantastical stories are also told through this form. Tales of the birth of their God "Biruba" are found in simple and earthy lines. Once every year the Dhangars return home to honour 'Biruba'. They spend their time with their families and beloved ones. The Dhangari Gaja dance is performed to please their God for His blessings. Dhangars dance in traditional Marathi dresses - dhoti, Angarakha and Pheta with colourful handkerchiefs. Dancers move around a group of drum players.

Dhanmondi Lake : Dhanmondi Lake a prominent depression within Dhaka metropolitan area. It is situated in the middle of dhaka City (about 23°43'N latitude and 90°26'E longitude). It lies within the vicinity of Dhanmondi residential area. Originally Dhanmondi Lake was an abandoned channel of the 'Karwan Bazar Nadi' ('Karwan Bazar' is commonly spelled and pronounced as 'Kawran Bazar'), previously known as the 'Carevan River', whose alignment was possibly along Begunbari Khal-Green Road-Kalabagan-Dhanmondi Lake to the turag river. Part of this lake still functions as a storm water drain and falls into the Begunbari Khal.

Expansion of urbanisation in this area during Pakistan period has changed the natural water system in this place. Dhanmondi residential area was developed in 1956 with 240.74 ha of land including the lake. The lake is about 16% of the total area of Dhanmondi and has been playing a vital role in maintaining the only drainage system of Dhanmondi and adjacent areas. It also shows some trellis pattern together with the dendritic pattern of drainage system. The lake offers attractive panoramic views to many thousands of people who live in the vicinity.

Dhanraj Pillay : Dhanraj Pillay (born July 16, 1968) is a former field hockey player and captain of the Indian hockey team. He was born in Pune. Presently, Pillay also plays for a club team named Maratha Warriors in the Premier Hockey League.

Dhanraj is the recipient of India's highest sporting honour, the Rajiv Gandhi Khel Ratna award for the year 1999-2000. He was awarded the Padma Shri, a civilian award in 2000. He is the only Indian to play in four Summer Olympics, four World Hockey Cups, four Champions Trophies, four Asian Games, and four Asia Cups.

Dhanushkodi : Dhanushkodi was a city at the southern tip of the Rameswaram island, at the eastern coast of the Tamil Nadu state of India.

Dhanushkodi is situated in the South-East of Pamban, the Dhanushkodi railway line was destroyed in the 1964 cyclone from Pamban Station and a trainload of passengers was washed into the sea.. Even though the railway line was laid between Rameswaram and Dhanushkodi, it was in course of time covered by six sand dunes and it was abandoned. One has to reach Dhanushkodi on foot along sea shore or in jeeps on sand dunes. It is said that Pilgrimage to Kashi will be completed only after the worship at Rameswaram besides a holy bath in Dhanushkodi at the Confluence of Mahodadhi (Bay of Bengal) and Ratnakara (Indian Ocean).

Dhar : Dhar is a town in the Malwa region of western Madhya Pradesh state in central India. It is the administrative headquarters of Dhar District. The town is located 33 miles west of Mhow, 908 ft. above sea level. It is picturesquely situated among lakes and trees surrounded by barren hills, and possesses, besides its old walls, many interesting buildings, both Hindu and Muslim, some of them containing records of a great historical importance.

Dharamsala : Dharamsala or Dharmsala, (literally; "Rest House") is a town in the northern Indian state of Himachal Pradesh. Dharamsala is located in the Kangra valley, in the Dhauladhar mountains. It became the capital of the Kangra District in 1852. Dharamsala has been connected with Buddhism for a long time, with many monasteries having been established there in the past. In the 8th century, however, these monasteries are believed to have declined, with Hinduism experiencing a revival. The local Gaddi people are now almost all Hindu.

Dharla River : Dharla river is one of the trans-boundary rivers of Bangladesh. It enters the country at Lalmonirhat through Changra Bandha of Patgram. In its upper course, it is known as the Jaldhaka or Singimari. Near Patgram upazila, it again flows back to India and continues an easterly course. Suddenly it turns south and enters Bangladesh for the second time through Kurigram and then follows a meandering course.

Dharla is a tributary of the Brahmaputra river. The main channel of this river originates in Kuch Bihar (India). It flows into the Brahmaputra a few kilometres southeast of Kurigram town. In Rangpur district, it has a small tributary called the Nilkumar, formerly a larger river. Kurigram town stands on the right-bank of the Dharla. It is known as the Dhola in Rangpur and has low and shelving banks and is particularly liable to changing its course. It is a swift river in the rainy season, but a braided stream in winter. The Dharla becomes wide and turbulent during the rainy season and resorts to erosion. In 1947 it completely washed the old site of Kurigram town.

Dharma Mittra : Sri Dharma Mittra is a Yoga teacher, and a student of Sri Swami Kailashananda Maharaj. According to Yoga Journal magazine, he's best known for creating the "Master Yoga Chart of 908 Postures," but his "influence on the yoga world extends far beyond the nearly 50,000 copies of that poster that have been printed since Mittra completed the laborious project in 1983." He has been teaching since 1967, and is Director of the Dharma Yoga Center in New York City.

Dharma Mittra is considered by some to be one of the original independent teachers, starting many on the path of studying, and teaching Yoga. He began teaching Yoga before various diverging styles became popular, and is considered by some to have remained true to the original practice of the third limb of Raja Yoga, asana, or the postures of ashtanga. Having initiated tens of thousands of individuals into the practice of Yoga, Dharma Mittra's students and admirers call him the "Teacher's Teacher" and the "Rock of Yoga."

Dharmapuri District : The district occupies an area of 9622 km^2 and has a population of 2,833,252 (as of 2001). It is bounded on the north by Krishnagiri District, on the east by Tiruvannamalai and Viluppuram districts, on the south by Salem District, and on the west by Karnataka's Chamarajanagar District. Dharmapuri District was created in 1966, when it was separated from Salem District. Krishnagiri District was formerly part of Dharmapuri, becoming a separate district in 2004. Dharmapuri city is also called thakadoor. Dharmapuri is famous for mango fruits. Hogenakkal is the famous tourist place in Dharmapuri district.

Dharmar and Hamchi Dances : These are energetic and fast tempoed dances are performed by the Siddis or Abysinnians who came from Africa centuries ago.

Dharmaraksita : Dharmaraksita was one of the missionaries sent by the Mauryan emperor Ashoka to proselytize the Buddhist faith. He is described as being a Greek in the Mahavamsa, and his activities are indicative of the strength of the Hellenistic Greek involvement during the formative centuries of Buddhism.

Dharmasthala : Dharmasthala is perhaps the most highly revered and best known Temple town in Karnataka. Located amidst the picturesque Western Ghats on the banks of the Nethravathi, it is about 100 km from Udupi. This holy place is the home of the Sri Manjunatheshwara

Temple, where devotees of all caste and creed visit and which is well known for charity. Sri Manjunatheshwara Temple is a temple devoted to Shiva and houses a lingam of gold. The temple is unusual in that it is run by a Jain administration and poojas are conducted by Madhva priests.Everyone enjoys the generous hospitality without any distinction of caste, creed or class whatsoever. On an average the flow of pilgrims is about 10,000 people everyday. A mechanised and clean kitchen provides free food for all pilgrims can feel comfortable at the guest houses, which have all modern amenities.

More than 25 institutions from primary schools to professional colleges are run in and around Dharmasthala. Old and decrepit temples have been renovated, taking care to preserve the traditional architecture. Ancient manuscripts and paintings have been painstakingly restored and preserved for posterity. A museum of beautiful antique objects, which is both educative and fascinating, has been established. A car museum houses a rare collection of vintage cars. Every year, a Sarva Dharma Sammelan (multi religious meet) is held at Dharmasthala, which attracts spiritual leaders from various faiths and schools, and patrons of art and literature, from far and wide. This is also among of the few pilgrim centers in India which provides free boarding and lodging to all the visiting devotees. The exponentially increasing number of visitors is a proof of the good work being done here.

Dharmavir Bharati : Dharmavir Bharati (1926–1997) was a renowned Hindi writer and known to many as the editor of the magazine Saaptahik Hindustan. Amongst his famous works are 'Suraj ka saatva ghoda' (The Seventh Steed of the Sun), and the lyrical play 'Andha-Yug'. The former is a short novella with seven relatively independent plots, but each woven together in an integrated whole. It has at places scathing wit, and may be read as meta-fiction or as an allegory. The latter is a moral allegory that draws its rubric from the Mahabharata but conveys a timeless message about degeneration of values in human society. He also wrote some very insightful essays, and some prominent essay anthologies are Thele par Himalaya and Pashyanti.

Dhebar Lake : Dhebar Lake, also known as Jaisamand Lake, is a lake in Udaipur District of Rajasthan state in western India. It has an area of 50 km² (20 square miles) when full, and was created in the 17th century when Rana Jai Singh of Udaipur built a marble dam across the Gomati River. The Jaisamand Wildlife Sanctuary protects 52 km², mostly teak forest, on the shore of the lake.

Dhenkanal : Dhenkanal District is an administrative division of Orissa, India. It has an area of 4599.5 square kilometers and a population of 1,087,973. It is bordered by Keonjhar in the north, Jajpur in the east, Cuttack in the south and Angul in the west. Dhenkanal town, the district headquarters has a cluster of temples, archaeological remains and a mediaeval fort.

A former princely state, Dhenkanal has a long history. Hari Singh Vidyadhar who was a commander of Gajapati Pratprudra deva defeated the local Bhanja kings and occupied and Dhenkanal and Karamul, its capital in 1529 AD. Subsequently, 18 generations kings ruled over Dhenkanal & brought about many administrative, political, socio-economic, and cultural evolutions tothe district. In 1947, after Indian Independence, the princely State of Dhenkanal merged in the Indian Union, and subsequently with Orissa in 1948. Most of this district is covered with dense forest and a long range of hills, which are home of wild elephants and tigers. Primarily agricultural, the principal forest products of the district are timber, bamboo, firewood and kendu leaf, and raw materials used for medicine.

Dhepa River : Dhepa river is an offshoot of the Karatoya-Atrai (Buri Tista) river. The river originated from the right-bank of the Atrai near Mohanpur (25 53'N latitude, 88 43'E longitude) in the greater Dinajpur district and flowed southeast direction. Then it turned south near Setabganj, Bochaganj and after following a meander course up to Poi-Chak (25 38'N latitude and 88 37'E longitude) the river debouches into the Punarbhaba. The total length of the river is about 40 km and navigable throughout the year for local boats. The Dhepa is totally free from tidal influence.

Dhirajlal Hirachand Ambani : Dhirajlal Hirachand Ambani, one of the leading Indian businessmen, was born on December 28, 1932 in Chorwad, Gujarat. Popularly known as Dhirubhai Ambani, he heads The Reliance Industries, India's largest private enterprise.

Dhirubhai started off as a small time worker with Arab merchants in the 1950s and moved to Mumbai in 1958 to start his own business in spices. After making modest profits, he moved into textiles and opened his mill near Ahmedabad. Dhirubhai founded Reliance Industries in 1958. After that it was a saga of expansions and successes.

Reliance, acknowledged as one of the best-run companies in the world has various sectors like petrochemicals, textiles and is involved in the production of crude oil and gas, to polyester and polymer products. The companies refinery at Jamnagar accounts for over 25% of India's total refining capacity and their plant at Hazira is the biggest chemical complex in India.

The company has further diversified into Telecom, Insurance and Internet Businesses, the Power Sector and so on. Now the Reliance group with over 85,000 employees provides almost 5% of the Central Government's total revenue. Dhirubhai has been one among the select Forbes billionaires and has also figured in the Sunday Times list of top 50 businessmen in Asia. His industrious nature and willingness to take on any risk has made him what he is. In 1986 after a heart attack he has handed over his empire to his two sons Anil and Mukesh. His sons are carrying on the successful tradition of their illustrious father.

Dhokla : Dhokla (also called Khaman) is a fast food from the Indian state of Gujarat. The dish can be made of ground chana dal (chickpeas) soaked overnight; other recipes call for flour. This paste is spiced by adding chile pepper, ginger, and baking soda, then left for fermentation for four to five hours. The dhokla is then steamed for about ten minutes on a flat dish and cut into cake-like pieces. It is usually served with green chutney and chopped onions, or some grated coconut. Dhokla can also be fried further with mustard for extra spiciness.

Dhol : The dhol is a drum widely used in Persia,Armenia, the Indian/Pakistani province of Punjab and Gujarat.

Dhol is said to have been invented by the Persian/ Afghanis. When they migrated to North India, it was incorporated into Gujarati, Punjabi, Rajasthani and other North Indian cultures. Nowadays, it is popular in modern Punjabi music.

The dhol is a rather bulky double-sided barrel drum played mostly as an accompanying instrument to the traditional Punjabi dance of Bhangra, the traditional dance of Gujarat, Raas, and the religious music of Sufism, Qawwali. In Qawwali music, the term dhol is used to describe a similar, but smaller drum used with the smaller tabla, as a replacement for the left hand tabla drum.

Dholak : The Dholak (sometimes dholaki) is a classical North Indian hand drum. A dholak may have traditional lacing or turnbuckle tuning. The dholak has a simple membrane on the right-hand side. The left-hand membrane has a special coating on the inner surface. This coating is a mixture of tar, clay and sand (dholak masala) which lowers the pitch and provides a well-defined tone.

The dholak is the main accompaniment instrument of the Qawwali. The Dholak is often used in Filmi Sangeet or Indian film music.

Dhola-ri-Dhani : This is a typical setting recreated with the entire rustic ambience and charm of an ethnic Rajasthani village, situated at Kompally on Medchal Road. It is in Hyderabad.

Dholavira : It is a small village situated near the north-western extremity of Khadir in Gujarat, which is a large island in the great Rann of Kutch. The village is approachable from Bhuj via Rappar by a good road on which plies a regular bus service. Nearest Airport Bhuj, Distance from Bhuj to Dholavira 140 Km. Kuntasi situated in Maliya taluka & Rajodi near Gondal were centres of ancient Harappan civilization. (2200 BC to 1500 BC) The excavations at these centres can fill many gaps in knowledge about the palaeology—day to day life of Harappan people These are sites of extra ordinary insight for those interested in ancient civilization & archeology. Kuntasi was a trading emporium & an active port when the waters of the Gulf were extended to it.

Dholka : Dholka is a town in western India. It is located in Ahmedabad District of Gujarat state. In the middle ages, Dholka was the seat of the Vaghela family, who were feudatories of the Solanki rulers of Gujarat. As the Solankis went into decline, the Vaghelas rose in power, ruling Gujarat from 1243 to the Muslim conquest in 1297. They restored stability to Gujarat for the latter half of the 13th century, and the Vaghela kings and their officials were dedicated patrons of the arts and temple-building. Dholka is also known for Jain Temple Kalikund Tirth. Every year lots of Jain families visit this Temple.

Dholpur : Dholpur (also Dhaulpur) is a city in eastern Rajasthan state of India. It was formerly the capital of the princely state of Dholpur, and is the administrative headquarters of Dholpur District. The present town of Dholpur, which dates from the 16th century, stands somewhat to the north of the site of the older town built in the 11th century by Raja Dholan (or Dhawal) Deo, a Tomara rajput chieftain; it named Dholdera or Dhawalpuri after him.

In 1450, Dholpur had a raja of its own; however, the fort was taken by the Delhi Sultanate under Sikander Lodi in 1501 and transferred to a Muslim governor in 1504. In 1527, after strenuous resistance, the fort fell by Babur and came under the sway of the Mughals along with the surrounding country. It was assigned by Emperor Akbar to the province of Agra. A fortified sarai built in the reign of Akbar still stands in the town, within which is the fine tomb of Sadik Mohammed Khan (d.1595), one of his generals.

During the dissensions which followed the death of the Mughal emperor Aurangzeb in 1707, Raja Kalyan Singh Bhadauria obtained possession of Dholpur. His family retained it until 1761, after which it was taken successively by the Jat Maharaja Suraj Mal of Bharatpur; by Mirza Najaf Khan in 1775; by the Sindhia in 1782; and finally, by the HEIC in 1803. It was restored by the HEIC to Sindhia under the Treaty of Sarji Anjangaon, but in consequence of new arrangements, was again occupied by the British. Finally, in 1806, the territories of Dholpur, Ban and Rajakhera were handed over to Kirat Singh of Gohad, in exchange for that Jat chieftains own state of Gohad, which was ceded to Sindhia. From this point begins the history of the princely state of Dholpur, a vassal of the British during the Raj. Please refer to the main article Dholpur.

Dhoper Chop : Dhoper chop is a Kolkata speciality snack dish, initially prepared in the canteens of Jadavpur University. "Chop" in Bengali cuisine refers to breaded fries. "Dhop" is believed to have initially been a nonsense rhyming word to go with chop. "-er" is a possessive marker in Bengali.

A dhoper chop is actually a batter fry (and not a breaded fry) of a vegetable sandwich. The vegetable in question is usually mocha (the banana flower). The dish is usually served with a sweet sauce on the side, like Papaya chutney.

"Dhoper chop" is also a Bengali colloquialism which means "stuff and nonsense". "Dhop" also means "stuff and nonsense" and may also be used in the sense of "fib". The usage possibly came from disgruntled dhoper chop eaters who found scanty vegetable stuffing inside a large fluffy fry.

Dhoti : The Dhoti is the original and timeless garment of men's wear in India. A rectangular piece of unstitched cloth, it is wrapped in a complex manner about the waist and legs. It is usually white or cream in color, although colourful hues are often used to create more vivid ensembles. There are more than 60 different ways of draping the this garment.

In northern India, the garment is worn with a Kurta on top, the combination known simply as "Dhoti Kurta". In southern India, it is worn with an Angavastram (another unstitched cloth draped over the shoulders) or else with a "Chokka" or "Jubba", a local version of the kurta. The Lungi is a similar piece of cloth worn in the same manner, though it is used only informally and never formally. It is also primarily worn by people of the lower classes and particularly popular in southern India as well as in Sri Lanka, Malaysia etc.

Dhrupad : Dhrupad is the oldest surviving genre of classical singing in India. Its name, from dhruva-pada, seems to mean "the eternal verse", and its foremost characteristics are a somber, dignified, devotional mood, its very slow tempo and slow melodic development. Like all Indian classical music, dhrupad is modal, with a single melodic line and no harmonic parts. The modes are called raga, and each raga is a complicated framework of melodic rules.

Dhrupad, as we know it today, has a repertoire of short songs (two to sixteen lines) which are performed by a solo singer, or a small number of singers in unison, to the beat of a double-headed barrel drum, the pakhawaj. The songs are mostly in praise of Hindu deities, but in recent centuries, Islamic or simply regalist lyrics have been written and added to the repertoire. The song itself, which is known as the dhrupad, is preceded in performance by a wholly improvised section, the alap, without accompaniment of the drum.

Traditionally, the only instrument used for playing dhrupad was the been, which is technically a fretted stick zither with strings set along a bamboo or wooden neck with a large gourd mounted at each end. The word "been" is a colloquial form of the Sanskrit "veena", the generic word used for plucked-string instruments all over India.

Dhule : Dhule is a city in northwestern state Maharashtra of India. It is the administrative headquarters of Dhule District. It lies in the Khandesh region, which forms the northwest corner of southern India's Deccan Plateau, in the valley of the Tapti River (a.k.a. Tapi River). It is situated along banks of Panzara river. It is a center for cotton-textile manufacturing, with both spinning and weaving operations. The nearest international airport is Mumbai, and has its own domestic airport at Gondur. Dhule became part of the Mughal Empire in 1601, during the reign of Akbar. In the 18th century Dhule came under Maratha rule. In 1818, Dhule was annexed by the British, and was included in the Bombay Presidency. When under the British Empire, Dhule city was designed by Sir Vishveshwarraya. After Indian independence in 1947, Bombay Presidency became Bombay State, which in 1960 was divided along linguistic lines into the new states of Maharashtra and Gujarat.

Dhundhar : Dhundhar is a region of Rajasthan state in western India. Also known as Jaipur region, It includes the districts of Jaipur, Dausa, Sawai Madhopur, and Tonk and the northern part of Karauli District. The region lies in east-central Rajasthan, and is bounded by the Aravalli Range on the northwest, Ajmer to the west, Mewar region to the southwest, Hadoti region to the south, and Alwar, Bharatpur, and Karauli districts to the east.

The southern and central portions of the region lie in the basin of the Banas River and its tributaries, including the Dhund River, which gives its name to the region. The northern portion of the region is drained by the Ban Ganga River, which originates in Jaipur district and flows east to join the Yamuna in Uttar Pradesh state.

The region was governed by the Kachwaha dynasty from the 12th century until after India's independence in 1947. The Kachwaha kingdom, whose first capital was at Amber, was later known as Jaipur, after the new capital established in 1727 by Maharaja Jai Singh II, who ruled from 1700 to 1743.

Dhundiraj Govind Phalke : Dada Saheb Phalke is known as the 'father of Indian Film Industry'. He was born in 1870. Phalke laid the foundation for the start of a regular feature film industry in the country. He has produced about 175 films. His famous films are 'Satyavan Savitri', 'Mohini Bhasmasur' and 'Raja Harichandra'. The outbreak of World War I plunged Phalke into extreme financial crisis. In 1917, he made a grand reappearance with the revised version of Raja Harischandra and India's first big box office hit 'Lanka Dahan'.

Phalke has been honoured by naming an award for the outstanding works in the field of films. It is called Dadasaheb Phalke Award.

Dhurang (Dhuring) Dance : This dance is performed by the Doms and the Bhotiyas and is connected with the death ceremonies. Its objective is to liberate the soul of the dead person from evil spirits.

Dhyan Chand : Dhyan Chand made great contribution in enhancing prestige of Indian Hockey in the eyes of the world. He was born on 29th August 1906, in Allahabad (Uttar Pradesh). He joined army at the age of sixteen. He started playing hockey in army and was included in the Indian Hockey team for the 1928 Amesterdam Olympics.

By his superior play, Dhyan Chand was held in high esteem with in the country as well as abroad. Dhyan Chand helped his country in winning gold medals in hokey in 3 successive Olympics games; Amesterdam Olympics (1928), Los Angles Olympics (1932) and Berlin Olympics(1936). He was the captain of the gold medal winner Indian Hockey team in the historic 1936 Berlin Olympics. Dhyan Chand scored 101 goals at the Olympic games and 300 goals in other international matches and his record is unbroken.

Dhyan Chand had a wonderful command in wielding the hockey stick and this earn him the title " Hockey Wizard". India won one gold medal in Hockey at

Amersterdom Olympics and out of a total of 28 goals scored by Indian hockey, 11 were scored by Dhyan Chand alone. He died on December 3,1979.

Diana Hayden : Diana Hayden, the 1997 Miss World was born in 1973 in Hyderabad, Andhra Pradesh. She was the only Miss World to have won a hat-trick at the pageant—Miss Photogenic, Miss Beachwear and Miss World 1997.

A tomboy as a teenager, Diana grew up to be a ravishing beauty. Diana' family split up at her very young age, but her family including her mother and brother was still very close-knit. After completing her schooling at St Ann's High School, Secunderabad, she graduated from Osmania University in English through correspondence. Diana shifted to Mumbai to pursue her career goals. She then moved to Bangalore working for the event management company Encore and then again to Bombay.

Diana had a brief stint in modelling and did a couple of fashion shows in Bangalore and Mumbai. Then she started work in the public relations division of BMG Crescendo, the music company where she helped handle the careers of artistes like Anaida and Mehnaz. It was Anaida who forced her to send her pictures for the Miss India Contest and the rest is history.

The self made perfectionist made India proud by bagging the world crown. As Miss World, she became the name and face for L'Oreal and ambassador for CRY (Child Relief and You). She has completed a 5 weeks course on Shakespeare at the Royal Academy of Dramatic Arts in London and is engaged in a year long training at Drama Studio, London.

Diana describes herself as a very steady person, enjoying herself, doing what she loves most in the world. She has a passion for music and dance. But, her first love is reading. She likes horse riding and playing chess. Diana actively supports an orphanage in Hyderabad, CAP (Child And Police), a rehabilitation project under Dr. Reddy's Foundation, which deals with the police taking off children from the streets and educating them. Diana continues to do International modelling assignments.

Dibang Valley : The Dibang Valley is a district of Arunachal Pradesh named after the River Dibang or the Talon as the Idus call the river, originates in the mountains of China and flows through the length of the valley, named after it. The major population of this district consist of the Adis (padams) and the idus.the upper Dibang Valley is inhabited by Idu people only.

The Idus have a story narrating the first journeys undertaken in course of migration. The story conveys names and location of the Cheethu-Huluni or the twelve rivers that the Idu people came over in the region and settled around.The first accounts of the Idus or the Mishmis as the Ahoms called them are found in the narrations given by the neighbouring Ahoms.The Mishmis inhabited the deep jungles of what is now the Dibang valley.

The district has been divided further into lower and upper Dibang Valley for administrative convenience.The headquarters of the two districts are Roing and Anini respectively. Roing is a newborn town in the plains of the Mishmi hills roughly aging only twenty years. It is a beautiful place with picturesque nature and beautiful climate. However Anini is a hilly place lying in the mountains close to the frontiers of China.

Dibru—Saikhowa National Park : Dibru—Saikhova is the largest national park of Assam, spread over an area of 650 sq. km. It is located at about 13 kms north of Tinsukia town and about 515 kms from Guwahati and is bounded by the Brahmaputra river and Arunachal hills in the north and Dibru and Patkai hills on the south. This was declared a wildlife Sanctuary in 1986 by the government of Assam by uniting two Reserve forest, viz., Dibru and Saikhowa including some other areas. It was elevated to the National Park status in 1999 restricting its core area to 340 sq. km. with a large buffer zone.

Dibru Saikhowa National Park is one of the 19 (nineteen) biodiversity hotspots in the world. It mainly consists of semi wet evergreen forests, tropical moist deciduous forest, bamboo, cane brakes and grasslands. Situated in the flood plains of Brahmaputra, at an altitude of 118 m above sea level, Dibru-Saikhowa is a safe haven for many extremely rare and endangered species of wild life including over 300 avifauna both endangered and migratory, as well as various species of shrubs, herbs and rare medicinal plants.

Didihat : Didihat is a deep Himalayan tourist destination situated 54 km from Pithoragarh in the state of Uttaranchal,India.The small hilly town is full of pure natural beauty with lush green flora at an altitude of 1725 m. Didihat is situated on the hill top plain of 'Digtarh' and river Charamgad or Bhadigad streaming below. Below the town there is a fertile 'Haat valley'. Administratively it is a tehsil and subdivision of the Pithoragarh district. Tehsil Didihat is divided into three developmental blocks—Didihat, Kanalichhina, and Berinag. Historically this region was ruled by feudal Raika Malla kings of Sirakot. Till the time of King Har Malla, this region was under Doti Kingdom of Nepal.

Digaru Mishmi Buiya Dance : The Digaru Mishmis in Arunachal have two types of dances called Buiya and Nuiya. The Buiya dance has two types of movements and it is performed for entertainment while the Nuiya is a ritual-dance performed by a priest. Buiya dance is performed on any festive occasion like the Duiya, Tazampu and Tanuya festivals which are performed for the prosperity and good health of the performer and his household. This dance may also performed after a feast arranged by a family to entertain the fellow villagers who co-operate with it opening a new field. The dance is performed in the passage which runs along one side of the house from the front to the rear. Men and women take part in this dance. There is no limit to the age of the dancers although generally children and old persons do not take active part in the dance itself but merely sit by, as spectators.

Dilip Balwant Vengsarkar : Dilip Balwant Vengsarkar (born April 6, 1956 in Rajapur, Maharashtra) was an Indian cricketer. He was one of the most stylish batsmen of his time. He was also known by the nickname 'Colonel'. Vengsarkar made his international cricket debut against New Zealand at Auckland in 1975-76 as an opening batsmen. India won this Test handsomely, but he did not have much success.

He was a member of the 1983 World Champion's team. He had a magnificent run of scores between 1985 and 1987, where he scored centuries against Pakistan, Australia, England, West Indies and Sri Lanka, many of them in successive games. At this pinnacle of his career, He was rated as best batsmen in the Coopers and Lybrand rating. He also scored a century at Lord's in 1986 and thereby attaining the distinction of scoring three consecutive Test match centuries at Lord's. For his effort to help India win the Test series in England (a rare feat in itself) he was awarded the Man of the Series award. He was also nominated one of the five Wisden Cricketers of the Year in 1987.

Vengsarkar took over the captaincy from Kapil Dev after the World Cup 1987, despite criticism that he missed the all important semi-final match due to a relatively minor finger injury. His captaincy period was turbulent and he lost the job following a disastrous tour of the West Indies in early 1989 and a stand-off with the Indian cricket board (BCCI). For his contribution to the Indian cricket the Government of India decorated him with the Padma Shri honor.

Dilip Kumar : Dilip Kumar (born December 11, 1922) is an Indian film actor and Member of Parliament (Rajya Sabha). He is the recipient of India's highest award for cinematic excellence, the Dadasaheb Phalke Award and also the Nishan-e-Imtiaz, Pakistan's highest civilian award.

Dilip Kumar was born Yusuf Khan in Peshawar (now Pakistan) in a Pathan family of twelve children. His father relocated to Bombay (now Mumbai), He initially was working in Devlali where he was spotted by a filmmaker and then the young Yusuf Khan became involved in the Bollywood film industry. A Hindi novelist suggested that he use a screen name, Dilip Kumar. His first film. Jwar Bhatta, was released in 1944.

Dilkusha : Dilkusha an are adjacent to the present Bangabhaban in Dhaka. It is now a commercial place. The area was once adorned with a Rang Mahal built by Mirza Mohammad. A big canal, later on turned into a lake and known as Motijheel, used to run through it. With the passage of time, the whole area came to be known by that name. Mir Mukim, the Daroga of Mir Jumla's naval force, had his residence in the area to the west of the Bangabhaban.

Dilwara Temples : The Jain Dilwara temples of India are located about 2½ kilometers from Mount Abu, Rajasthan's only hill station. These temples dating back from the 11th to the 13th century AD are world famous for their stunning use of marble.

The five legendary marble temples of Dilwara are the sacred pilgrimage of the Jains. They are an overwhelming blend of simple beauty and exquisite elegance. The marble temples have an opulent entranceway. The simplicity in architecture verily reminds one that Jainism as a religion "encouraged honesty and frugality". The temples reside amidst mesmerizing surroundings of mango trees and wooded hills. A high wall, shimmering luminous in the sunlight, shrouds the temple complex.

Although the Jains built some beautiful temples at other places in Rajasthan, none come close to these in terms of architectural perfection. The ornamental detail spread over the minutely carved ceilings, doorways, pillars and panels is simply marvellous and has to be seen to be believed. For the people who come to perform pooja here, there are facilities to take bath and get ready. The facilities use solar power to heat up the water for bath and other usage. There are guided tour hours for tourists which are posted outside the temple.

Dimapur : Dimapur is Indian state of Nagaland's largest city. The name Dimapur comes from the Kachari dialect. Etymologically di means "river", ma means "big" and pur means "city", in effect it means "the city near the great river." It is also the headquarters of Dimapur District. It is located at 25°54'45 N, °93'4430.

The main city has a population of 110,000 inhabitants(2001 census).Apart from the main city, Dimapur has a vast urban sprawl which continues upto the satellite township of Chumukedima, also called Nichuguard.This agglomeration has an estimated population of around 220,000 and is one of the fastest growing Indian cities.Its population has more than tripled in the last two decades. Unlike other places in the state, this city has a heterogeneous mix of people from all over India, and for which it is also known as "mini India." Besides the dominant Naga tribes who comprise about 50% of the city's population,other prominent groups include Bengalis, Assamese, Nepalese, Biharis, Marwaris, Punjabis and also Tamils.In the last two decades Tibetan traders have also settled in the city.

Dimapur is the magnet around which the economic and developmental activities of the state are centred. An important commercial centre for the region, it is one of the fastest developing cities in the North-East. It is also a gateway to Nagaland and Manipur. The National Highway 39 that connects Kohima, Imphal and the Myanmar border at Moreh runs through Dimapur.

Dimsa Dance of Araku Valley : The Araku valley is the most charming hilly region in Visakhapatnam district. Valmiki, Bagata, Khond and Rotia tribes inhabit this valley and other areas of this district. The favourite dance of these tribes is Dimsa which is performed by old and young men and women, during the month of chaitra i.e. in March/April, during weddings and other festivals. During festivals people go from one village to another to participate in the dance and are honoured with community feasts. People of different villages enjoy such festivities and dances called 'Sankidi Kelbar'. Dimsa Dance not only provides amusement to the dancers and spectators but also develops friendship and fraternity between people of different villages. The instruments accompanying Dimsa are Mori Kiridi, Tudumu, Duppu and Jodukommulu.

Dina Thandi : Daily Thanthi (or Dina Thandi) is a leading daily newspaper published in Tamil Nadu, India. It was founded by Sri Si. Pa. Aditanar, with its first edition from Madurai in 1942. The publication spread over Tamil Nadu and the neighbouring states of Pondicherry and Karnataka. Daily Thanthi became one of the largest Tamil language dailies by circulation within a few years; it has been a leading Tamil daily since the 1960s. It has today 14 editions. It is the highest circulated Tamil language daily in Bangalore and Pondicherry, and one of the largest in Tamil Nadu. Daily Thanthi's editorial policy is neutral. The publication does not support any one political party or government. The language is simple and easily understandable. Daily Thanthi's circulation during July-December 2004 was 790,900 copies (certified by ABC).

Dindi and Kala (Dahikala) : These are religious devotional dances which describe the playful attitude of Lord Krishna. Dindi is a small drum, like a 'Tamate'. The musicians in the centre, comprising of a 'Mridangam' player and a vocalist, give the dancers surrounding them the necessary musical background. This is usually performed on the Ekadashi day in the month of Kartik.

Dindigul : Dindigul is a city in the Tamil Nadu state of southern India. It is the administrative headquarters of Dindigul district. It gets it name from Thindu - pillow kal- Rock, pillow like rock which is a landmark of the City. Dindigul, also known as "The City of Locks and Tannery", is a fast growing tier-4 city in India. Its attracting a great deal of education sector investments.

Din-i-Ilahi : Din-i-Ilahi or Divine Faith, was a syncretic religion propounded by the Mughal emperor Akbar, intended to merge the best elements of the religions of his empire (primarily Hinduism and Islam; elements were also taken from Christianity, Jainism and Zoroastrianism), and thereby reconcile the sectarian differences that divided his subjects.

Akbar was the first Mughal ruler who tolerated religions other than Islam; in fact, not only did he tolerate them, he encouraged debate on philosophical and religious issues. This led to the creation of the Ibadatkhana, or Hall of Worship, at Fatehpur Sikri. From the discussions he led there in 1575, Akbar concluded that no single religion could claim the monopoly of truth. This inspired him to create the Din-i-Ilahi in 1581. Various Muslim clerics responded by declaring this to be blasphemy.

The Din-i-Ilahi, as propounded by Akbar, combined mysticism, philosophy and nature worship. It also recognized no gods or prophets. The religion had few followers; the only person other than Akbar who was a Din-i-Ilahian until their death was Birbal, one of Akbar's ministers. Raja Mansingh, his commander-in-chief refused conversion, saying that he recognised only two religions, Hinduism and Islam.

Dino Shafeek : Dino Shafeek (born 1929 in Dacca, East Bengal, British India; died March 10, 1984) was a Bangladeshi actor. He was probably best known for the part of 'Char Wallah Muhammed' in the BBC sitcom It Ain't Half Hot Mum, though he also appeared as a regular in the sitcom Mind Your Language. His first role was 'Akbar' in The Long Duel in 1967. His last role was 'Satvinder' in High Road to China in 1983.

Dir : The State of Dir was a small former princely state located in the modern North-West Frontier Province in Pakistan. The state ceased to exist in 1969 when it was incorporated into Pakistan. The area once occupied by the state (5,282 km^2) now forms two districts of Pakistan - Upper Dir and Lower Dir. The two districts were part of Malakand division until divisions were abolished as an administrative tier.

Diran : Diran is a mountain in the Karakoram region of the Northern Areas of Pakistan. This pyramid shaped mountain lies in the East of Rakaposhi (7,788m). Diran was first climbed in 1968 by three Austrians Rainer Goeschl, Rudolph Pischinger and Hanns Schell. Earlier attempts by a German expedition in 1959 and an Australian expedition in 1964 were unsuccessful.

Direct Action Day : Direct Action Day a.k.a (Affirmative Action Plan) on August 16, 1946 was a day to protest and voice the Muslim demand for Pakistan. This was planned as a peaceful day of civil disobedience. Direct Action Day, which, though peaceful all over India led to violence in Calcutta,Bihar and Noakhali where according to Lord Wavell's estimate 3000 Hindus and 7000 Muslims were killed. The figure has generally been corroborated by Sir Francis Tuker's account. Violence was then perpetrated against Muslims in Bihar the bloodbath which finally erupted across the country. Over 10,000 (upto 100,000 by non-official sources) Hindus, Buddhists, Sikhs and Muslims were killed. Following the Direct Action Day debacle and fearing the collapse of Muslim League coalition ministry with Scheduled Caste Federation in Bengal, Muslim League was forced to enter the Interim Government on Congress' conditions. Jinnah stayed out of the ministries, allowing Liaquat Ali Khan to head the League ministers.

In terms of a resolution of the Muslim League Council Meeting held during the period 27 July –29 July 1946, the Direct Action Day was intended to unfold "direct action for the achievement of Pakistan."

Dishdah : The dishdah is an overgarment worn by some Muslim women. It is an article of clothing worn in accordance with Islamic requirements for modesty of dress. The dishdash resembles a closed-front floorlength robe. The sleeves extend to the wrists. They are often decorated with ornate embroidery, however styles change according to region and personal taste. The dishdah covers the whole body with exception of hands, feet and head. It is nearly always worn with hijab, a wrap worn to cover one's hair.

Dispur : Dispur is the capital of Assam, a state in northeast India. This place that existed as a locality on the outskirts of Guwahati, took its place as the capital of

Assam in 1973. This was after Shillong, the erstwhile capital became the capital of the state of Meghalaya that was carved out of Assam. To the south of Dispur is the mythologically important site of Basistha Ashram and the Sankardeva Kalashetra, a cultural center created in the 1990s. Next to Dispur is the ancient township of Jatia.

Distaghil Sar : Distaghil Sar is a mountain in the Hispar Muztagh range in the Karakoram region of Northern Areas of Pakistan or Gilgit-Baltistan. Distaghil Sar was first climbed in 1960 by G. Starker and D. Marchart of an Austrian expedition led by Wolfgang Stefan.

Diu : Diu is an island lying off the south coast of Gujarat's Kathiawar peninsula, separated from the mainland by a tidal creek. It has an area of 40 km^2, and a population of 44,110 (2001 census). The town of Diu lies at the eastern end of the island, and is famous for its fortress and old Portuguese Cathedral. It is also a fishing town. The Indian Air Force has an air base here. The village of Ghoghla, which lies on the mainland opposite the eastern end of the island, is also part of the union territory.

In 1535 Bahadur Shah, the Sultan of Gujarat, concluded a defensive alliance with the Portuguese against the Mughal emperor Humayun, and allowed the Portuguese to construct a fortress and maintain a garrison on the island. The alliance quickly unravelled, and attempts by the Sultans to oust the Portuguese from Diu between 1537 and 1546 failed. The fortress, reconstructed by Dom Joao de Castro after the siege of 1545, still stands. The island was occupied by the Indian military on 19 December 1961. It is considered one of the most beautiful tourist locations in India. Famous destinations include the nearby Nagoa beach, one of the finest beaches in the country. The old fort, the church and the museum have a strong Portuguese taste.

Diwali : Diwali or Deepawali is a festival of lights symbolizing the victory of righteousness and the lifting of spiritual darkness. The word 'Deepawali' literally means rows of 'deepaks' or 'diyas' (clay lamps). It is celebrated 20 days after Dusshera on the 13th day of the dark fortnight of the month of Asvin (Oct-Nov). Continuing the story of Ram, this festival commemorates Lord Ram's return to his kingdom Ayodhya after completing his 14-year exile. Twinkling diyas and candles light up every home and firework displays are common all across the country. The goddess Lakshmi, who is the symbol of wealth and prosperity, is also worshipped on this day.

Lord Ganesh, the symbol of auspiciousness and wisdom, is also worshipped in most Hindu homes on this day. The occasion of Diwali sees the spring-cleaning and white-washing of houses; decorative designs or *rangolis* are painted on floors and walls. New clothes are bought and family members and relatives gather together to offer prayers, distribute sweets and to light up their homes.

Diwan-i-Am (Hall of Public Audience) : It is in Uttar Pradesh. It is 350 ft long, consist of cloisters surrounding a courtyard that contains the Hall of judgment. It was here that Akbar handed down the decisions, as the chief justice of his subjects, on various disputes, by sitting on his throne flanked by marble.

D K Pattammal : The vocalist Damal Krishnaswamy Pattammal is one of the most popular and respected Carnatic musicians. Along with her two contemporaries, M.S. Subbulakshmi and M.L. Vasanthakumari she forms the "Female Trinity of Carnatic Music".

Pattammal's sweet disposition and humble nature belie the fact that she started a few revolutionary trends in Carnatic music. She is the first Brahmin woman to have performed this music publicly, both on stage and on air.

(Brahmins rank as the (so-called) highest caste in India, and in the hyper-conservative 1930s society considered it taboo for a Brahmin woman to perform on stage.) Pattammal is also the first woman to have performed Ragam-Tanam-Pallavi on stage. Ragam-Tanam-Pallavi (or Pallavi) is the most difficult concert item in Carnatic music. Before Pattammal, it classed as a male stronghold. Not only did Pattammal boldly venture into Pallavi-singing, but she performed some very complex Pallavi-s in intricate Talas impressively enough to earn the respect of her male peers. For this reason, she became dubbed "Pallavi Pattammal". Today, hearteningly, many women Carnatic musicians perform Ragam-Tanam-Pallavi as the main item in their concerts.

Pattammal has received many awards and titles throughout her career. Most notably these include the Sangeetha Kalanidhi (considered the highest accolade in Carnatic music) in 1970, the Padma Bhushan from the Government of India in 1971, and the Padma Vibhushan, India's second-highest civilian honor, in 1998. However, she herself treasures the title 'Gana Saraswathi' bestowed on her by the formidable musician Tiger Varadachariar.

Dnyaneshwar : Dnyaneshwar (1275-1296) (alson known as Jnanadeva or Jnaneshvar) was a Hindu saint and poet who lived in Alandi Maharashtra, India at the end of the thirteenth century. Besides writing nearly a thousand Marathi abhangas, his major works are the Bhagvat Deepika/dnyanadevi, (popularly known as the Dnyaneshwari), a commentary on the Bhagavad Gita written in Marathi and the Anubhavamrita / Amritanubhava, is the work in which he has stated his own philosophy, sometimes called as Chitvilaasavaada. His writing is a combination of scholarly Intelligence and poetic beauty. He is called the founder of Bhakti tradition, that is, devotional worship, in Maharashtra known as

Bhagavata Dharma. His Dnyaneshwari is one of the three sacred books or Prasthanatrayì of Bhagavata Dharma.

Doctrine of Lapse : The Doctrine of Lapse was an annexation policy devised by Lord Dalhousie, who was the Governor General of India between 1848 and 1856. According to the Doctrine, any princely state or territory under the direct influence (paramountcy) of the British East India Company (the dominant imperial power in the subcontinent), as a vassal state under the British Subsidiary System, would automatically be annexed if the ruler was either "manifestly incompetent or died without a direct heir". The latter ignored a long-established right for an Indian sovereign without an heir to choose their successor. In addition, the British decided if potential rulers were competent enough.

At the time of its adoption, the Company had absolute, imperial administrative jurisdiction over many regions spread over the subcontinent. The company took over the princely states of Satara (1848), Jaitpur and Sambalpur (1849), Nagpur and Jhansi (1854) and Awadh (Oudh) (1856) using the Doctrine. With its increasing influence, discontent simmered amongst many sections of the society and the largely indigenous armed forces, who rallied behind the deposed dynasties, during the First War of Independence (known by British as Sepoy Mutiny of 1857).

Doddabetta Peak : Doddabetta Peak is the highest peak in Ooty, at 2623 meters. It is the most popular Tourist part in Ooty. From the Doddabetta Chamundi Hills can be viewed. Dodda betta got its name from the tribes 'dodda' living there.

Dogra : The Dogra are an ethnic group in South Asia. Some two million Dogras live in South Asia, predominantly in the Jammu region of Jammu and Kashmir but also in the adjoining areas of Punjab, Himachal Pradesh, and other parts of Kashmir. They speak their own language, Dogri, which is similar to the Hindko language of Azad Kashmir and it is related to the Punjabi language. Dogras primarily practice Hinduism.

Dokra : Tribal in origin, the Dokra metal craft is common to the tribal belts of Madhya Pradesh, Orissa, Bengal and Andhra Pradesh. In Andhra Pradesh this craft is found in Chittalbori and Ushegaon in Adilabad District. What makes Dokra unique is that no two pieces are alike. Deftly created by hand, the objects have an individualistic touch. Figurines, horses, drummers, peculiar shaped spoons and hauntingly original tribal Gods can be seen in Dokra. Primarily made from brass scrap, the objects also have a core of clay preserved within the metal casting, unlike other metal work.

Dol Purnima : In Bengal, Holi is celebrated as Dol Purnima. This festival is dedicated to Sri Krishna. On this auspicious day, an image of Krishna, richly adorned and besmeared with coloured powder, is taken out in procession, in a swinging palanquin, decorated with flowers, leaves, coloured clothes and papers. The procession proceeds forward to the accompaniment of music, blaring of conch shells, trumpets and shouts of 'Jai' (victory). Dol Purnima becomes all the more significant for Bengalis, because this is also the birthday of Chaitanya Mahaparabhu (1485-1533). He was a great Vaishnava saint, who popularized modern sankirtana. He elevated the passion of Radha and Krishna to a high spiritual plane. He underlined emotional at the cost of the ceremonial side of devotion. Followers of Chaitanya School of Vaishnavism, believe Chaitanya to be the manifestation of Krishna. Chaitanya Mahaprabhu believed that the essence of Sadhana is always the loving remembrance of Hari.

Dola Jatra : Beginning with the Purnima or the full moon day in the lunar month of Phalguna. The Radha and

Krishna images from the Vaishnava temples begin the ritual journey to some important centres of congregation or Melana. With Holy or sprinkling of red 'abir' powder and chanting of bhajan and kirtan, the devotees come in a procession with images of Radha and Krishna carried in the Vimanas to the site of the fair. The deities pay a visit to several villages on their outing and receive homage and offerings from devotees. At the site of the fair chanting if spiritual songs and recitation of the Bhagavata and other scriptures are usually organised.

Dolphin's Nose : The captivating symbol of Visakhapatnam that charms the young and old alike is the headland Dolphin's Nose.

Dona Paula : It is 7 Kms away from Panaji. This small palm fringed beach with Casuarina groves is very peaceful. The small town has several resorts.

Dongargarh : Dongar means mountains while garh means fort. Like most places of pilgrimage, dongargarh also has legend behind it. Roughly 2200 years ago, Raja Veersen, a ruler of this kingdom, was childless and upon the suggestions of his royal priests, went to Mahishmatipuri (mandla) to perform some puja and construct a temple. Within a year, the princess gave birth to a son whom they named Madansen. Raja Veersen considered this a blessing of lord Shiva and Parvati and constructed a temple here. Raja madansen went on to have a son named Kamsen, under whose rule the kingdom flourished and it came to be known as Kamakhaya Nagari. Now the place is known as dongargarh. The Maa Bamleshwari Devi temple is of great spiritual importance. Situated at a height of 1000 ft, this is the main temple at dongargarh. One has to climb 1100 stairs to reach here.

Donyi-Polo : Donyi-Polo is a religion in Arunachal Pradesh, formed in order to unify all the Animistic beliefs of the tribes in this area. It is also spelt as Danyi Piillo. The practise of the religion traditions passed on from generation to generation orally. Believers worship the sun and the moon, besides other things like bamboo and bushes found in the jungles. They also believe in Abo-Teni, the primal man who came from Tibet. Influenced by Hinduism in the recent years, the religion also has some forms of religious mantras.

Doom : A revolt by the subject of a particularly cruel or ruthless local Rana or Raja is known as 'Doom'. To attract the royal attention to their grievances the people in the area struck work and departed peacefully into the nearby forest, which brought all activity in the region to a standstill and forced the ruler to take measures to redress their grievances. This custom was always followed peacefully and there was no violence of any kind.

Doordarshan : Doordarshan is a public broadcast terrestrial television channel run by Prasar Bharati, a board nominated by the Government of India. It is one of the largest broadcasting organisations in the world in terms of the infrastructure of studios and transmitters. Doordarshan had a modest beginning with the experimental telecast starting in Delhi in September, 1959 with a small transmitter and a makeshift studio. The regular daily transmission started in 1965 as a part of All India Radio. The television service was extended to a second city – Mumbai (then Bombay) only in 1972. Till 1975, only seven cities were covered by Doordarshan and it remained the only television channel in India. Television services were separated from radio in 1976. Each office of All India Radio and Doordarshan were placed under the management of two different Director Generals in New Delhi. Finally Doordarshan as a National Broadcaster came into existence.

Dorah Pass : The Dorah Pass, also spelled and pronounced Durah Pass, connects Badakshan in

Afghanistan with Chitral in Pakistan. The Dorah Pass is more than 14,000 feet high. It crosses the Hindu Kush. It became important during the Soviet invasion of Afghanistan because the Soviets were unable to stop the flow of arms and men back and forth across the pass. Almost the entire Munji speaking population of Afghanistan fled across the border to Chitral during the War in Afghanistan.

Dosa : Dosa (Dose in Andhra state, Dosay in Karnataka state, Dhosai in Tamil Nadu state, Dosha in Kerala state) is a common south Indian food which comes in many varieties, flavours and with various accompaniments. Ideally a breakfast item, it is also eaten as a 'tiffin' all through the day.

It is prepared by laying a thin circular film from a batter of rice and lentil flour mixed with water on a flat, preheated pan, and frying it with a dash of edible oil or ghee. It gets evenly fried on one side to obtain a brownish tinge. The other side is partially fried next by turning the dosa over. The end product is neatly folded and served. The crispness, the colour, the amount of batter used and the time for which the batter was allowed to ferment prior to cooking determine the variety of dosa you eat. It is like a crêpe in shape and thickness, but usually crispier.

A stuffing inside a folded dosa is not uncommon. A common variety—masala dosa or Mysore masala dosa is essentially a freshly cooked, crisp dosa stuffed with mashed potatoes lightly cooked with fried onions and spices. Sometimes the onions are mixed into the batter itself- in which case it becomes an onion dosa. Cracking an egg onto a dosa as it is frying turns it into an 'egg dosa'.

Dover Lane Music Festival : Dover Lane Music Conference, one of the largest Indian Classical musical events is being held in Kolkata for the past five decades. The music conference which started as a humble get together of some music lovers in the by lanes of South Kolkata has now turned into one of the culturally most important event of the year. This festival provides a wonderful platform for the younger generation to come and perform with the best in the art. Every year number of youngsters come and display their skills in front of a huge crowd.

The festival is conducted at Nazrul Mancha in South Avenue in Kolkata every year between January 22 and 26. The auditorium with a seating capacity of 3,500 is filled with music enthusiasts and lovers from around the country. The music maestros from all over the country get together and create magic in front of an enormous crowd which is a real treat for music lovers. For the six days during which this event is held the city of Kolkata enjoys the presence of a number of music maestros. The people of Kolkata consider this festival as a heritage event.

Dow Medical College : The most respected medical school in Pakistan, Dow Medical College is one of the oldest education institutions of the country. It has produced a large number of well-trained physicians, who are now spread all over the world, establishing themselves as authorities in different areas of medicine. The college is situated in Karachi, the largest city of the country; however, it was first established in Hyderabad as a small college.

Dow University of Health Sciences : The most respected medical school in Pakistan, Dow Medical College is one of the oldest education institutions of the country. It has produced a large number of well-trained physicians, who are now spread all over the world, establishing themselves as authorities in different areas of medicine. The college is situated in Karachi, the largest city of the country; however, it was first established in Hyderabad as a small college. Until 2003, Dow Medical College was an affiliate institution of the University of Karachi. The adminsitrators and faculty as well as influential alumni of the college as well as sister institutions (Sind Medical College and Ojha Insitute of Chest Diseases) had had been trying, for several years, to have the provincial government merge these institutions and create a health sciences university. This effort finally succeeded in 2003 and the college and its sister institutes now enjoy full university charter, together known as the Dow·University of Health Sciences.

Draksharama : Draksharama is one of the Pancharama Kshetras which is located at Draksharamam town near Kakinada city in East Godavari District of Andhra Pradesh in South India. Lord Shiva is known as Bhimeswara Swamy here. The temple is situtated on the eastern bank of Godavari River. The consort of Lord Bhimeswara is Manikyamba. The Sivalinga at this place is installed and established by Lord Surya. Maha Shivaratri, Devi Navaratrulu, Karthika Masam, Dhanurmasam are the main festivals celebrated at this temple.

Drass : Drass is a tiny town in the Kargil District of Jammu and Kashmir, India. The town, reportedly the second coldest inhabited town in the world shot into prominence in the summer of 1999 following Pakistani backed incursions into the Indian Occupied Kashmir. The Kargil War saw the town being shelled by infiltrators and the war ended with Indian Army recapturing the areas surrounding the town and the kargil district.

Dravida Munnetra Kazhagam' (DMK) : 'Dravida Munnetra Kazhagam' (DMK) is a regional political party in the Tamil Nadu state of India. It was founded by C N Annadurai as a breakaway faction from Dravidar Kazhagam, headed by Periyar. The party is currently headed by M Karunanidhi, the former Chief Minister of the state.

The ideology of Dravidian parties is probably the only rational ideology that is indigenous to India, unlike Marxism, which has its origins in Europe. The movement was initially mooted as one that championed the cause of socially and economically disadvantaged sections of the society. It advocated concepts of rationality, self-respect and rejection of casteism and superstitious practices, prevalent in the Tamil society. Prominent members preached militant atheism. The movement was sympathetic to the claim that there were two separate races in India, the Aryans and Dravidians, and the movement claimed to represent the latter.

DMK championed the cause of Tamil and used its national clout to make Government of India declare Tamil as classical language. In the enrichment of Tamil literature, the writers belonging to DMK had an important role, although it needs to be pointed out that their contributions have tended to be more of expressions of dissent and disgruntlement at what was perceived as social injustice and domination of certain communities, in the social sphere, and of the Northern parts of India, in the political sphere, and substitution of less often used Tamil words for borrowed-assimilated popular ones for administrative and oratorical purposes, in the linguistic sphere. The DMK is also sympathetic and formerly allied to the Liberation Tigers of Tamil Eelam in Sri Lanka. The DMK has split into the AIADMK, the PMK and the MDMK. Of the three, the AIADMK is the strongest rival party.

Dravidar Kazhagam : Dravidar Kazhagam or Dravida Kazhagam (Dravidian Organization) was the first fully Dravidian party in India. It was a radical party formed by Periyar in the erstwhile Madras Presidency. Its original goals were to eradicate the ills of the society that existed at that time including untouchability and on a grander scale to obtain a "Dravida Nadu" or Dravidian nation mainly from the Madras Presidency. The founders were motivated by questionable theories that the Brahmins of the north and Aryans were wreaking havoc on the local Dravidian populace. The DK thus became the first fully Dravidian party and would in turn give birth to two other dravidian parties, the DMK and AIADMK over the course of time.

Dravidian Mural Paintings : Dravidian mural paintings are the frescos depicting South Indian mythology and legends, which are drawn on the walls of temples in South India. The masterpieces of Dravidian mural art include—the Shiva Temple in Ettumanoor, the Ramayana murals of Mattancherry Palace and Vadakkumnatha kshetram. St. George Syrian Orthodox Church of the nasranis, depicting Biblical narrations. The fresco paintings of Kerala is called as "Fresco-secco". Its features are the lime medium and technique in which the prepared walls are painted only after it gets completely dry. It is derived probably from the ancient art of Kalamezhuthu. It adheres to the principles of the 'Shilparatna', the principal text on Indian painting techniques. It specifies that white, yellow, red, black and terreverte or Syama are the pure colours to be used as pure colours or in combination to make murals.

Dravidians : The terms Dravidians and Dravidian Race are sometimes given to the peoples of southern and central India and northern Sri Lanka who speak Dravidian languages, the best known of which are Tamil, Telugu, Kannada, Malayalam and Tulu.

The Dravidian family of languages includes approximately 26 languages that are mainly spoken in southern India and Sri Lanka, as well as certain areas in Pakistan, Nepal, and eastern and central India, as well as in parts of Afghanistan and Iran. Dravidian languages are spoken by more than 200 million people, and they appear to be unrelated to languages of other known families. A few scholars include the Dravidian languages in a larger Elamo-Dravidian language family, which includes the ancient Elamite language of what is now southwestern Iran; but this is not accepted by most of the Dravidianists.

Dream Valley Resorts : Nestled amidst lush green environs and located at Gandipet in Hyderabad, Dream Valley Resorts is a water theme park with waterslide, cascading waterfalls, water squirts, a 9-hole golf course and go-kart track.

Dree—Apatani Festival : This is a festival of Arunachal Pradesh. The Apatanis observe a series of agriculture rites and festival by sacrificing domestic fowls, animals and eggs in different times, starting from the sowing to the harvesting periods for ensuring of bumper yield of crops in the year such as Dree, Tamu, Metri, Chandii and Yahung etc. Chandii Tamu rite is performed during the sowing period, Dree during every growing periods of crops and Yahung just before the harvest.

The literary meaning of 'Dree' is one who borrows or purchases food grains from others in order to meet out the shortage by addition to one's old and new stock of food grains. During Dree festival, a few rites are performed to worship and appease Gods and Goddesses, who protect the crops, and ensure well-being of man. These divinities include Tamu God, Metii God, Sky God and Danyi Pilo (sun and moon). They are worshipped by offering sacrifices of fowls, dogs, pigs, chickens, eggs, mithuns and cows. The divinities associated with Dree are collectively knows as 'Dree or Dri Wuhi' (Gods). For conduction of ritual of Dree, one or two persons are appointed permanently or temporarily from each clan of the village. These persons are known as Dree Kholi or Dree Gora.

Dronacharya Award : Dronacharya Award is an award presented by the government of India for excellence in sports coaching. The award comprises of a bronze statuette of Dronacharya, a scroll of honour and a cash component. The award was instituted in 1985. As the best sportsperson award is named Arjuna Award, it is appropriate that the coaching award is named after Dronacharya, as he was the Guru of Arjuna.

Drum Dance : This is a professional dance-form from Jalore. Five men with huge drums around their necks, some with huge cymbals, accompany a dancer who holds a naked sword in his mouth and performs vigorously by twirling three painted sticks.

Dudh Kosi : Dudh Kosi is a river in eastern Nepal. The river begins just east of Gokyo Lakes and flows south to Namche Bazaar where it meets the Bhote Kosi. Continuing south, the Dudh Kosi exits Sagarmatha National Park and passes to the west of Lukla. The Lamding Khola joins the Dudh Kosi to the southwest of Surkya and continues its southerly course to the extreme southeast corner of Nepal.

Dudhadhari Math : The founder of this "math" (temple) was shri Balbhadra Das Mahantji. He was a great devotee of lord Hanuman. It is believed that when he started worshipping a piece of stone as an idol of lord Hanuman, everyday a cow, Surhi would come and bathe the stone with milk. Popular belief is that Mahantji Drank this milk after the stone was bathed and stopped eating everything else. Since Mahantji's food became "Dudh-ahari" (meaning food consisting of milk), the math came to be named so.

Dudhkumar River : Dudhkumar river is the Raidak or the Sankosh river of West Bengal (India) enters Bangladesh near Pateshwary and is renamed as the

Dudhkumar. The river receives the Gadadhar and the Gangadhar as tributaries at Pateshwary and travels along a 52 km long meander course and joins the Brahmaputra at Kurigram Sadar upazila. Most of the main course of the Dudhkumar lies in India. The river is free from tidal influence, but often overflows

Dudhsagar : Dudhsagar literally meaning The Sea of Milk, is a waterfall situated on the Goa-Karnataka border, at a distance of 60 kilometers from Panaji and 10 kilometers from Kulem Railway Station (Indian Railway station code QLM). This beautiful waterfall is accessible by train and rough road. Water plummets hundreds of feet in large volume, in cascades, forming one of the most spectacular of all natural phenomena in Goa. It is a major part of the Goa ecosystem. It is also a popular destination for hikers and trekkers.

Dudhwa National Park : Situated in kheri district the park was set up in 1968 covering an area of 498sq.km. The rail head and the nearest town is Dudhwa which is 4km from the park. The nearest airport from the park is Amausi (Lucknow) at a distance of about 250km.

Dudwara : Dudwara is a primarily farming community in the Kathua district in the Indian state of Jammu and Kashmir. Dudwara is southward and uphill from the river Bhini. Dudwara's small handicraft industry does not fully support the resident's needs - they depend on money sent in from family members who work all over India and send money back home.

Dumhal (Ras Dhamali) : This dance is performed by the men-folk of the Wattal tribe of Kashmir on specific occasions. The performers wear long colourful robes and tall conical caps, which are studded with beads and shells.

Dupatta : Dupatta is a long scarf that is essential to many Indian and Pakistani women's suits. Some "dupatta suits" include the salwar kameez, the trouser suit, and the kurta. The dupatta has long been a symbol of modesty in South Asian dress. It traditionally is worn across both shoulders. However, the dupatta can also be worn like a cape around the entire torso. The material for the dupatta varies according to the suit: cotton, georgette, silk, chiffon, and more. The other names for dupatta are chunri and chunni.

The use of the dupatta has definitely undergone a metamorphosis over time. In current fashions, the dupatta is frequently draped over one shoulder, and even over just the arms. Another recent trend is the short dupatta often seen with kurtas and Indo-Western clothing. Essentially, the dupatta is often treated as an accessory in current urban fashion. Nevertheless, the dupatta remains an integral part of Indian clothing and Pakistani clothing.

Durand Line : The Durand Line is a term for the poorly marked 2,640 kilometer border between Afghanistan and Pakistan. After being defeated in two wars against Afghans, the British succeeded in 1893 in imposing the Durand Line dividing Afghanistan and what was then British India (now the North-West Frontier Province and Balochistan of Pakistan). Named for Sir Mortimer Durand, the foreign secretary of the British Indian government, it was agreed upon by representatives of both Afghanistan and the British Empire, but deeply resented by the Afghan Emir Abdur Rahman Khan. One of the two representatives of the Afghan government was the Ahmadi Sahibzada Abdul Latif of Khost. The border was drawn intentionally to cut through the Afghan tribes whom the British feared and may have tried to disunite.

Durg : Durg is a town in Chattisgarh, India. It has a population of 231,182 (2001 census) and is part of the Bhilai agglomeration. Durg lies about 11 km from Bhilai and 35 km from the state capital Raipur. It is also the headquarters of Durg District. It is second largest district of Chattisgarh.

Durga Puja : In Manipur, Durga Puja is celebrated in Mera (October) month. The main centre of worship of Durga Puja is the Kali temple of Imphal town. The images of goddess Durga are made at several places in Mandapas and in public places. The Mandapas are decorated during these days and Puja is held in praise of the goddess. The Brahmins recite stories of Puranas, Krishna, Radha and Chaitanya. The idol of goddess is carried in a procession on the last day.

Durgamma Festival : This festival is celebrated in Andhra Pradesh. It is celebrated for four days in the month of Bhadrapada. On the first day, the water for worship is brought from a near by river Majira. On the second day, a buffalo intended for sacrifice is taken to the river. After worshipping the water-goddess, the buffalo is washed there. It is then decorated and brought to the temple in a procession to the accompaniment of music. The next day the buffalo is sacrificed and after that devotees sacrifice innumerable jowls, goats, rams and buffaloes. In the evening, the ground in-front of the temple is cleaned and a heap of cooked rice and mutton is kept as offering to the deity. An unbaked earthen pot is buried up to its neck and a winnow is placed over it.

A woman sits on the winnow and apparently possessed predicts future events. A man representing Poturaju, the brother of Durgamma, is smeared with turmeric and vermilion and decorated round his head, neck and waist with margosa leaves. He goes round the temple and kills a sacrificial lamb by biting its throat. On the last day, devotees go round the temple with Bomalu (puppets). Carts and bullocks decorated with flowers and coloured sarees are taken round the temple. Prasadam is distributed. A fair is held here during the festival.

Durgapur : Durgapur is an industrial township in the state of West Bengal, India. Durgapur is the vision child of Dr. Bidhan Chandra Roy the first Chief Minister of the state of West Bengal in Independent India. It was primarily designed by Joseph Allen Stein Stein, designer and planner, along with Benjamin Polk, an American architect living in Calcutta. Durgapur is well known for engineering and chemical industries and well planned residential townships. The main employment sectors in this city are the two steel plants belonging to Steel Authority of India Limited (SAIL). One is the Durgapur Steel Plant (DSP) and the other is the Alloy Steel Plant (ASP). Although these plants had their share of troubled times in the past both these plants are doing fairly well now.

The success of these plants has resulted in setting up of a large number of ancillary industries in this region. Other major employers in Durgapur include the thermal power plants of Damodar Valley Corporation popularly known as D.V.C., the Central Mechanical Engineering Research Institute (CMERI), Philips Carbon Black (PCBL), Graphite India Limited, Birla Cements etc. A software technology park is also proposed to be built here. There is also a very informative website i.e, durgapuronline.com - for almost everything you ever need to know about the city. It has the Durgapur Barrage which is the main source of water for cultivation in Bardhaman district.

Durgasagar : Durgasagar with an area of about 2,500 hectare, is the largest pond or dighi of southern Bangladesh. It is located at Madhabpasa village of babuganj upazila, about 11 km away from barisal town. Locally it is known as Madhabpasha Dighi. According to a desire of Rani Durgavati, mother of Raja Joynarayan, the dighi was dug in 1780 (1187 BS). Initially there were four pucca ghats each having 15m width. Due to the lack of proper maintenance jungles gradually surrounded the dighi.

However in 1975, government renovated it to some extent. There are coconut trees around the dighi which together with the dighi are bounded by brick-walls. There are two gates each on the eastern and western sides of Durgasagar. In the middle of the dighi, there is an island with bushes. migratory birds usually come here during winter. The surrounding areas of the dighi has now been turned into a picnic spot. Presently, Barisal Development Board is looking after it.

Durgiana Temple : In Orissa, the temple is dedicated to goddess Durga and dates back to 16th century. This Hindu temple also draws its share of visitors. A large temple is dedicated to Hindu deities Laxmi (The Goddess of wealth) and Narayan. (The Preserver of Universe). All dignitaries visiting Golden Temple make it a point to visit Durgiana Temple also.

Durpin Hill : Durpin Hill is one of the two hills (the other being Deolo Hill) connected by a ridge on which the town of Kalimpong stands. The hill is 1,372 metres (4,501 feet) above mean sea level and is located south west of the town. The hill commands a panoramic view overlooking the town of Kalimpong, the snow clad Himalayan ranges of West Sikkim, the Teesta River and its valleys and the Jelepla Pass in the distance. A golf course is also present just off the summit.

Durrani : Durrani or Abdali tribe is one of the two largest Pashtun tribes of Afghanistan and is also found in large numbers in western Pakistan. They are estimated to be roughly 20% of the population of Afghanistan and number around 7 million there with another 1-2 million found in Pakistan and hundreds of thousands also live in northeast Iran. The Durrani are the most "Persianized" of Pashtun tribes, often bilingual in Dari (or Afghan Persian), as well as arguably being among the most urbanized and educated of the Pashtuns in Afghanistan.

Dussehra : Celebrated by all Hindus of India on the tenth day after Navratri (September or October), Dussehra is celebrated as the day of Rama's victory over king Ravana, or as a day on which the Goddess Kali destroyed the buffalo-demon and liberated the world. The Dussehra festival celebration at Jagdalpur is unique in its perspective and significance. It is a mixture of Hindu and tribal beliefs. To quote Grierson, "Primitive cults are influenced by Hinduism, but also react on it, and it seems to have been part of the policy of Bastar chiefs to identify themselves as much as they could with the religious life of their subjects, save those in the Abujhmar hills. Much of the long Dussehra ritual at Jagdalpur is celebrated from tribal ideas".

Another important feature of this festival is that an underlying spirit of participation, cutting across caste and creed, prevails. During the celebrations, along with Danteshwari Mai, representing the Hindu Goddess Durga or Kali, a number of lesser powers and tribal deities, some indigenous and others borrowed from Hinduism, are also worshipped.

The custom of celebrating Dussehra starts with worship at the temple of Kachhingudi, a local goddess. A seven year old girl of the weaver caste is chosen and ceremonially married to the priest of the shrine. This girl symbolizes the goddess. After a while she goes into a trance and is asked to grant the safe conduct of the celebration.

Dutch East India Company : The Dutch East India Company (Vereenigde Oostindische Compagnie or VOC in Dutch, literally "United East Indies Company") was established on March 20, 1602, when the Estates-General of the Netherlands granted it a monopoly to carry out colonial activities in Asia. It was the first multinational corporation in the world and it was the first company to issue stocks.

The VOC consisted of 6 Chambers (Kamers) in Amsterdam, Middelburg (for Zeeland), Enkhuizen, Delft, Hoorn and Rotterdam. Delegates of these chambers convened as the Heeren XVII (the Lords Seventeen). To the counsel of Heeren XVII, eight delegates were from the Chamber of Amsterdam, four from Chamber Zeeland and one from each of the smaller Chambers. Access to the seventeenth seat was rotated among the Chamber of Zeeland or one of the smaller Chambers. Amsterdam had thereby the decisive voice. The Zeelanders were particularly suspicious at the start up of the VOC for this reason. The fear was not unfounded, because in practice it meant that indeed Amsterdam stipulated what happened.

By 1669, the VOC was the richest private company the world had ever seen, with over 150 merchant ships, 40 warships, 50,000 employees, a private army of 10,000 soldiers, and a dividend payment of 40%.

The company was in almost constant conflict with the English; relations were particularly embittered after the Amboyna Massacre in 1623. During the 18th century, its possessions were increasingly focused on the East Indies. After the fourth war between the United Provinces and England (1780–1784), the VOC got into financial trouble, and in 1798, the company was dissolved, four years after the end of the Estates-General. The East Indies were awarded to the Kingdom of the Netherlands by the Congress of Vienna in 1815.

Dutch India : The Dutch (Dutch East India Company) established trading posts on different parts along the Indian coast. For some while, they controlled the Malabar east coast (Cranganore/Cranganor/Kodungallor, Cochin de

Cima/Pallipuram, Cochin, Cochin de Baixo/Santa Cruz, Quilon (Coylan), Cannanore, Kundapura, Kayankulam, Ponnani) and the Coromandel south coast (Golkonda, Bimilipatnam, Jaggernaikpoeram/Kakinada, Palikol, Pulicat, Porto Novo/Parangippettai, Negapatnam) and Surat (1616-1795). They conquered Ceylon, nowadays Sri Lanka (1658 - 1796), from the Portuguese. The Dutch also established trading stations in Travancore and coastal Tamil Nadu as well as at Rajshahi Pipely,Hougli/Chinsura,Baleshwar/ Bellasoor, Murshidabad in present Bangladesh and Ava, Arakan, Syriam in present Burma/Myanmar. Ceylon was lost at the Congress of Vienna in the aftermath of the Napoleonic Wars, where the Dutch having fallen subject to France, saw their colonies raided by Britain. The Dutch, later became less involved in India, as they had the Dutch East Indies, (now Indonesia) as their prized possession.

Dwaraka Pitha : The Dwaraka Pitha or Dwaraka matha is situated in the coastal city of Dwaraka, Gujarat — which itself is a popular destination of pilgrimage for the Hindus, dedicated to Krishna. It is one of the four cardinal mathas said to have been founded by Adi Sankaracarya, and is the pascimamnaya matha, or western matha. It is also known as the Kalika Matha, and, as per the tradition initiated by Adi Shankara, is in charge of the Sama Veda. The current head or Shankaracharya of this order is Swami Svarupananda Sarasvati, who also claims to head the corresponding northern matha at Jyotirmath.

Dwarka : Dwarka is a city in Gujarat, India. Dwaraka is rated as one of the seven most ancient cities in the country. The legendary city of Dwarka in Hindu mythology was the dwelling place of Krishna. It is believed that, due to damage and destruction by the sea, the city of Dwarka has submerged six times and the current city is the 7th city of Dwarka. Recent archealogical findings have shown that there existed a city resembling the city described in Mahabharata. It is located in the Jamnagar District of Gujarat. It is on the mouth of the Gomti River into Gulf of Kutch. The city lies in the westernmost part of India.

E

East Bengal : East Bengal was the name used during two periods in the 20th century for a territory that roughly included the modern state of Bangladesh. Both instances involved the violent partition of Bengal. The province of East Bengal was administered by ceremonial Governor and an indirectly-elected Chief Minister. During the year from May 1954 to August 1955, executive powers were exercised by the Governor and there was no Chief Minister.

East Bengal Communist Party (EBCP) : The Communist Party of Pakistan (CPP) was formed in 1948 in the second congress of the Communist Party of India (CPI). The East Pakistan Communist Party (EPCP) was also established at the same time with its headquarters located in Dhaka. It had very little links with the CPP and functioned more as a secret organisation, although it was not banned until 1955. The EPCP broke into EPCP (Marxist-Leninist or pro-Chinese) and EPCP (pro-Soviet) in 1966. By 1970, the EPCP (ML) had fragmented into four parties: EPCP (ML), East Bengal Communist Party (EBCP), Coordination Committee of Communist Revolutionaries (CCCR), and East Bengal Workers Movement (EBWM). Over the years these parties have fragmented mostly into small-armed factions or cliques, and as many as 18 of them can be traced.

East Bengal Regiment : The East Bengal Regiment is an infantry regiment of the Bangladesh Army. It was formed in 1948 following India's independence from Britain. As part of the agreement, the Muslim population were given their own state of Pakistan, made up of West Pakistan and East Pakistan. The infantry of the new Pakistan Army was made up exclusively of men from the main, west part of the country. As a consequence, it was necessary to raise a regiment in the east; so two companies of Bengali pioneers from the Bihar Regiment were regimented into the 1st Battalion, East Bengal Regiment, with the 2nd Battalion being formed soon after. Between 1948 and 1971, a total of eight battalions were raised, with the 5th, 6th and 7th in West Pakistan.

In March 1971, in response to a crackdown on locals in East Pakistan, the five battalions of the East Bengal Regiment mutinied and initiated the Bangladesh War of Liberation. The East Bengal Regiment formed the core of the liberation forces, which became known as the Mukti Bahini. Further units were raised to replace those that remained stranded in West Pakistan. Following the foundation of Bangladesh, these units formed the core of the new army. However, the 7th Battalion was incorporated as 44th Battalion, Frontier Force Regiment in the Pakistan Army, which led to the raising of the 10th Battalion in 1971. The East Bengal Regiment is the largest formation of the army, with battalions in each of the fifteen infantry brigades. The regiment also provides three battalions to Bangladesh's peacekeeping commitments overseas, as Bangladesh is one of the largest providers to the UN.

East Deccan Dry Evergreen Forests : The East Deccan dry evergreen forests are an ecoregion of southeastern India. The ecoregion includes the coastal region behind the Coromandel Coast on the Bay of Bengal, between the

Eastern Ghats and the sea. It covers eastern Tamil Nadu state and southeastern Andhra Pradesh state.

The East Deccan dry evergreen forests cover lie in the rain shadow of the Western Ghats and Eastern Ghats, which block the rain-bearing summer southwest monsoon. Rainfall averages 800 mm/year, and mostly falls during the highly variable northeast monsoon between October and December.

The ecoregion covers an area of 25,500 square kilometers (9,800 square miles), extending from Ramanathapuram District of Tamil Nadu to Nellore District of Andhra Pradesh. Much of the ecoregion is densely settled, and has been substantially altered by human activity, including agriculture, grazing, and forestry, over the centuries. The ecoregion is home to the metropolis of Chennai (Madras), and a number of other cities, including Pondicherry, Thanjavur, Kanchipuram and Nellore. It is estimated that 95% of the original forest cover has been cleared, and the species composition of the remaining forests have been altered by intensive human use.

Unlike most of the world's tropical and subtropical dry broadleaf forests, whose trees tend to lose their leaves during the dry season to conserve moisture, the East Deccan dry evergreen forests retain their leaves year round. Only two other ecoregions exhibit a similar pattern, the Sri Lanka dry-zone dry evergreen forests and the Southeastern Indochina dry evergreen forests.

The ecoregion is home to two important wetlands, Kaliveli Lake north of Pondicherry in Viluppuram District of Tamil Nadu, and Pulicat Lake north of Chennai. Kaliveli lake is the one of the largest wetlands in peninsular India, and is deemed a wetland of national and international importance by the IUCN. It is a seasonal wetland, with a gradient from freshwater to brackish water, and is an important feeding and breeding ground on migratory bird flyway. It is currently threatened by encroachment by agricultural fields, wildlife poaching, loss of the surrounding forests, and increases in commercial prawn farming.

East Garo Hills : East Garo Hills is an administrative district in the state of Meghalaya in India. The district headquarters are located at Williamnagar. The district occupies an area of 2603 km^2 and has a population of 247,555. The East Garo Hills district was formed in 1976, after the erstwhile Garo Hills district of Meghalaya was re-organised with a view to bring the administration closer to the people.

The district headquarter-complex of the district, christened as Williamnagar after the name of Captain Williamson A. Sangma the founder Chief Minister of the State of Meghalaya. Williamnagar is located on the vast plainlands along the bank of the Simsang River, at Simsanggre. These plainlands are in a sense historical, as it was here that the Garos made their last major resistance to the British intrusion into Garo Hills during the year 1837. The legendary Garo leader Pa Togan Nengminja Sangma was felled by the British, in skirmish, at Chisobibra, quite close to Wiliamnagar, on 12th December 1837.

The district falls under the Tura Parliamentary Constituency which Purno Agitok Sangma has been representing at the Lok Sabha (the House of the People), the Lower House of the Indian Parliament since 1975. Purno Agitok Sangma has been a former Union Minister and has the distinction of being the only unanimously elected Speaker of the Lok Sabha.

East Godavari : East Godavari District is situated on the northeast of Andhra Pradesh state, India. The District headquarters is Kakinada. The distance from state capital Hyderabad is 564 km.

East Godavari District is bounded on the north by Visakhapatnam District and the state of Orissa, on the east and south by the Bay of Bengal, on the west by West Godavari District, and on the northwest by Khammam District.

East India : East India is a region of India consisting of the states of West Bengal, Orissa, and often Jharkhand and Bihar. It is geographically between North India and North-East India, and shares many cultural and linguistic characteristics with Bangladesh, which formed part of this region before Partition. The Indo-Aryan languages spoken in this region descend from that of the ancient kingdom of Magadha.

Durga is a particularly popular deity in this region. Bengali culture, and to a certain extent that of Orissa, has been profoundly influenced by the Bengal renaissance and subsequent cultural development. Kolkata is the great metropolis of the region.

East Kameng : The East Kameng district is located in Arunachal Pradesh. It shares an international border with Tibet in the north, a state border with Assam and district borders with West Kameng, Papumpare and Kurung Kumey, who bifurcated from Lower Subansiri on April 1, 2000.

Like West Kameng, the East Kameng district experiences an arid tundra or a cool temperate climate in the north to a humid subtropical climate in the southern sub-himalayan hills bordering Assam. Owing to its climatic diversity, plants that are suitable climate such as apples, oranges, etc planted in orchards.

East Kameng is inhabited by various tribes of similar origin with distinct cultures and beliefs, practising the

Donyi-Polo religion. The most populous of these, the Nishi, are scattered throughout the entire district. Other tribes, especially the Miji, Sullung and the Aka, are found in regions near the Kameng river.

Since independence, much of the population has relocated to the district capital, Seppa. With the coming of modernism, festivals such as the Sarok of the Aka, Nyokum of the Nishi, Jonglam-Ponklam and Chindang of the Miji and the Gumkum-Gumpa are celebrated in full flair in Seppa.

East Kameng is a worthwhile place to visit. One of these is the Pakhui Wildlife Sanctuary, a place where it shows a wide range of wildlife. Seppa, the capital, hosts beautiful tribal dance festivals that adds colors to the natural landscape. Cool and clear as they were, tourists can also take a good look at the view of the mighty Himalayas from the hill stations of Bameng, Chayangtajo and Pakke-Kessang.

East Khasi Hills : East Khasi Hills is an administrative district in the state of Meghalaya in India. The district headquarters are located at Shillong. The district occupies an area of 2752 km^2 and has a population of 660,994 (as of 2001). The place is was notorious for anti social activities but within these past few years it has become a peaceful place. Wonderful place for tourists it has an abundance of natural beauty.

East Pakistan : East Pakistan was a former province of Pakistan which existed between 1955 and 1971. It replaced the former province of East Bengal and occupied the area now known as Bangladesh.

East Pakistan Communist Party : East Pakistan Communist Party (Marxist-Leninist), a communist party in the erstwhile East Pakistan. EPCP(M-L) was founded in

1969 when the general secretary of the pro-China National Awami Party (Bhashani), Mohammed Toha, broke away. EPCP(M-L) had a programme of People's Democratic Revolution and launched armed struggle. EPCP(M-L) opposed both the Pakistani rulers and the Awami League.

East Siang : East Siang is an administrative district in the state of Arunachal Pradesh in India. The district headquarters are located at Pasighat. The district occupies an area of 4005 km^2 and has a population of 87,430 (as of 2001).

Various tribal groups of the Adi people live in various parts of the district. The local people traditionally follow Donyi-Polo, although a sizeable minority have embraced Christianity.

East Sikkim : East Sikkim is one of the four administrative districts of the Indian state of Sikkim. Geographically, East Sikkim occupies the south-east corner of the state. The capital of East Sikkim is Gangtok, which is also the state capital. It is the hub of all administrative activity in the state. The district occupies an area of 964 sq km with a population of 244, 790 (2001) individuals. The civilian region is administered by a district collector, appointed by the Union Government and the military area by a Major General.

Military wise, the district is a very sensitive area with the Indian army having control over most areas east of Gangtok and near its borders with People's Republic of China and Bhutan. Visitors to this region are restricted and just a few areas are open to tourists in the areas east of Gangtok. Popular tourist locales are the Tsongmo Lake, Baba Mandir and the Nathula Pass. The Nathula Pass formed the offshoot of the ancient Silk Route which connected Lhasa to India. The pass and the famous Baba Mandir are open to Indian nationals only. To enter this region a special pass — The Inner Line Permit has to be obtained one day prior to departure. This pass is made through local tourist offices. Other tourist areas include Gangtok and the famous Phodong Monastery north of Gangtok and the internationally famous Rumtek Monastery.

Eastern Chalukyas : Eastern Chalukyas were a South Indian dynasty whose kingdom was located in the present day Andhra Pradesh. Their capital was Vengi and their dynasty lasted for around 500 years from the 7th-century until c. 1130 C.E. when the Vengi kingdom merged with the Chola empire. The Vengi kingdom was continued to be ruled by Eastern Chalukyan kings under the protection of the Chola empire until 1189 C.E., when the kingdom succumbed to the Hoysalas and the Yadavas. They had their capital originally at Vengi near Eluru of the West Godavari district end later changed to Rajamahendravaram (Rajamundry).

Eastern Chalukyas were closely related to the Chalukyas of Vatapi (Badami) and were of Kannada origin. Throughout their history they were the cause of many wars between the more powerful Cholas and Chalukyas over the control of the strategic Vengi country.

The five centuries of the Eastern Chalukya rule of Vengi saw not only the consolidation of this region into an unified whole, but also saw the efflorescence of Telugu culture, literature, poetry and art during the later half of their rule. It can be said to be the golden period of Andhra history.

Eastern Ghats : The Eastern Ghats are a discontinuous range of mountains along India's eastern coast. The Eastern Ghats run from West Bengal state in the north, through Orissa and Andhra Pradesh to Tamil Nadu in the south. They are eroded and cut through by the four major rivers of southern India, the Godavari, Mahanadi, Krishna, and

Kaveri. These ranges run parallel to the Bay of Bengal; the Deccan Plateau lies to the west of the range, between the Eastern Ghats and Western Ghats, and a coastal plain lies between the eastern Ghats and the Bay of Bengal. The Eastern Ghats are not as high as the Western Ghats. As with the Western Ghats, these mountain ranges also have their local names, e.g. the Velikonda Range of Andhra Pradesh.

At their southern end, the Eastern Ghats form several ranges of low hills. The southernmost of the Eastern Ghats are the low Sirumalai and Karanthamalai hills of southern Tamil Nadu. North of the Kaveri river are higher Kollimalai, Pachaimalai, Shevaroy (Servaroyan), Chitteri, Palamalai, and Mettur hills in northern Tamil Nadu state. The climate of the higher hill ranges is generally cooler and wetter than the surrounding plains, and the hills are home to coffee plantations and enclaves of dry forest. The hill station of Yercaud is located in the Shevaroy Hills. The Bilgiri Hills, which run east from the Western Ghats to the Kaveri river, forms a forested ecological corridor that connects the Eastern and Western Ghats, and allows the second-largest wild elephant population in India to range between the South Eastern Ghats, the Biligiri and Nilgiri hills, and the South Western Ghats.

Eastern Highlands Moist Deciduous Forests : The Eastern Highlands moist deciduous forests is a tropical moist broadleaf forest ecoregion of east-central India. The ecoregion covers an area of 341,100 square kilometers (131,700 square miles), extending across portions of Andhra Pradesh, Chhattisgarh, Jharkhand, Madhya Pradesh, Maharashtra, and Orissa states.

The Eastern Highlands moist deciduous forests extend from the Bay of Bengal coast in northern Andhra Pradesh and southern Orissa, across the northern portion of the Eastern Ghats range and the northeastern Deccan Plateau, to the eastern Satpura Range and the upper Narmada River valley.

The forests of the ecoregion are sustained by the moisture-bearing monsoon winds from the Bay of Bengal, which lies to the southeast. The ecoregion is bounded on the north and west by tropical dry deciduous forest ecoregions, including the Central Deccan plateau dry deciduous forests to the southwest and west, the Narmada valley dry deciduous forests to the northwest, and the Chota Nagpur dry deciduous forests to the north and northeast. The drier Northern dry deciduous forests ecoregion, lying west of the Eastern Ghats range, is completely surrounded by the Eastern Highlands moist deciduous forests, in the rain shadow of the Ghats, which partially block the moisture-laden monsoon winds off the Bay of Bengal. The humid Orissa semi-evergreen forests ecoregion lies to the northeast in the coastal lowlands of Orissa.

The ecoregion's forests are dominated by Sal (Shorea robusta), in association with Terminalia, Adina, Toona, Syzygium, Buchanania, Cleisanthus, and Anogeissus. The flora of the ecoregion shares many affinities with the moist forests of the Western Ghats and the eastern Himalayas.

The ecoregion is considered globally outstanding by the World Wildlife Fund for its assemblage of large mammals, including tiger (Panthera tigris), wolf (Canis lupus), gaur (Bos gaurus), and sloth bear (Melursus ursinus). The Asian Elephant (Elephas maximus) has been extirpated from the ecoregion.

Eastern Highlands Moist Deciduous Forests : The Eastern Highlands moist deciduous forests is a tropical moist broadleaf forest ecoregion of east-central India. The ecoregion covers an area of 341,100 square kilometers (131,700 square miles), extending across portions of Andhra

Pradesh, Chhattisgarh, Jharkhand, Madhya Pradesh, Maharashtra, and Orissa states.

The Eastern Highlands moist deciduous forests extend from the Bay of Bengal coast in northern Andhra Pradesh and southern Orissa, across the northern portion of the Eastern Ghats range and the northeastern Deccan Plateau, to the eastern Satpura Range and the upper Narmada River valley.

The forests of the ecoregion are sustained by the moisture-bearing monsoon winds from the Bay of Bengal, which lies to the southeast. The ecoregion is bounded on the north and west by tropical dry deciduous forest ecoregions, including the Central Deccan plateau dry deciduous forests to the southwest and west, the Narmada valley dry deciduous forests to the northwest, and the Chota Nagpur dry deciduous forests to the north and northeast. The drier Northern dry deciduous forests ecoregion, lying west of the Eastern Ghats range, is completely surrounded by the Eastern Highlands moist deciduous forests, in the rain shadow of the Ghats, which partially block the moisture-laden monsoon winds off the Bay of Bengal. The humid Orissa semi-evergreen forests ecoregion lies to the northeast in the coastal lowlands of Orissa.

Edhi Foundation : Abdul Sattar Edhi founded the Edhi Foundation in 1947. Today, he is the head of the organization. His wife Bilquis, a nurse, oversees the maternity and adoption services. The Edhi Foundation provides 24-hour emergency assistance across the nation of Pakistan and abroad. The Foundation provides, among many other services, shelter for the destitute, free hospitals and medical care, drug rehabilitation services, and national and international relief efforts. According to the Guinness Book of World Records, as of 1997, Edhi Foundation's ambulance service is the largest volunteer ambulance service in the world. He also personally holds the world record for having gone the longest time working without having taken a holiday. As of when the record was set, he still has not taken a day off work.

Edicts of Ashoka : The Edicts of Ashoka are a collection of 33 inscriptions on the Pillars of Ashoka, as well as boulders and cave walls, made by the Emperor Ashoka of the Mauryan dynasty during his reign from 272 to 231 BCE. These inscriptions are dispersed throughout the areas of modern-day Pakistan and northern India, and represent the first tangible evidence of Buddhism. The edicts describe in detail the first wide expansion of Buddhism through the sponsorship of one of the most powerful kings of Indian history. According to the edicts, the extent of Buddhist proselytism during this period reached as far as the Mediterranean, and many Buddhist monuments were created.

The inscriptions proclaim Ashoka's beliefs in the Buddhist concept of dharma ("righteousness") and his efforts to develop the dharma throughout his kingdom. Although Buddhism and the Buddha are mentioned, the edicts of Ashoka tend to focus on social and moral precepts rather than religious practices. No mention is made of the philosophical dimension of Buddhism, such as the Four Noble Truths or the Eightfold Path. This could possibly be because Ashoka wanted to remain simple in his message to the public, because these notions may have been formalized at a later date, or some combination of the two.

In these inscriptions, Ashoka refers to himself as "Beloved of the Gods" and "King Priya-darshi." The identification of King Priya-darshi with Ashoka was confirmed by an inscription discovered in 1915. The inscriptions found in the eastern part of India were written in the Magadhi language, using the Brahmi script. In the western part of India, the language used is closer to Sanskrit, using the Kharoshthi script, and one bilingual edict (Edict 13) was written in Greek and Aramaic.

The inscriptions revolve around a few repetitive themes: Ashoka's conversion to Buddhism, the description of his efforts to spread Buddhism, his moral and religious precepts, and his social welfare program.

EDUSAT : EDUSAT or GSAT-3 was launched in September 2004 by the Indian Space Research Organisation. EDUSAT is the first Indian communication satellite built exclusively to serve the educational sector. It is mainly intended to meet the demand for an interactive satellite-based distance education system for the country. EDUSAT carries five Ku band transponders providing spot beams, one Ku-band transponder providing a national beam and six Extended C-band transponders providing national coverage beams. Mr. Vilas Palsule, Sr. Scientist from ISRO, Ahmedabad has put in lot of sincere work to make Edusat a success which has ushered in a new never seen before changes in the system of education in India. Extent of use of Edusat is not clear.

Eenadu : Eenadu, headquartered in Hyderabad, India, is the largest circulated Telugu news daily in the state of Andhra Pradesh. According to NRS (National Readership Studies) 2005 it has got a readership of 1,13,49,000 and is the third most read daily in India. Eenadu (meaning "Today" in Telugu) was founded by the Indian media baron Ramoji Rao in 1974. It has played a role in both crowning or dethroning governments in Andhra Pradesh. It has also successfully adapted the latest publishing and communication technologies into the Telugu language. Eenadu's rapid expansion enabled diversification of its portfolio by venturing into numerous other markets such as finance and chitfund (Margadarsi), foods (Priya Foods), film production (Usha Kiron Films), film distribution

(Mayuri Films), and a group of television channels (ETV). All the businesses are organized under Ramoji Group.

Eid Gah Mosque : This grand mosque of Multan is located on the main Multan-Lahore highway in the Northeast of the city. It was built in 1735 AD by Nawab Abdul Samad Khan when he was the governor of Multan. It is a very spacious mosque provided with a vast courtyard and a huge prayer chamber measuring two hundred and fifty feet long and fifty-four feet broad crowned by seven domes. Its exterior was faced with glazed blue tiles and interior was ornamented with colorful mosaics. After independence it was found insufficient to accommodate the increased number of people so its courtyard was enlarged further.

Eid ul-Adha : Eid ul-Adha occurs on the tenth day of the Islamic month of Dhul Hijja. It is one of two Eid festivals that Muslims celebrate. Eid ul-Adha is celebrated by Muslims worldwide as a commemoration of Prophet Ibrahim's willingness to sacrifice his son for God. Muslims believe that God revealed in a dream to Ibrahim (Prophet Abraham) to sacrifice his son Isma'il. Ibrahim and Isma'il set off to Mina for the sacrifice. As they went, the devil attempted to persuade Ibrahim to disobey God and not to sacrifice his beloved son. But Ibrahim stayed true to God, and drove the devil away. As Ibrahim prepared to sacrifice his son, God stopped him and gave him a sheep to sacrifice instead. The story is also a part of the other Abrahamic religions.

Eid ul-Fitr (Eid) : Eid ul-Fitr is an Islamic holiday that marks the end of Ramadan, the month of fasting. Fitr means "to break" and therefore symbolizes the breaking of the fasting period and of all evil habits. On the day of the celebration, a typical Muslim family gets up very early and attends special prayers held only for the occasion in big mosques, in large open areas, stadiums or arenas. The festivities and merriment start after the prayers with visits to the homes of friends and relatives and thanking the Creator for all blessings. Eid is a time to come together as a community and to renew friendship and family ties. This is a time for peace for all Muslims in the world to devote to prayers and mutual well-being.

It is a joyous occasion with important religious significance. Happiness is observed at attaining spiritual uplift after a month of fasting. Muslims dress in holiday attire. After attending the special congregational prayer in the morning, worshippers greet and embrace each other in a spirit of peace, love, and brotherhood. Visiting friends and relatives is common. For Muslims, Eid ul-Fitr is a joyful celebration of the achievement of enhanced piety. It is a day of forgiveness, moral victory and peace, of congregation, fellowship, brotherhood and unity. Muslims are not only celebrating the end of fasting, but thanking their God for the help and strength that they believe he gave them throughout the previous month to help them practice self-control. Common greetings during this three-day festival are the Arabic greeting "Eid mubarak", "Eid saeed" or its Urdu variation "Eid mubarak ho!" which, loosely translated, means "Happy Eid!". In many parts of Southeast Asia, it is common to greet people with "Selamat Hari Raya" which means "Happy Eid" in Malay.

E K Nayanar : Erambala Krishnan Nayanar (December 9, 1919 - May 19, 2004) was an Indian politician leader of the Communist Party of India (Marxist) in Kerala and the Chief Minister. He held the post three times 1980-81, 1987-91 and 1996-2001. He holds the distinction of serving in the post for the longest period of time - 11 years, spanning 4009 days. He was a member of the Polit Bureau of CPI(M).

Nayanar was born in Kalyassery in Kannur district of Kerala as the son of Govindan Nambiar. He belonged to a family of freedom fighters and revolutionaries. One of his cousins was K.P.R. Gopalan, one of the prominent Communist revolutionaries. He joined the Communist Party of India in 1939. He participated in the Kayyoor-Morazha peasant uprisings and was forced to go underground to evade arrest. When the Communist Part of India split in 1964, Nayanar joined sides with the CPI(M).

In 1967 he was elected to Lok Sabha from Palghat (now Palakkad). He was elected to Kerala Assembly six times. Among the legislative constituencies he won from were Irikkur, Malampuzha, Trikaripur and Thalassery. He became the Chief Minister of Kerala for the first time on January 25, 1980. His term ended in 1981. He served a four-year term starting from 1987 and a full five-year term in 1996. Nayanar died on May 19 2004 in New Delhi following a heart attack.

Ekambaranatha Temple : Ekambaranatha Temple is one of the oldest temples in the city or Kanchipuram. Notable for its architecture, the temple bears the work of practically every dynasty that ruled Kanchipuram. Reaching a height of 57 meters, the temple's gopuram is one of the tallest in South India. One notable feature of the temple is the Aayiram Kaal Mandapam, or the "hallway with a thousand pillars." The temple's inner walls are decorated with an array of 1,008 Siva Lingams. The sthala-virutcham is a 3,500 year old mango tree whose branches are said to yield four different types of mangoes.

Eklingji : Eklingji is a temple complex in Udaipur District of Rajasthan in western India. It is located 22 km north of Udaipur. Begun in 971, the temple complex was built by the Guhila (later called Sesodia) dynasty of Mewar, in honor of their presiding deity Eklingji, a form of Lord Shiva. The beautifully sculpted temple complex includes 108 temples within its high walls. The main temple dates to the 15th century, rebuilt from the ruins of an earlier destroyed temple. It is made of marble and granite, and has an enormous double-storied, elaborately-pillared hall or "mandap" under a vast pyramidal roof, with a four-faced image of Lord Shiva in black marble. Another temple in the complex is the Lakulish Temple, built in 971, it is the only temple of the Lakulish sect in the whole of India

Ekushey Padak : Ekushey Padak a national award introduced in memory of the martyrs in the Language Movement. This padak is awarded to individuals in recognition of their substantial contribution in their respective fields in national life. The criteria of consideration for the award consists of contribution to the field of literature, journalism, education, art and culture, song, dance, fine art, dramatic performance, sculpture, etc. Each award includes taka twenty five thousand in cash, a gold medal of three tolas weight (18 carret standard), and a certificate of honour. The government honoured the four Language Movement martyrs Abul Barkat, Rafiq Uddin Ahmed, Abdus Salam and Abdul Jabbar with Ekushey Padak (posthumously) in 2000 AD.

Elamo-Dravidian Languages : The Elamo-Dravidian languages are a hypothesised language family which includes the living Dravidian languages of India and Pakistan, in addition to the extinct Elamite language of ancient Elam, in what is now southwestern Iran. Linguist David McAlpin has been a chief proponent of the Elamo-Dravidian Hypothesis. In addition to Elamite and the Dravidian languages, some speculate that the extinct language or languages of the Indus Valley Civilization, also known as the Harappan Civilization, may be part of the Elamo-Dravidian language family.

Electoral College of Pakistan : The President of Pakistan is chosen by an electoral college. According to article 41(3) of the Constitution of Pakistan, this electoral college consists of the Senate, the National Assembly, and the Provincial Assemblies. Members of the National Assembly and Provincial Assemblies are directly elected by the people in competitive multi-party elections. Members of the Senate are indirectly elected by the provincial assemblies.

Electoral College of Pakistan : The President of Pakistan is chosen by an electoral college. According to article 41(3) of the Constitution of Pakistan, this electoral college consists of the Senate, the National Assembly, and the Provincial Assemblies. Members of the National Assembly and Provincial Assemblies are directly elected by the people in competitive multi-party elections. Members of the Senate are indirectly elected by the provincial assemblies.

Elephant Festival : A festival when the mighty mammals claim the centre stage. They stride majestically parading their decorated trunks and tusks. The festival begins with a procession of elephants, camels and horses, followed by folk dancers at their entertaining best. Spectators are enthralled with the elephant-polo matches. The sight of these heavy animals running to win the famous elephant race is truly amazing. The most hilarious highlight of the festival is a tug of war between elephants and men. A special show is also held after which a prize for the best decorated elephant is announced.

Elephant Stables : A set of large stables, to house the ceremonial elephants of the royal household. The area in front of them was a parade ground for the elephants, and for troops. This is another structure that shows definite Islamic influence in its domes and arched gateways. The guards' barracks are located right next to the elephant stables.

Ellora : The world-heritage listed cave temple of Ellora, about 30km from Aurangabad, are the culmination of Deccan rock-cut architecture in Maharashtra. There are 34 caves cut out of the sloping side of the low hill. Another 28 caves have been discovered later by the archeological Survey of India. The masterpiece of Ellora is the Kailash Temple. It is the world's largest monolithic sculpture, sculpted out of a rock by 7000 labourers over a 150 year period. The shrines are not exclusively Buddhist, but of Hindu and Jain faiths as well. Entry to Ellora is free.

Eluru : Eluru is a town in the state of Andhra Pradesh, India. It is the headquarters of West Godavari district and has a population of 189,772 (agglomeration 215,343] (2001 census). Eluru is situated on the National Highway connecting Vijayawada and Visakhapatnam. Eluru was ealier called Helapuri and has a rich cultural and political history. It was believed to a capital of the Vishnukundinas at one time.

Kolleru Lake a big fresh water lake found near Eluru. It is known for its well established educational institutes like C.R.Reddy College.

Emergency in India : The Emergency in India was a 18-month period between 1975 and 1977, when President Fakhruddin Ali Ahmed, upon advice by Prime Minister Indira Gandhi, declared a state of emergency under Article 352 of the Constitution of India, effectively allowing her to rule by decree, suspending elections and civil liberties. It was the most controversial period in the history of independent India.

Opponents had long made allegations that Indira's party, Congress, had practiced electoral fraud to win the 1971 elections. The Gandhian socialist Jaya Prakash Narayan (JP) had been agitating in Bihar for a change in provincial government, and increasingly sought to direct popular action against the government at the Centre through satyagrahas.

JP and his supporters sought to unify students', peasants', and labour organisations in a 'Total Revolution' to nonviolently transform Indian society. Indira's party was defeated in Gujarat by a coalition of parties calling itself the Janata Party (People's Party), and even faced an all-party, no-confidence motion in Parliament.

On June 21, 1975, Justice Jagmohanlal Sinha of the Allahabad High Court found the Prime Minister guilty of using government machinery for election purposes, and ordered her to be removed from her seat in Parliament and banned from running for an additional six years.

Her conviction was actually upon a small technicality—an official in the Prime Minister's Office had failed to submit his resignation in time before officially beginning work on Indira's election campaign in 1971. However, strikes in labor and trade unions, student unions and government unions swept across the country. Protests led by Narayan and Morarji Desai flooded the streets of Delhi close to the Parliament building and the PM's residence.

President Fakhruddin Ali Ahmed declared a State of Emergency. Apart from being a political ally of Indira, the President in India acts mostly upon the advice of the Prime Minister. In her own words, Indira brought democracy "to a grinding halt".

Elections for the Parliament and state governments were postponed. Invoking article 352 of the Indian Constitution, she granted herself extraordinary powers and launched a massive crackdown on civil liberties and political opposition. The Government cited threats to national security, as a recent war with Pakistan had just been concluded. The strikes and protests had paralyzed the government and hurt the economy of the country greatly. Indira herself had the right to appeal to the Supreme Court of India and had no legal obligation to resign until then.

But in face of massive political opposition, desertion and disorder across the country, she took the advice of a few close party loyalists and her younger son Sanjay Gandhi, who had become a close political advisor.

As the constitution requires, Indira advised and President Ahmed approved the continuation of Emergency over every six-month period until her decision to hold elections in 1977. President Ahmed signed the decree, invoking a state of emergency under the Constitution. The Government used police forces across the country to arrest thousands of protestors and strike leaders. J.P. Narayan, Morarji Desai, Charan Singh, Jivatram Kripalani, Atal Bihari Vajpayee, Lal Krishna Advani and other protest leaders were immediately arrested. Organizations like the Rashtriya Swayamsevak Sangh and opposition political parties were banned.

Indira attempted to re-write the nation's laws with the help of the Parliament, where the Congress controlled over a two-thirds majority. She felt her powers were not amassing quickly enough, so she utilized the President to issue "extraordinary laws" that bypassed parliament altogether, allowing her to rule by decree. She constructed a 20-point economic program to increase agricultural and industrial production, improve public servics and fight poverty and illiteracy. Also, she had little trouble in making amendments to the constitution that exonerated her from any culpability in her election fraud case, declaring President's Rule in Gujarat and Tamil Nadu where anti-Indira parties ruled (state legislatures were thereby dissolved and suspended indefinitely), and jailing thousands of opponents.

It is suggested that official intelligence sources told the Prime Minister that her administration was popular across the country. It has also been known that Indira feared that Field Marshall Sam Manekshaw, then Chief of Army Staff threatened to depose her if she did not immediately call elections, even though Maneckshaw denied any intentions in a later interview to The Times of India. The Janata Party alliance of political parties opposed to Indira swept the polls, winning a majority in Parliament. Many Congress Party loyalists deserted Indira, who herself lost her constituency seat. Morarji Desai became the first non-Congress Prime Minister of India.

The efforts of the Janata administration to try government officials and Congress politicians for Emergency-era abuses and crimes were largely a flop due to a disorganized, over-complex and politically-motivated process of litigation. Although special tribunals were organized and scores of senior Congress Party and government officials arrested and charged, including Indira and Sanjay Gandhi, police were unable to submit sufficient evidence for most cases, and only a few low-level officials were convicted of any abuses.

The people lost interest in the hearings owing to their continuous fumbling and complex nature, and the economic and social needs of the country grew more important to them. An impression was created that corruption and political subversion stalled the process of justice. Indira's emergency rule lasted 19 months, and its legacy remains intensely controversial.

EMS Namboodiripad : Elankulam Manakkal Sankaran Namboodiripad (June 13, 1909–March 19, 1998), popularly knows as EMS was an Indian communist leader and the first Chief Minister of Kerala.

Namboodiripad was one of the architects of unified Kerala. He was renowned as a brave and committed socialist, historian and a marxian theorist. EMS was born on June 13, 1909 in Perinthalmanna taluk of the present Malappuram district. In his early years itself, he was associated with V.T. Bhattathiripad, M.B. Bhattathiripad and many others to fight casteism and reactionary conservatism which existed in the Namboothiri community. He became one of the office bearers of Valluvanadu Yogaskshema Sabha, an organisation of progressive Namboodiri youth. During his college days, he was deeply associated with the Indian National Congress and Indian Independence Struggle. In 1934, he joined the Congress Socialist Party, a socialist wing within Indian National Congress. Later he was elected as the Kerala State Congress secretary. His commitment to socialist ideals and compassion towards the downtrodden working class made him join the ranks of the Communists, for which he had to go in hiding for many years.

India achieved its independence in 1947 and the state of Kerala was formed in 1956, making him the first communist leader anywhere to head a popularly elected government. In 1957, EMS led the Communists to victory in the first popular election. Soon he introduced the revolutionary Land Reform Ordinance and Education Bill. His government was dismissed by the central government using the controversial article 356 of the Indian Constitution.He influenced Kerala society by his visions on decentralization of power and resources (People's Plan) and the Kerala Literacy Movement. When the Communist Party of India split in 1964 EMS sided with the CPI(M) and became an important leader of that party.

Enamul Haque : Enamul Haque Jr. (born December 5, 1986 in Sylhet) is a Bangladeshi cricketer. He currently plays for his home team, Sylhet Division. He is a right-handed batsman and bowls a slow left-arm delivery. His Test debut occurred against England in at Dhaka in 2003. His best bowling occurred in the second Test against Zimbabwe in January 2005. He hit 7 wickets for 95 runs in the first innings, and 5 wickets for 105 runs in the second, making this the first and only ten wicket haul he has bowled. His highest batting score is a 24 not out which he achieved against Zimbabwe.

Enchey Monastery : The Enchey Monastery is an old Buddhist monastery situated just above the township of Gangtok, capital of Sikkim state India. An important seat of the Nyingma order, the Enchey Monastery is built on the site blessed by Lama Druptob Karpo, a tantric master known for his power of flying. This 200 year old monastery has in its premises images of Gods, Goddesses and other religious objects. Every year around January "Chaam" or religious masked dance is performed.Lama Drupthob Karpa is supposed to have built a small hermitage at the spot he reached after he flew from Maenam Hill in South Sikkim. Later during the reign of Sikyong Tulku (1909-1910), the present monastery was built in the shape of a Chinese Pagoda. Following the Nyingma order, it has around 90 monks. The annual Puja(worship) is celebrated with dances on the 18th & 19th days of the twelfth month of the lunar calendar.

English : English is a West Germanic language which is the dominant language in the United Kingdom, the United States, many Commonwealth nations, and other former British colonies Including India Pakindtan and Bangladesh. It is also a dominant or official language in many countries formerly under British rule. It has lingua franca status in many parts of the world, due to the military, economic, scientific, political and cultural influence of the British Empire in the 18th, 19th and early 20th centuries and that of the United States from the early 20th century to the present. Through the global influence of native English speakers in cinema, airlines, broadcasting, science, and the Internet in recent decades, English is now the most widely learned second language in the world.

Engro : Engro is a Pakistani fertilizer and chemicals company which is listed on the Lahore Stock Exchange. Its production is based in Daharki. Engro was formed by a novel (then for South Asia) employee buyout from the erstewhile shareholders, Exxon. The deal was led by Shaukat Raza Mirza serving then as the CEO of Exxon Pakistan.

Eqbal Ahmad : Eqbal Ahmad (1933/34 - May 11, 1999) was a Pakistani writer, journalist, and anti-war activist.

He was strongly critical of the Middle East strategy of the United States as well as what he saw as the "twin curse" of nationalism and religious fanaticism in such countries as Pakistan. Ahmad was born in the village of Irki in Bihar. When he was a young boy, his father was murdered over a land dispute in his presence. During the partition of India in 1947, he and his elder brothers migrated to Pakistan.

Eravikulam National Park : Eravikulam National Park is a 97 km^2 national park located along the Western Ghats in the Idukki district of Kerala in India, between 10°05′N—10°20′N latitude and 77°0′E—77°10′E longitude.

The terrain consists of high altitude grasslands interspersed with sholas. Eravikulam National Park harbours the largest surviving population of Nilgiri tahr (Hemitragus hylocrius). Nilgiri Tahr is endemic to the southern Western Ghats.Its relatives are the Himalayan tahr(Hemitragus jemlahicus) and Arabian Tahr(hemitragus jayakiri).The estimated population of Nilgiri tahr inside the park is about 750. Wild dog, leopard and tiger are the main predators. Apart from tahr, other little known animals such as Nilgiri marten, small clawed otter, ruddy mongoose, and dusky striped squirrel are also found. Elephants make seasonal visits.

Ernakulam District : Ernakulam District is a district of the state of Kerala in southern India. The district headquarters are at Kakkanad. The district includes the city of Kochi, Kerala's largest city and chief port. The present Ernakulam District includes Paravur, Aluva, Kochi, Kanayannoor, Muvattupuzha, Kunnathunadu, Kothamangalam taluks which come under Fort Kochi and Muvattupuzha revenue subdivision.

Erode : Erode District is one of the districts of northern part of Tamil Nadu State, South India, and Erode is the district headquarters. The District is bounded by Karnataka to the north, and by Kaveri River to the east. Across the Kaveri lie Salem, Namakkal and Karur districts. Dindigal District lies immediately to the south, and Coimbatore and The Nilgiris districts lie to the west. Erode District is landlocked (having no seacoast of its own) and is situated at between 10 36″ and 11 58″ north latitude and between 76 49″ and 77 58″ east longitude.

Erramala : The Erramala (also called Yellamala) are range of low hills in southern India, in Kurnool District of Andhra Pradesh state. The Erramala hills lie on the Deccan plateau, running east-west and dividing the basin of the Penner River to the south from the basin of the Krishna River to the north.

Eruvaka Purnima : This is a special festival celebrated mainly by the farmers and agriculturists in Andhra. It falls on the full moon day in the month of Ashadha. Agriculturists worship the yoke, the plough and the bulls with turmeric and kumkum. Coconuts are broken either at home or in the field, in-front of the yokes and bulls. They inaugurate the annual cultivation by ploughing five or nine rounds in their fields on this day, as it is supposed to be an auspicious day auguring fresh showers. They also cook Payasam, a small dish and enjoy it with their children and relatives.

In some parts of the country cultivators worship the bullock. They wash the cattle, smear and decorate the hooves and horns with oil and a variety of colours and feed them with Pulagam (rice, green gram dal and sesame cooked together). The bodies are also decorated gaily with coloured circles and designs. Little bells are tied to their horns and necks and they are driven out into the open space to wander and run about. The tillers take home a part of the festoon that is tied to the village gate, after the cattle pass under it as a talisman for the ensuring year. Children collect seeds a week in advance and sow them in the corners of the temple. By the festival day, the young plants sprout and a few of these tender plants are taken home by the tillers and kept in their granaries for a prosperous crop during the coming year. The gaily dressed people and the colourfully decorated cattle make the village a grand spectacle of colour and pageantry.

Esraj : The esraj (also called israj or dilruba) is a string instrument found in two forms throughout the north, central, and east regions of India. It is a young instrument by Indian terms, being only about 200 years old. The dilruba is found in the north, where it is used in religious music and light classical songs in the urban areas. The esraj is found in the east and central areas, particularly Bengal, as well as Bangladesh. It is used in a somewhat wider variety of musical styles than is the dilruba.

The esraj is mostly used as an accompanying instrument. It is the accompanying instrument of choice for Rabindra Sangeet singing. However, it has also been used as a solo instrument to interpret Hindustani Classical Music, mostly in the Vishnupur tradition. The most famous exponent of the esraj has been Pandit Ranadhir Ray, who died in 1988.

Ethnological Museum : Ethnological Museum located in the Agrabad Commercial area in Chittagong. It was established in order to foster mutual understanding and fellow-feeling among all the ethnic groups of Bangladesh.

Established in 1974, the ethnological museum has at this moment 11 galleries to exhibit the various aspects of lifestyle of the 29 ethnic groups of the country, including twelve ethnic groups of Chittagong hill tracts. The exhibits represent all aspects of life and activities of the ethnic groups. The exhibits have been made lively and attractive by means of maps and photographs, models, wall paintings and by artificially creating the environment in which the tribes live. Besides there are plaques containing short introductory notes.

Eturnagaram Sanctuary : Eturnagaram Wildlife Sanctuary is one of the oldest sanctuaries of Andhra Pradesh. It is spread at a distance of 806 sq.km in Warangal district. It is located at a distance of 90 km. from Warangal.

ETV : ETV is one of the largest networks of satellite television channels in India. Based at Hyderabad, the network runs a group of 12 regional language news and entertainment channels. When the satellite TV revolution broke out in India during the late 1990s, the Telugu daily newspaper Eenadu started with its own channel called ETV. Initially launching a Telugu channel the network has later diverisfied into other Indian languages such as Bengali, Urdu, Kannada, Gujarati and Marathi. With 12 channels in regional languages of India, ETV has the largest news-reporting network in India, at the grassroot level. Managed by Newstoday Private Limited, the channels give news inbetween entertainment programs. 4 Hindi channels for Madhya Pradesh, Uttar Pradesh, Bihar and Rajasthan, and infotainment channels in Telugu, Kannada, Bangla, Marathi, Urdu, Gujarati—and a 24-hours news channel in Telugu constitute the bunch of ETV Channels.

European Colonies in India : European colonies in India were set up by several European nations beginning at the end of the 15th century. In 1498, the Portuguese set foot in Goa. Rivalry between reigning European powers saw the entry of the Dutch, British and French among others. The fractured debilitated kingdoms of India were gradually taken over by the Europeans and indirectly controlled by puppet rulers. By the 19th century, the British had assumed direct and indirect control over most of India.

The Portuguese were the first Europeans to arrive in India in 1498. The closing of traditional trade routes in western Asia by the Ottomans and rivalry with the Italian states, set Portugal in search of an alternate sea route to India. The first successful voyage to India was by Vasco da Gama in 1498, when he arrived in Calicut, Kerala. He proceeded to Goa. The Portuguese established a chain of outposts along India's west coast and on the island of Sri Lanka in the early 16th century. Goa was their prized possession and, the seat of Portugal's viceroy who governed Portugal's empire in Asia. Portugal's northern province included settlements at Daman, Diu, Chaul, Baçaim, and Mumbai. Mumbai was given to the British crown in 1661 as part of the dowry of Catherine of Braganza. The rest of the northern province, with the exception of Daman and Diu, was lost to the Marathas in the early 18th century. Dadra and Nagar Haveli was occupied in 1779. Dadra and Nagar Haveli was occupied by India in 1954, and Goa, Daman, and Diu were annexed to India in 1961.

Ezhimala Hill : Ezhimala (286 m above sea level) is in Kannur district of Kerala, south India and was the capital of the ancient Mooshika kings and is considered to be an ancient historical site. It is a conspicuous, isolated cluster of hills, forming a promontory, 38 km north of Kannur. A flourishing sea port and centre of trade in ancient Kerala, it was one of the major battle fields of the Chola-Chera war of the 11th century. It is believed that Lord Buddha had visited Ezhimala.

Ezhimala : Ezhimala, the capital of the ancient Mooshika kings, is considered to be an ancient historical site. It is a conspicuous, isolated cluster of hills, forming a promontory, 38 km north of Kannur town. A flourishing sea port and centre of trade in ancient Kerala, it was one of the major battle fields of the Chola-Chera war of the 11th century. It is believed that Lord Buddha had visited Ezhimala. An old mosque, believed to contain the mortal remains of Shaikh Abdul Latif, a Muslim reformist, is also located here. The hill is noted for rare medicinal herbs. There is an old tower of great antiquity here, the Mount Deli Light House. It is maintained by the Indian Navy and is a restricted area. The beach sand is of a different texture and the sea is bluer than in other areas. At the Ettikulam bay, one can enjoy watching dolphins. Bordered by sea on three sides, Ezhimala is set to occupy a prominent place in the Naval history of the country, consequent to the proposal for commissioning the Naval Academy there.

F

Faisal Mosque : King Faisal Mosque (Shah Faisal Masjid) is one of the largest mosques in the world, located in Islamabad, the capital city of Pakistan. It is a well-known mosque in the Islamic world and is renowned for both its immense size and its architecture.

In 1976, construction began on the mosque, funded by the government of Saudi Arabia, costing over 130 million Saudi riyals. King Faisal of Saudi Arabia was instrumental in the funding, and it was thus dedicated to him after his assassination. It was completed in 1986, and used to house the International Islamic University. The small mausoleum of General Muhammad Zia-ul-Haq is located right outside of the mosque

Faisalabad : Faisalabad is the third largest city in Pakistan with an estimated population of 6.4 million. It is an important industrial centre located in the Punjab province, west of Lahore. The city-district of Faisalabad is bound on the north by the districts of Gujranwala and Sheikhupura, on the east by Sahiwal district, on the south by Toba Tek Singh district and on the west by Jhang district.

The city was founded in 1892 by the Lieutenant Governor of the Punjab, Sir Charles James Lyall and was originally named Lyallpur after him as acknowledgement of his contributions in the colonisation of the area. The city centre of Lyallpur was designed by Captain Poham Young, to imitate the Union Jack with eight roads radiating from a large clock tower in the centre to eight separate bazaars. The farmland around the city was improved by irrigation with new canals and new inhabitants were attracted by promises of land. The city grew into a strong industrial and agricultural centre and by 1947 was a major urban area. The name of the city was changed to Faisalabad in honour of the late King Faisal of Saudi Arabia who had been assassinated.

Faisalabad has a strong industrial base including textiles, jewelery, home furniture, and phramaceuticals, assisted by the expanding transport network which includes newly built motorways to Lahore and Rawalpindi. The city is also home to numerous colleges and universities such as the Agricultural University and Punjab Medical College.

Faiz Ahmed Faiz : Faiz Ahmed Faiz, (1984 - 1911) is considered by many to be a poet in the great tradition of Urdu poets like Ghalib and Iqbal. He was born in Sialkot, in the Punjab in pre-independence India (in what is now Pakistan). He remained in Pakistan after the partition of 1947, and died in Lahore.

Faiz was a member of the Anjuman Tarraqi Pasand Mussanafin-e-Hind (Progressive Writers' Movement), and an avowed Marxist. In 1962 he was awarded the Lenin Peace Prize by the Soviet Union. In the 1930s Faiz Ahmed Faiz married a British women Alys Faiz. They had two daughters. Alys Faiz's influence on Faiz's life and poetry is reputed to have been great.

Faizabad : Faizabad is a city on the banks of river Saryu in the state of Uttar Pradesh, India. Faizabad has a sister city Ayodhya, birthplace of Lord Ram. Lord Ram was the king of Ayodhya and is worshipped as a God. Faizabad was the fist capital of Nawabs of Oudh. Asaf-ud-daula, son of Nawab Shuja-ud-daula made Lucknow the capital of Oudh. Faizabad and Ayodhya have a great heritage and have many monumental sites. The city of Ayodhya is known for its temples of Hindu religion. In Faizabad city there are many monuments of Nawabs, like tomb of Bahu Begum, Gulab-bari and many more. Ayodhya is also the birth place of first Tirthankar of the Jain religion, Shri Rishabh Dev. He is known as the father of Jain religion.

Fakhruddin Ali Ahmed : Born on May 13, 1905 at Hauz Qazi area of Old Delhi with a silver spoon in his mouth, Fakhruddin Ali Ahmed was one of those few Muslims who by virtue of his service to the country under the leadership of Mahatma Gandhi reached the pinnacle of honour as the President of the Indian Republic, the fifth in the roll.

Shri Fakhruddin's grandfather, Shri Khaliluddin Ali Ahmed, of Kacharighat near Golaghat town in the Sibsagar district, Assam, married in one of the families who were the relics of Emperor Aurangzeb's bid to conquer Assam. Ali Ahmed's father Col. Zalnur Ali, of the Indian Medical Service, had to leave Assam while he was a bachelor doctor following an incident in Shillong. Col. Ali and one of his Assamese contemporaries, Col. Sibram Bora, were allotted seats at a function in the Shillong Club away from the European guests. The two Assamese Colonels boycotted the function in protest against the segregation meted out to them. This naturally enraged the European bosses who transferred Col. Zalnur Ali to distant North-West Province. This provided him with an opportunity to come in contact with the Nawab of Lohari in Delhi whose daughter he married. Here was born Fakhruddin Ali Ahmed.

Educated first in the Bonda Government High School in U.P., Fakhruddin matriculated from the Delhi Government High School then under the Punjab University. He was sent to England for higher education in 1923 in order to groom him for the I.C.S., though his mother was opposed to his son being sent abroad. He joined the Catherine College of Cambridge University and was called to the Bar from Inner Temple of London. He could not compete for the I.C.S. examination due to illness. On return to India he started legal practice in the Lahore High Court in 1928. In October that year, Col. Zalnur Ali, accompanied by his Barrister son, Fakhruddin, paid a visit to Gauhati ostensibly to look after his paternal property which included a few hundred acres of land in and around Gauhati. Obviously, the Ahmed family's link, snapped on the Colonel's posting in N.W.P. was thus re-established after several years. Two years later Fakhruddin Ali Ahmed revisited Gauhati and came in contact with the leaders of the Congress in Assam and in 1931 enrolled himself as its primary member. This was a turning event in the life of Ahmed.

In the Congress hierarchy Ali Ahmed enjoyed an enviable position being a member of the Congress Working Committee for several years. In the Great Split of the Congress (1969), Ali Ahmed remained with Indira Gandhi, may be his deep-rooted association with the Nehru family made him adhere to Indira Gandhi's leadership till his death. He was elected to the highest post of the land—the Presidentship of the Indian Republic on 29 August, 1974, but his tenure in the office was cut short (1977) by his sudden death due to a heart attack which he suffered on his return from a tour of the South-East Asian countries only a day before. In the wake of the Emergency Ali Ahmed became the target of criticism of his detractors. It was alleged that he put his signature as President to the order on promulgation of Emergency on 25 June, 1975 at the behest of the Prime Minister, though he assured at the time of his election to Presidentship that he would not be a yes-man of the Cabinet. Notwithstanding this criticism, Ali Ahmed's personality, integrity and ability in administration were never questioned.

Suave and sober, Ali Ahmed seldom allowed anger and prejudices to get better of him, at the same time, he did not compromise with unprincipled issues. These traits of his character were apparently the key to his success in the public life and enabled him to acquire a respectable position in the society. Towards the end of his political career, he was, however, accused of being communal by certain quarters, but this accusation was hardly warranted. Mention of an incident in this connection would perhaps be relevant. In 1935, when Mohammad Ali Jinnah, Liaquat Ali Khan, Nazimuddin and a few starwarts of the Muslim League came to Assam to campaign against Fakhruddin Ali Ahmed who was pitted by the Congress against a Muslim League candidate in the Assembly poll, a common friend at the instance of Sir Mohammad Saadullah suggested that Fakhruddin Saheb should pay a courtesy call to the Muslim League leaders at Gauhati.

Liaquat Ali, however, reacted to the suggestion somewhat tersely saying that he would not shake hands with a Kafir meaning Ali Ahmed. Thus, the suggestion was scotched. It is apparently difficult to believe that he could be communal with a long record of service to the country under the banner of the Congress. It is, nonetheless, a fact that he tried to bring to the Congress fold a number of Aligarh Muslim University educated youths of his community whose communal outlook was a public knowledge. If this had created an impression in certain quarters that Fakhruddin Ali Ahmed was communal, that was entirely a different matter. But his love for the country and faith in secularism were profound and therefore, were not in doubt in the least.

Though politics was Ali Ahmed's forte, his deep interest in sports and other extra-mural activities was well-known. Himself a tennis player and golfer, he was elected President of the Assam Football Association and the Assam Cricket Association for several terms; he was also the Vice-President of the Assam Sports Council. In April, 1967 he was elected President of the All India Cricket Association besides being a member of the Delhi Golf Club and the Delhi Gymkhana Club since 1961. His love for music and finer arts was no less; he was deeply interested in poetical works of Ghalib. His travels in the USSR, the USA, the UK, Japan, Malaysia and many Arab countries as a Minister and afterwards as the President of India widened his urbane outlook that endeared him to all sections of the people, irrespective of caste, creed and avocation. Elegantly dressed he was always courteous but firm in what he considered to be just and fair and presented himself as a Moghul, as it were, which quality he perhaps inherited from his maternal side.

At forty Ali Ahmed married Abida (21) of a respectable family of U.P. educated in Aligarh Muslim University. When negotiations for the wedding were under way Ahmed was undergoing a jail term in Jorhat as security prisoner. At a certain stage of the negotiations Abida's family wanted to know what the prospective bride groom was doing. The answer came from one of the relatives of the would-be bridegroom: Fil hal to jail men Hai (At present he is in jail). But Destiny so ordained that Fakhruddin Ali Ahmed and Abida were happily married on 9 November, 1945. Begum Abida Saheba was elected to the Lok Sabha in 1981 from a U.P. constituency in a by-election. Ali Ahmed passed away on 11 February, 1977 in the Rashtrapati Bhavan leaving behind wife, two sons and a daughter.

Fakhruddin Mubarak Shah : Fakhruddin Mubarak Shah (1338-1349) one of the founders of an independent kingdom in Bengal with its capital at sonargaon. He assumed power on the death of the Tughlaq governor Bahram Khan (1338) of whom he was the silahdar (armour-bearer). He captured Comilla and Noakhali and extended his sway up to Sylhet in the north and Chittagong in the south (1340), and ruled over a territory comprising the whole of the eastern and southeastern part of Bengal. Having supremacy over the Padma, Meghna and Jamuna (Jumna) he fought successfully with his fleet of war-boats against Sultan alauddin ali shah of lakhnauti, checked the onrush of Haji Iliyas of southwest Bengal, and tightened his grip over the kings of Tipperah and of Arakan.

Mubarak Shah constructed a trunk road connecting Chittagong with Chandpur opposite the outpost of Sripur, raised embankments in Chandpur, built mosques and tombs in Chittagong. ibn batuta visited Sonargaon during his region in 1346. The traveller felicitates Fakhruddin as a distinguished sovereign who loved strangers, particularly the fakirs and sufis. The importance of Fakhruddin lies in the fact that with him started the independent sultanate of Bengal which lasted for two hundred years (1338-1538).

Fakir Dance : This dance is performed by the followers of Madar Pir on the occasion of his urs. Long-haired devotees, wearing long, loose garments, gather at the pir's mausoleum at the end of Chaitra (March-April) and burn candles and incense. A bamboo, draped in red with a fly-whisk on top, is dedicated to the pir as his symbol. One devotee carries the bamboo on his shoulder; others follow him. They wear bells round their ankles. A fire is lit and meat is burnt on it as offering to the pir. The devotees dance around the fire, swaying their heads to the beat of the music.

Fakir-Sannyasi Resistance : Fakir-Sannyasi Resistance against the east india company dominance in Bengal began from the early 1760s and subsided in the 1790s. The East

India Company regulations had disturbed the ways of life of the religious mendicants like the Muslim fakirs and Hindu sannyasis in several ways. Both the groups of mendicants lived on alms provided by their followers. The company rulers, who little understood the religious institutions of the country, took their alms collection drive for unauthorised impositions on the village people. The government thus issued decrees banning collection of alms by the organised groups like the fakirs and sannyasis. In response, they started a resistance movement against the feringhee rulers. The resistance movement got ready support from the peasantry who were hard pressed under the new land revenue policy of the company government.

The resisting fakirs belonged to the Madaria tarika, a sufi sect which flourished in Bengal under the leadership of Shah Sultan Hasan Suriya Burhana in the second half of the seventeenth century. The sannyasis were the Vedantic Hindu yogis belonging to the Giri and Puri groups of ek-dandi sannyasism. Both the fakirs and sannyasis were armed bands living in khankahs and akhdas. In rituals and practices there was good deal of affinity between the sufi fakirs and yogi sannyasis and that contributed to their common alliance against the British.

Fakrul Alam : Dr Fakrul Alam is a Bangladeshi academic and translator. He is Professor of English at the University of Dhaka, and has written widely on literary matters. Among his publications are book-length studies of Daniel Defoe and Bharati Mukherjee. Alam is perhaps best known for his translation of Jibanananda Das, the great Bengali poet. Earlier translators, most notably Chidanananda Dasgupta and Clinton B. Seely, had tried to convey the elusive quality of Das's poetry to an Anglophone audience. When Alam's volume Jibanananda Das: Selected Poems came out in 1999 on the occasion of the poet's birth centenary, it was greeted with widespread acclaim. The book has proved to be popular with readers since then. The first edition having sold out, a second, expanded edition was published in 2003. Alam's work is now regarded as perhaps the best (and certainly the most wide-ranging) translation of Das in the English language.

Falak Sher : Falak Sher (also known as Falak Sar) is a mountain in Pakistan (elevation 5918 m). It is considered the highest peak of Swat Kohistan in the Hindu Kush mountains.

This mountain was climbed for the first time by W.K.A Berry and C.H. Tyndale-Biscoe of New Zealand in 1957 from its North ridge. The second ascent was made by Dr. Wolf Gang Stephen who also climbed Dastigil Sar and also Malika Parbat. Carlo Pinelli attempted another peak in the Hindu Raj which is the only 6000 of this part of Hindu Kush. They named it Maingol Sar.

Falgu River : Falgu River is one of the tributary of the river Ganges. Gaya and Bodh Gaya are the most famous and important locations on the banks of the Falgu River. Gaya is a sacred city for Hindus, and Bodh Gaya is one of the holiest places for the Buddhists. In certain ancient texts, Falgu River finds mention as the Niranjana River.

There is reference to the city of Gaya and the Falgu River in the Hindu epic of Ramayana. Hindu mythology states that Sita who was wife of Lord Rama has cursed the Falgu River. This is an interesting story and the mythology states that on account of this curse, Falgu River lost its water, and the river is simply a vast stretch of sand dunes.

An eye witness account of Falgu River state: "Across the road was the Falgu river, a mile wide, flatter and drier than the Sahara." But the mass of water is available below the sand dunes. If one digs even a meter, the water sips out and a small crater full of water is formed. In some places, water flows are also available

Falooda : Falooda is a South Asian refreshment drink made by using milk, vermicelli, sabja (basil seeds), tutti frutti and sugar along with huge amounts of ice cream. The popular flavours in which falooda is available include rose, mango, chocolate, fig, and many others.

Falooda is very popular throughout North India/ Pakistan and is easily available in hotels and on beach stalls. A variant is falooda kulfi, where falooda and kulfi are served together with a syrup. The most common flavour added to falooda is rose, which is taken from the syrup. Some people also use milk to enhance the drink.

Farakka Barrage : Farakka Barrage constructed by India, about 18 km upstream near Monohorpur, to save Calcutta Port from silting, but in the process causing widespread and devastating effects, especially in southwestern Bangladesh.

Farashganj : Farashganj an area in dhaka city developed around the French market established in 1780 with permission from Naib Nazim Nawab Nawajish Mohammad Khan. Farashganj was originally named Frenchganj as the French (Farashis) had settled in the area. The French settlement started with seizure of the English Factory by the French in 1750. This, however, created a crisis, which was resolved by the intervention of Naib Nazim Jasarat Khan. The factory became known as Dhaka Factory years before the fall of the last Muslim ruler of Bengal in 1757, but Farashganj continued to flourish. In the area, French merchants established wholesale trading posts for spices like raw turmeric, ginger, garlic and chilli. Apart from being the French area in Dhaka city, Farashganj is known for a number of old and historic buildings. These include the ruplal house built along the riverfront, the

Mahalla Farashganj with its long gateway in which stands Bibi ka Rauza, the oldest husaini dalan in Dhaka, and the Farashganj Nil Kuthi (Indigo House), one of the largest of the kind, now used as a venue for wedding receptions.

Farida Khanum : Renowned Pakistani Ghazal singer. Farida Khanum has been given the title "Malika-e-Ghazal" (Queen of Ghazal) in tribute to her singing talents. Farida Khanum currently resides in Lahore and performs at select musical gatherings. In 2005 she was awarded the Hilal-e-Imtiaz (Pakistan's highest civilian honors) by the President of Pakistan President General Pervaiz Musharraf. Farida Khanum who hails from Punjab was born in Calcutta and raised in Amritsar. She migrated to Pakistan after partition. Her sister Mukhtar Begum and the renowned maestro of Patiala Gharana, Ustad Ashiq Ali Khan trained her in initial years. She usually sticks to classical Raagas and minimalist accompaniment.

Faridabad : Faridabad is a major industrial city and population center in Haryana state, northern India. It is located in Faridabad District. the city was founded in 1607 by Shaikh Farid, treasurer of Jahangir, with the object of protecting the highway which passed through the town. Shaikh Farid built a fort, a tank and a mosque which are in ruins. Later, it becomes the headquarters of a pargana which was held in jagir by the Ballabgarh ruler. Faridabad became 12th district of Haryana State on 15th August, 1979.

Faridkot : Faridkot (1981 pop. 42,423) is a town in Punjab state of India, in Faridkot District. It has been named after the great Sufi Saint Baba Sheik Farid Shakarganj, whose verses are mentioned in Guru Granth the holy book of Sikh religion. Previously it was called Mokhalpur. Industries of the town include cotton handling, from ginning to baling to weaving, as well as manufacture of machine tools, sewing machines, and bicycles.

The ruling dynasty of Faridkot claimed descent from Jaisal, who founded Jaisalmer in Rajasthan in 1156. The town was founded in the 16th century by his descendant Bhallan of the Burai Jats. His nephew Kapur converted to Sikhism and founded the state of Kot Kapura in Punjab in 1705. A dispute between his grandsons led to the division of the state in 1763. The older brother, Sardar Jodh Singh Brar, retained control of Kot Kapura, and his younger brother, Sardar Hamir Singh Brar, was given Faridkot.

The state was captured in 1803 by Ranjit Singh, but was one of the Cis-Sutlej states that came under British influence after the 1809 Treaty of Amritsar. During the Sikh wars in 1845, Raja Pahar Singh aided the British, and was rewarded with an increase of territory. The state had an area of and its 642 square miles, and a population of 124,912 in 1901. It was bounded on the west and northeast by the British district of Ferozepore, and on the south by the state of Nabha.

Farmagudi : Farmagudi is a town in Goa, in India. It belongs to the Ponda taluka. It is located three km. from the main Ponda City on the way towards Panjim. It is located on a plateau. (GVM's) Higher Secondary School, GVM's College of Commerce & Economics, Ponda Education Society's Higher Secondary School, College and The Goa Engineering College is there.

Farooq Abdullah : Farooq Abdullah (1937-), the son of Shaikh Abdullah, has served as chief minister of Jammu and Kashmir on several occasions. Farooq Abdullah has been for autonomy to Jammu and Kashmir within the constitution of India and formalising the Line of Control (LoC) as the international border.

Farooq Abdullah was a novice in the political arena of Jammu and Kashmir when he was appointed president of National Conference in Srinagar on August 21, 1981. His prime qualification was that he was the son and heir of the nationalist Kashmiri leader Sheikh Abdullah. Power came easily to him but he had been handed over a state where deep dissatisfaction was brewing. Anti-India feelings were running high.

Though charges of corruption were rampant against him, he returned to power in 1987 in the elections which were believed to be massively rigged. He forged an intricate alliance with the Congress and returned as interim chief minister in 1987. 1989 saw a massive Muslim uprising in the state against the leadership and paramilitary forces were deployed to control the dangerously escalating violence.

Farooq Abdullah resigned and President's Rule was imposed on the state. In September 1996, Farooq returned to power when fresh assembly elections were held. He allied with the BJP led government in the centre and his son and political heir, Omar Abdullah held a position in the union cabinet. In 2003, Farooq's government was trounced in the polls by an INC-PDP alliance led by Mufti Mohammed Sayeed.

Fateh Jang : Fateh Jang is small town located nearly 20 kilometers from Islamabad, Pakistan. The new location of the Islamabad International Airport has been selected at Fateh Jang and the construction will start in 2006. Fateh Jang is located in Attock District.

Fateha-e-Yazdaham : Fateha-e-Yazdaham a religious festival of Muslims observed on the eleventh (yazdaham, Persian for eleventh) of the Islamic lunar month of Rabi-u-Sani, commemorating the death of Hazrat Abdul Qadir Jilani (R), the founder of the qadiriah Sufi order.

Observances include reading the Holy quran, holding milads, discussing the life of Hazrat Abdul Qadir Jilani (R), asking for God's blessings through du'a-munajat or supplications (individual and collective), and distributing tabarruk (consecrated food), specially prepared for the occasion. Sessions of qawwali are held in certain areas of Old Dhaka on this occasion. It is an optional holiday in educational institutions.

Fatehpur Sikri : Fatehpur Sikri served as Akbar's political capital from 1571 until 1585 when it was abandoned, ostensibly due to lack of water. It is regarded as the emperor's crowning architectural legacy and indeed there are no shortage of palaces, halls, and masjids to satisfy his creative and aesthetic impulses typical of Mughals. Brilliant innovations in land revenue, coinage, military organisation, and provincial administration emerged from the Fatehpur Sikri years. Fatehpur Sikri shared its imperial duties as a capital city with Agra, where a bulk of the arsenal, treasure hoards, and other reserves were kept at its' Red Fort for security.

During times of crisis, the court, harem, and treasury could be removed to Agra, located 26 miles or less than a day's march.

Fath Khan's Tomb : Fath Khan's Tomb lies within the gaur citadel in its eastern part within the kadam rasul enclosure. It was built in imitation of a vernacular do-chala hut. It is generally regarded as the tomb of Fath Khan, the son of Dilir Khan, a general of Aurangzeb sent by him to subdue shah niamatullah, the patron saint of shah shuja. Although no contemporary historian has mentioned Fath Khan, tradition has it that this is the tomb of Fath Khan who fell ill in Gaur after arrival with his father, and possibly died here.

Fath Shah's Mosque : Fath Shah's Mosque is situated in the dargah complex in Nagar Sadipur village of Mograpara Union of Sonargaon, Narayanganj. The area is considered to be a part of the medieval capital of sonargaon. Restoration and repair works to the mosque have unfortunately, caused the disappearance of many of its original features. But some are still left to attest its archaeological importance.

The mosque is entirely covered with plaster and is washed white with lime. The outer surface of the walls, just below the bent cornices, is variegated with rectangular panels in the usual Mughal fashion. The central mihrab, contained within a rectangular frame, has a cusped arch with spearhead ornamental motifs. A frieze of blind merlons tops the frame, which has now been painted.

The mosque has at present two inscriptions—one over the central doorway and the other now fixed on the wall of the graveyard opposite the mosque. The Persian inscription over the doorway records the date as 1112 AH/ 1700-01 AD. The other inscription is in Arabic and gives the date as 889 AH/1484 AD. It is likely that the mosque was originally built during the reign of Sultan jalaluddin fath shah in 1484 and subsequently thoroughly repaired or rebuilt with a new roof of dome and vaults in the Mughal period in 1700-01. The apparent Mughal features are thus due to later renovation works.

Fathang : It was in the nature of land revenue for cultivated land in Mizoram. A chief had jurisdiction over a certain tract of land (ram). When a villager would cultivate a land in the ram of a chief he would pay a predetermined measure of paddy to the chief. The earlier measure of heaps was replaced by that of empty Kerosene caus or tins. Normally fathang was fixed at six tins (twenty litre kerosene tins) of unhusked paddy. In lieu, two rupees in cash could also be paid.

Fatima Jinnah : Fatima Jinnah was the sister of Quaid-i-Azam Muhammad Ali Jinnah, the founder of Pakistan and an active political figure in freedom movement against British Raj.

Dr. Fatima Jinnah was born on July 31, 1893 in Karachi. Of a family of seven brothers and sisters, she was the closest to Muhammad Ali Jinnah. Her illustrious brother became her guardian upon the death of their father in 1901. Encouraged by her brother but opposed by the rest of her family, she received excellent early education. She joined the Bandra Convent in Bombay in 1902. In 1919 she got admitted to the highly competitive University of Calcutta where she attended the Dr. Ahmad Dental College. After she qualified, Miss Jinnah went along with her idea of opening a dental clinic in Bombay in 1923.

Miss Fatima Jinnah initially lived with her brother for about eight years till 1918, when he got married to Rutanbai. Upon Rutanbai's death in February 1929, Miss Jinnah wound up her clinic, moved into Jinnah's bungalow, and took charge of his house; thus beginning the life-long companionship that lasted till her brother's death on September 11, 1948.

Fauj-i-Khas : The Fauj-i-Khas was a brigade of the army of Punjab in the time before the First Anglo-Sikh War. It was the Maharaja Ranjit Singh who started to hire European officers to train and command parts of his army. The Fauj-i-Khas was a model brigade trained and equipped after European model under the command of General Jean-Baptiste Ventura. The Fauj-i-Khas had 4 battalions of infantry, 2 regiments of cavalry and a troop of artillery. The cavalry was built on a British model and the infantry on French pattern. This was the first unit in the army to be equipped European-style. Impressed by its performance, the Maharaja ordered a total reorganisation of his whole regular force on the model of Fauj-i-Khas in 1835. This alarmed the British, who had come to see the emerging military power of Punjab as a threat, to such a degree that they in 1837 issued orders to be vigilant and try to arrest any French officer travelling in disguise to join Ranjit Singh's army.

Faxian : Faxian was a Chinese Buddhist monk, who, between 399 and 412 travelled to India to bring Buddhist scriptures. His journey is described in his work A Record of Buddhistic Kingdoms, Being an Account by the Chinese Monk Fa-Hien of his Travels in India and Ceylon in Search of the Buddhist Books of Discipline.

On Faxian's return to China he landed at Laoshan in modern Shandong province, 30km east of the city of Qingdao. After landing, he proceeded to Shandong's then-capital, Qingzhou, where he remained for a year translating and editing the scriptures he had collected. His work is not only one of the world's greatest travel books, but is filled with invaluable accounts of early Buddhism, and the geography and history of numerous countries along the so-called Silk Roads at the turn of the 5th century CE.

Fazal Din's Group : Fazal Din's Group is a group of family owned concerns with a joint turnover of over 25 million USD, with approximately 1200 Employees. The activities of the Group are entirely in the Healthcare field covering a Chain of Pharmacies, Marketing of Healthcare Devices, Electro-medical Equipment, Manufacturing of IV Solution & Pharmaceutical Preparations and joint venture participation in the production of Pharmaceutical Preparations.

Fazal Ilahi Chaudhry : Fazal Ilahi Chaudhry (January 1, 1904 - June 2, 1982) was President of Pakistan from August 14, 1973 until his resignation on September 16, 1978. Fazal Ilahi Chaudhry was born in the city of Gujrat in the Punjab province on January 1, 1904. He studied at Aligarh University and later Punjab University from where he got a law degree, and went into practicing law.

Upon the independence of Pakistan, Chaudhry got involved in the new government, moving up to high ranking positions in the National Assembly. He would end up joining the Pakistan Peoples Party and would be made President in 1973, when the head of the PPP, Zulfiqar Ali Bhutto was made Prime Minister.

Chaudhry was largely a figurehead, and was the first President with less power than the Prime Minister. This was due to the new constitution of 1973 that gave power to the Prime Minister. Previously, the President had been the chief leader of Pakistan, having the power to appoint Prime Ministers. Fazal Ilahi Chaudhry would remain President until 1978, when he would resign after the military took control of the government under General Muhammad Zia-ul-Haq. Chaudhry died on June 2, 1982.

Fazal-e-Akbar : Fazal-e-Akbar born in November 1903, graduated in Arts from St. Xavier College, Calcutta. He graduated in Law from University of Calcutta and was called to Bar from Lincoln's Inn, London in 1930. He started his career as a Lawyer at Fort William High Court in 1931. From 1931 to 1943 he also taught Jurisprudence at University of Calcutta. In 1943 he was appointed District and Sessions Judge, in which capacity he worked till 1946. After Partition he became Special Officer of the Judicial Department and Registrar East Pakistan High Court. In 1949 he was elevated as the Judge of the High Court of East Pakistan. Justice Fazal-e-Akbar was deputed as Chairman Railway Tribunal in 1950 and Chairman University Commission in 1954. He was elevated to the Supreme Court of Pakistan in May 1960. Justice Fazal-e-Akbar became the sixth Chief Justice of Pakistan replacing Dr. Justice S.A. Rehman on June 4, 1968. He retired on November 17, 1968.

Fazl Ghazi : Fazl Ghazi said to be one of the chieftains (Barabhuiyas) of pre-Mughal Bengal. Bhawal was his domain. Fazl Ghazi belonged to the Ghazi family which had originally settled at Chaura on the western bank of the Lakhya, about a mile north of present Kaliganj in Gazipur district. He was eighth in descent from Pahlwan Shah who fought for the cause of Islam about the beginning of the fourteenth century. Pahlwan Shah's son Karforma Sahib was a holy man who acquired the pargana of Bhawal as fief through a sanad of the ruler of Dehli.

Fazle Rabbi, Khondkar (1848-1917) wa a writers and Muslim nationalist, born at Salar in Murshidabad district, West Bengal. His father, Khondkar Obaidul Akbar, was mir munshi of the nawab of Murshidabad. The family traces its lineage back to Khorasan in Iran. Fazle Rabbi was educated in Persian and entered the service of the nawab of Murshidabad as dewan. In 1869 he went to London as a clerk. The British government honoured him with the title of 'Khan Bahadur'.

Fazle Kaderi Muhammad Abdul Munim : Justice Abdul Munim (1924-2001) was a former Chief Justice of Bangladesh. Born on 1 December 1924 in Dhaka district FKMA Munim joined the Dhaka High Court Bar in 1951. After practising in the High Court for some years he went to London for higher studies and obtained LL.M and Ph.D degrees from the University of London in 1958 and 1960 respectively. In 1959, Munim was called to the bar as a Barrister-at-Law from the Linclon's Inn.

After his return from London, Abdul Munim started legal practice and was enrolled as a senior advocate of the Supreme Court of Pakistan in 1964. He was a member of the then East Pakistan Bar Council and of the Pakistan Bar Council constituted under the Legal Practitioners and Bar Council Act, 1965. He was appointed Advocate General of East Pakistan in 1970. In the same year he was elevated to the position of a judge in the Dhaka High Court.

After the emergence of Bangladesh Munim was appointed a judge of the High Court. But soon he was appointed secretary of the Ministry of Law Justice and Parliamentary Affairs, and was closely associated with the drafting of the constitution of Bangladesh. Shortly after he returned to the High Court Division as a judge. He was elevated to the Appellate Division of the Supreme Court of Bangladesh in 1976. Munim was appointed the Chief Justice of Bangladesh in 1982 from which office he retired in November 1989. Justice Munim was appointed chairman of the Bangladesh Law Commission in 6 August 1996, but he had to resign from this post on 31 December 1997 on health ground.

Fazle Lohani : Fazle Lohani (born 1928- died 30 October 1985) was a television talk and variety show host from Bangladesh. He was the host of the popular show Jodi Kichu Mone Na Koren aired on Bangladesh Television Lohani was born in the village Kaulia in what is now Sirajganj District. After working as a journalist, he went to England and worked for the BBC. Following his return, he persued a career as a journalist and writer. His directed and hosted the programme Jodi Kichhu... between 1977 until his death in 1985.

Fazlur Rahman Khan : Fazlur Rahman Khan (April 3, 1929 - March 27, 1982), born in Dhaka, Bangladesh, was a Bangladeshi-American structural engineer. After completing undergraduate coursework at the Bengal Engineering College, University of Calcutta (Now Bengal Engineering and Science University, Shibpur), Fazlur R. Khan received his bachelor's degree from the University of Dhaka in 1951 while placing first in his class. A Fulbright Scholarship and a government scholarship enabled him to travel to the United States in 1952 where he pursued advanced studies at the University of Illinois at Urbana-Champaign. In three years Khan earned two Master's degrees — one in structural engineering and one in theoretical and applied mechanics — and a PhD in structural engineering.

In 1955, employed by Skidmore, Owings and Merrill, he began working in Chicago, Illinois. He is noted for his efficient designs for Chicago's 100-story John Hancock Center and 108-story Sears Tower, the tallest building in the United States since its completion in 1974. One of the foremost structural engineers of the 20th century, Fazlur Khan epitomized both structural engineering achievement and creative collaborative effort between architect and engineer. He believed that "only when architectural design is grounded in structural realities—thus celebrating architecture's nature as a constructive art, rooted in the earth—can the resulting aesthetics ... have a transcendental value and quality."

Fazlur Rahman Malik : Fazlur Rahman Malik (September 21, 1919—July 26, 1988) was a well-known scholar of Islam; M. Yahya Birt of the Association of Islam Researchers described him as "probably the most learned of the major Muslim thinkers in the second-half of the twentieth century, in terms of both classical Islam and Western philosophical and theological discourse." Since Rahman's death his writings have continued to be popular among scholars of Islam and the Near East. His contributions to the University of Chicago are still evident in its excellent programs in these areas.

Federally Administered Tribal Areas (FATA) : The Federally Administered Tribal Areas (FATA) are areas of Pakistan outside the four provinces, comprising a region of some 27,220 km^2 (10,507 mi^2). The FATA are bordered by: Afghanistan to the west with the border marked by the Durand Line, the North-West Frontier Province and the Punjab to the east, and Balochistan to the south. The total population of the FATA was estimated in 2003 to be about 3,138,000 people, or roughly 2% of Pakistan's population. Only 2.7% of the population of the Tribal Areas resides in established towns. The Tribal Areas comprise seven Agencies: Khyber, Kurram, Bajaur, Mohmand, Orakzai, and North and South Waziristan. The main towns include Miran Shah, Razmak, Bajaur, and Wana.

Fei Hsin : Fei Hsin was one of the three officials who accompanied Admiral (Eunuch) Zheng-He during his voyages to the Indian Ocean in the early medival period. His description of the court of Bangla (Bengal) is an important source to reconstruct the history of medieval Bengal.

Fei Hsin's travelogue is about half the length of Ma Huan's, but within that limit he provides notices on forty-five places as compared with twenty-one countries described by ma huan. While 19 places are common to both writers, Fei Hsin gives accounts of twenty-six places which are absent in Ma Huan's travelogue; on the other hand, Ma Huan describes two countries which find no place in Fei Hsin. Fei Hsin is the first of the medieval writers to provide information, albeit at second-hand, of La'sa (probably at Muscat or near Bir Ali, 18.19E) in Arabia, and Mogadishu, Brava and Giumbo in East Africa. Although much shorter, his book complements Ma Huan's on many points. Fei Hsin adds that in Sri Lanka a memorial stone was set up; king Alagakkonara was defeated and captured and the Chinese mission to Bangla included soldiers, received a ceremonial welcome at the custom-station of Chittagong and was lavishly entertained by the very generous Sultan of Bangla in his magnificent court at the prosperous capital of Pandua.

Feni River : Feni river rises from the hill ranges of the Indian state of Tripura at 23 20'N and 91 47'E, flows southwest marking the boundary with the Chittagong Hill Tracts, then flows west, separating Tripura from Chittagong up to Aliganj and then emerges out of the hills and passes through the plains dividing Chittagong from Noakhali before falling into the Bay of Bengal at 22 50'N and 91 27'E. This river belongs to Bangladesh as it used to form the demarcation line between Chittagong, Noakhali and Tripura State of India. But since 1960, India is using the river, claiming their right up to the midstream.

The river is 116 km long from the source to the Bay of Bengal and 80.5 km of it up to Ramgarh is navigable throughout the year by small boats. During monsoon rains it remains full of water but with every heavy shower in its catchment area it becomes furious with rapid currents and whirling eddies at sharp turns. The Muhuri from Noakhali district, also called Little Feni, falls into it near its mouth but it has no important affluent from Chittagong district. The river is gradually silting up due to reckless extraction of Timber tree from the hill slopes and consequent heavy erosion of the hills

Fenny : Fenny is an Indian liquor made from either coconut or the juice of the cashew apple. Fenny also spelt as Feni originated in Goa, and the Goan fenny is generally considered superior, with the best brand being "Big Boss" (available both in coconut and (slightly more expensive) cashew versions). The other popular brands of Fenny are 'Cashyo' (the makers of which spell it as feni) and 'Reals' (pronounced as Reaals). Feni made from the cashew apple is known as Kaju feni (cashew feni).

Feroz Khan Noon : Sir Feroz Khan Noon was a politician from Pakistan. He was educated at Oxford University and belonged to one of the most influential landlord families of the Punjab. He held many posts in government both before and after the partition of India, and was an important figure in the Pakistan movement.

He was the High Commissioner of India to the United Kingdom from 1936 to 1941, and in 1947 he was sent as

Quaid-i-Azam Muhammad Ali Jinnah's special envoy to some countries of the Muslim world. This one-man delegation was the first official mission sent abroad by the Pakistani government. The aim of the mission was to introduce Pakistan, to explain the reasons of its creation, to familiarize the Muslim countries with its internal problems and to get moral and financial support from these countries. Noon performed the role assigned to him in a successful manner.

Noon was then Chief Minister of the Punjab state from 1953 to 1956, after which he assumed charge as the Foreign Minister of Pakistan until 1957. On December 16, 1957 he was elected as the 7th Prime Minister of Pakistan. He held this post till October 7, 1958, when martial law was enforced for the first time in Pakistan's history by General(Retd) Iskander Mirza.

Apart from politics, Feroz Khan Noon also proved his capabilities in the field of academics. He wrote five books, including his autobiography, From Memory. His wife Viqar-un-Nisa Noon, though not originally from Pakistan, spent her entire life working for the betterment of the people of Pakistan, and proved to be a great social worker. Feroz Khan Noon died on December 9, 1970 in his ancestral village of Nurpur Noon, near Sargodha.

Feroze Khan : Feroze Khan (September 9, 1904 – April 21, 2005) was, at the time of his death, the world oldest Olympic medal winner, following the death of U.S. athlete James Rockefeller in 2004. He was part of India's Olympic hockey team at the 1928 Summer Olympics in Amsterdam, the Netherlands, which won the gold medal for the event. In his later years, he moved to Pakistan where he served as a well-respected coach.

The cause of his death was not stated, although his son claimed that no illness was involved.

Fidai Khan : Fidai Khan was the subahdar of Bengal (1627-1628). His real name was Mirza Hedayetullah. He rose to prominence under the patronage of Mahabbat Khan and held the important post of Mir Bahr-i-Nawarah or Admiral of the Fleet of the Mughals. He was appointed subahdar of Bengal in 1627 at the death of Mukarram Khan. He remitted from Bengal a sum of five lakh rupees yearly for jahangir and an equal amount for Nur Jahan. From this time onward the personal tributes of the subahdars of Bengal were fixed at that sum. Fidai Khan ruled Bengal for about a year. Soon after the death of Jahangir, he was transferred from Bengal and was replaced by qasim khan jwini.

Filigree : "Standardisation is alien to them." So say admirers of the silversmiths of Karimnagar—the creators of silver Filigree. Because, the most fascinating aspect of silver Filigree is the element of newness and surprise. Every piece looks different, delicate and unique. In Filigree work, twisted silver wire is the material, and the articles have the trellis-like appearance of 'jali' (net) which endows them with a rare charm.

The silversmith crimps thin strips of fine silver into zigzag patterns and loops using it to fill up the ground of designs formed by thicker silver strips. The- strips and fine silver are then deftly soldered, carefully avoiding the trellis-like Filigree pattern. Leaves, flowers, trees, animals, and birds in the area of origin seem to be predominant. However, the versatility of the art is not restricted by tradition. The art has been extended from jewellery to other household articles like tea-trays, ornament containers, key chains and even cigarette boxes.

Fire Dance : This is a desert dance is performed by the Jasnathis of Bikaner in which the Jasnathi men and boys jump on to the fire to the accompaniment of drum beats.

Firozpur : Firozpur (or Ferozepur, Ferozepore) is a city in Firozpur District in Punjab, India. The city (1991 pop. 78,738) lies on the Sutlej River, near the Pakistani border and is a transportation hub and administrative center, founded by Firuz Shah Tughluq (1351-88), sultan of Delhi. Cotton and grain are traded, and there is some light manufacturing; the city has three colleges.

First Anglo-Sikh War : The First Anglo-Sikh War was fought between the Sikh kingdom of the Punjab and the British East India Company between 1845 and 1846. It resulted in partial subjugation of the Sikh kingdom.

Ranjit Singh, the strong ruler of the Punjab, died in 1839. Almost immediately, the kingdom fell into disorder. His unpopular legitimate son, Kharak Singh, was removed from power within a few months. After a succession of illegitimate sons died or were also deposed, a wife of Ranjit Singh named Rani Jindan became regent for her infant son Duleep Singh. Jindan's lover, Lal Singh, became Vizier, and Tej Singh became commander of the army. Sikh historians have stressed that neither Lal Singh nor Tej Singh were Sikhs, being high caste Hindus from outside the Punjab.

An alternate power source lay in the regimental panchayats within the army of the Punjab, which now claimed itself to be the Khalsa, or embodiment of the Sikh nation. British representatives in the Punjab described the regiments as preserving "puritanical" order internally, but also as being in a perpetual state of mutiny or rebellion against the central Darbar.

Meanwhile, immediately on the death of Ranjit Singh, the East India Company had begun increasing its military strength on the borders of the Punjab. Outwardly, they were taking precautionary measures against disorder in the Punjab. It cannot be denied that there was a desire to expand British influence and control into the Punjab. The unconcealed British military buildup had the effect of increasing tension within the Punjab and the Khalsa.

After mutual demands and accusations between the Sikh Darbar and the East India Company, diplomatic relations were broken. An East India Company army began marching towards Ferozepur, where a division was already stationed. This army was commanded by Sir Hugh Gough, the commander in chief of the Bengal Army, and Sir Henry Hardinge, the British Governor General.

In response, the Sikh army began crossing the Sutlej River on December 11, 1845, but they made no effort to surround or attack the division at Ferozepur. Meanwhile, a force under Lal Singh clashed with Gough's and Hardinge's forces at the Battle of Mudki onDecember 18. The British won an untidy encounter battle. Lal Singh was alleged to have fled the battlefield early.

On the next day, the British came in sight of the large Sikh entrenchment at Ferozeshah. Gough wished to attack at once, but Hardinge overruled him and ordered him to wait for the division from Ferozepur. When they appeared on December 21, Gough attacked. The well served Sikh artillery caused heavy casualties among the British, and their infantry fought desperately. On the other hand, the elite of the Sikh army, the irregular cavalry or Gorchurras, were comparatively ineffective against Gough's infantry and cavalry.

By nightfall, some of Gough's army had fought their way into the Sikh positions, but other units had been driven back in disorder. Hardinge expected a defeat on the following day and ordered the state papers at Mudki to be burned in this event. However, on the following morning, the British and Bengal Army units rallied and drove Lal Singh's troops from the rest of their fortifications. At this point, Tej Singh's army appeared. Once again, Gough's exhausted army faced defeat and disaster, but Tej Singh inexplicably withdrew.

Operations temporarily halted, mainly because Gough's army was exhausted and required rest and reinforcements. Although the Sikhs did not themselves attack, they remained on the British side of the Sutlej.

When hostilities resumed, a Sikh detachment crossed the Sutlej at Aliwal. A division under Sir Harry Smith was sent to deal with them. Sikh cavalry attacked him continually on his march and captured his baggage, but at the Battle of Aliwal on January 28, 1846, Smith won a model victory, eliminating the Sikh bridgehead.

Gough's main army had now been reinforced, and rejoined by Smith's division, attacked the main Sikh bridgehead at Sobraon on February 10. Tej Singh deserted the Sikh army early in the battle. Although the Sikh army resisted as stubbornly as at Ferozeshah, Gough's troops eventually broke into their position. The bridge behind the Sikhs broke, trapping them. None surrendered, and the British showed little mercy. This victory effectively broke the Sikh army.

In the Treaty of Lahore in 1846 the Sikhs were made to give up Kashmir and had to accept a British resident in Lahore. This effectively gave the East India Company control of the region's government. The Treaty also gave the Koh-i-Noor diamond to Queen Victoria.

Sikh historians have always maintained that, in order to retain their hold on power and maintain the figurehead rule of Duleep Singh, Lal Singh and Tej Singh embarked on the war with the deliberate intent of breaking their own army. In particular, Lal Singh was corresponding with a British political officer and betraying state and military secrets throughout the war. Lal Singh's and Tej Singh's desertion of their armies and refusal to attack when opportunity offered, seem inexplicable otherwise.

First Battle of Panipat : The first battle of Panipat took place in northern India, and marked the beginning of the Mughal Empire. In 1526, the forces of Zahir al-Din Muhammad Babur, the ruler of Kabul and of Timurid descent, defeated the much larger army of Ibrahim Lodi, the ruler of the large North Indian Delhi Sultanate.

The battle was fought near the small village of Panipat, in the present day Indian state of Haryana, an area that has been the site of a number decisive battles for the control of Northern India since the twelfth century. It is estimated that Babur's forces numbered about 12,000 men and he had between 15 to 20 pieces of field artillery. These guns proved decisive in battle because Ibrahim Lodi's lacked any field artillery. Babur was an inspirational leader of men and commanded a well disciplined army.

In contrast, Ibrahim Lodhi was loathed by many of his commanders and feudatories because of his legendary cruelty and avarice; his army, which really consisted of separate feudal contingents, loosely held together, started disintegrating under the bombardment of Babur's forces. Ibrahim Lodi died on the field of battle, abandoned by his feudatories and generals, most of whom would change their allegiance to the new master of Delhi.

The battle marked the foundation of the so called Mughal or Mogul empire in India—the word means Mongol and alludes to the Turko-Mongol origins of Baburs and his officers, although the majority of his troops would probably have had been of mixed Central Asian descent. The other significance of the battle is that it marked the beginning of large scale use of fire arms in Indian warfare as artillery is used for the first time in india.

Firuz Minar : Firuz Minar one of the most famous of the surviving monuments of Bengal built according to an inscription by Saifuddin Firuz Shah (1488-90 AD), the second ruler of the Abbyssinian Slave dynasty. Built in brick, 26m high with a base diameter of 6m, it stands outside the citadel of gaur as its eastern side on the north-eastern edge of a large mound that is probably the site of the mosque to which it was once attached. The minar thus resembles the Qutb Minar at Delhi, being a madhana, and at the same time a victory tower proclaiming the victory and glory of the sultan and of the religion to which he and the community belonged.

The position of the minar in the centre of the city suggests that it must have been a place for assemblase, that is to say, a central esplanade for spending time and enjoying the city view from its top. It should perhaps be mentioned here that a minar of such a height was unnecessary for muadhdhan's call, since a minar was not regarded as an inevitable adjunct to a mosque. In fact, after early Islam the existence of a minar, either attached to a mosque as madhana, or built singly, amounted to symbolising the glory of the land and its builder. The Firuz Minar at Gaur could not be otherwise, and is in line with its predecessors in India or outside, particularly in Iran.

The minar resembles the chhota pandua minar, also a madhana and a victory tower in receding storeys and tile decoration. The independent existence of the minar has led to the contention that the tower was not a madhana. But the walls found in the mound on the southwestern side of the tower appears to prove sufficiently that there existed a mosque at one time. The door of the minar is on its southwest side and points toward the middle of the mound which must have been the central doorway of the mosque. The position of the minar in relation to the destroyed mosque is, in fact, the same as that of the position of the Bayana and Vijaymandargarh minars to their mosques.

Firuz Shah Tughlaq : Firuz Shah Tughlaq (also known as Firoz Shah Tughluq) was a Muslim ruler of the Tughlaq Dynasty (1351 - 1388). He succeeded his cousin Muhammad bin Tughluq following the later's death from a fatal illness, but due to widespread unrest Firuz's realm was much smaller than Muhammed's. Firuz was forced by rebellions to concede virtual independence to Bengal and other provinces. He was known as an iconoclast.

He was the first Muslim ruler to think of the material welfare of his people. Many rest houses, gardens and tombs were built. A number of madrasas (schools) were opened to encourage education. He set up hospitals for the free treatment of the poor. He provided money for marriage of girls belonging to poor families.He also commissioned many public buildings in Delhi. He built over 300 villages and dug 5 major canals for irrigation. More land came under cultivation. Plenty of grains and fruits were grown.

Hindu religious works were translated form Sanskrit to Persian. He had a large personal library full of manuscripts in Persian, Arabic and other languages. He brought 2 Ashokan Pillars from Meerut and Topara, carefully wrapped in silk cloth, to Delhi. He re-erected one of them in his palace at Firoz Shah Kotla.

He had about 1,80,000 or 180,000 slaves, who had been brought from all over the country, trained in various arts and crafts. They however turned out to be undependable.

Firoz Shah's death led to many rebellions. His lenient attitude had weakened the sultan's position. His successor Ghiyas-ud-Din Tughluq II could not control the slaves and the nobles. The army had become weak. Slowly the empire shrank in size. After 10 years of his death, Timur's invasion devastated Delhi.

Flute : Flute is one among the three celebrated musical instruments of India (the other two are veena and mridanga). It has various names such as bansuri, venu, vamshi, kuzhal, murali and so on.

The flute was used in the Vedic period. In ancient India, flute was commonly used in the religious music of the Buddhists. It is used both as an accompaniment to vocal music and as a part of instrumental ensembles.

Flute is a cylindrical tube made of bamboo with uniform bore and closed at one end. Flutes are of different kinds and their lengths and number of holes vary. The length can vary from eight inches to two and a half feet. There is a mouth hole in every flute. In addition to it there are 6 to 8 holes arranged in a straight line. The range of the flute is about 21/2 octaves. Long flutes have a rich, deep and mellow tone whereas in small flutes the tone is high pitched.

The flute is held in a horizontal position with a slight downward inclination. The two thumbs are used to hold the flute in position. The three fingers of the left hand, excluding the little finger and the four fingers of the right hand are used to manipulate the finger holes.

The player blows into the mouth hole, thus setting in vibration, the column of air inside the tube. The lowest octave of the scale is produced by altering the effective length of the tube by covering the holes with the finger. The player can produce any interval by opening or closing the available holes with his fingers.

Bamboo flutes used in the north are longer than those used in the south. South India and Bengal are popular for horizontal flute. Vertical flutes are popular in the north and the west. These are held vertically and played through a mouthpiece. There are a number of artists who have excelled at this instrument. The most notable person are Pandit Hariprasad Chaurasya.

Food Street : Food Street in Gawalmandi, Lahore is a centre of traditional Pakistani food. The site is surrounded by centuries old buildings and places like Landa Bazaar, Mayo Hospital and Baansan-wala Bazaar. The food street is open to traffic in the morning but as the sun sets, the street is blocked off. Hungry visitors arrive and stay till very late at night, enjoying some of the best local food available in Lahore.

Fort Gobind Garh : In the south-west of the city, has been taken over by the Indian army and is now off limits. It was built in 1805-09 by Ranjit Singh, who was also responsible for constructing the city walls.

Fort William : Fort William the most impressive edifice in calcutta of the military power of the British Raj in the East. It still continues to serve as a citadel of the Indian army in Eastern India. There were actually two Fort Williams, the old and the new. The old fort goes back to the early days of the east india company. Sir Charles Eyre started the construction of the southeast bastion and the adjacent walls. His successor John Beard added the northeast bastion around 1701. He began the Factory or the Government House in 1702 in the middle of the fort and on completion in 1706, it was named after King William of England.

Forward Bloc Today : AIFB struggles for socialism in India but they consider that their ideology differs from that of Communist Party of India (Marxist) and Communist Party of India, as they build their socialism on foreign ideologues as Marx and Lenin, whereas the socialism of AIFB is the Indian socialism of Netaji. AIFB has branches throughout the country, but the main strength of the party is concentrated in West Bengal. It is part of the Left Front government in there, and Forward Bloc has various ministers in the state government. The party is also part of Left Front in Tripura, but since they've failed to win any seat in the State Assembly they don't have any minister in that government. Notably though AIFB is cooperating with CPI(M) in West Bengal, Tripura and on the national level, AIFB is not part of the Left Democratic Front in Kerala.

Fossil National Park : Established in the year1983. The fossil National park is located in the district of Mandala in an area of 0.27sq.km. The nearest town from the park is Shahpura at a distance of 13km. The nearest railhead and airport are at Jabalpur, 87km from the park. The park contains botanical fossils.

Fourteen Points of Mr Jinnah : In 1927 Jinnah led a successful demonstration against Simon Commission's exclusion of Indians. Later he entered into negotiations with Muslim and Hindu leaders on the issue of a future Indian constitution. The Muslim opinion wanted to continue with the separate electorates while the majority Hindu opinion was in favour of the joint electorates. Jinnah personally had opposed the separate electorates. He then charted a middle course between the Hindu position and the Muslim position and put forth a set of demands that he thought would satisfy both positions. These became known as the 14 points of Mr Jinnah.

—The form of the future constitution should be federal with the residuary powers vested in the provinces.

—A uniform measure of autonomy shall be granted to all provinces.

—All legislatures in the country and other elected bodies shall be constituted on the definite principle of adequate and effective representation of minorities in every province without reducing the majority in any province to a minority or even equality.

—In the Central Legislature, Muslim representation shall not be less than one-third.

—Representation of communal groups shall continue to be by means of separate electorate as at present, provided it shall be open to any community at any time to abandon its separate electorate in favor of a joint electorate.

—Any territorial distribution that might at any time be necessary shall not in any way affect the Muslim majority in the Punjab, Bengal and the North West Frontier Province.

—Full religious liberty, i.e. liberty of belief, worship and observance, propaganda, association and education, shall be guaranteed to all communities.

—No bill or any resolution or any part thereof shall be passed in any legislature or any other elected body if three-fourth of the members of any community in that particular body oppose such a bill resolution or part thereof on the ground that it would be injurious to the interests of that community or in the alternative, such other method is devised as may be found feasible and practicable to deal with such cases.

—Sindh should be separated from the Bombay presidency.

—Reforms should be introduced in the North West Frontier Province and Baluchistan on the same footing as in the other provinces.

—Provision should be made in the constitution giving Muslims an adequate share, along with the other

Indians, in all the services of the state and in local self-governing bodies having due regard to the requirements of efficiency.

—The constitution should embody adequate safeguards for the protection of Muslim culture and for the protection and promotion of Muslim education, language, religion, personal laws and Muslim charitable institution and for their due share in the grants-in-aid given by the state and by local self-governing bodies.

—No cabinet, either central or provincial, should be formed without there being a proportion of at least one-third Muslim ministers.

—No change shall be made in the constitution by the Central Legislature except with the concurrence of the State's contribution of the Indian Federation.

One newspaper headline described the 14 points as Muslims' irreducible minimum. These demands were rejected by the Congress Party, leaving Jinnah an isolated man even amongst the Muslims, who he had convinced to scale down their demands. He was then invited to attend the round table conferences, where he forwarded the Muslims' point of view as he understood it. However neither the nationalists nor the pro-British Muslim nobility were willing to listen to him. Years later he would remark to his Hindu friend Dalmiya of how he was able to finally bring the British lackeys, "Jee Huzoors"(yes men) and "nawabs" into line. But not in 1930-31 when his political career seemed all but over.

Foy's Lake : Foy's Lake artificial lake constructed by the assam-bengal railway in 1924 near Khulshi not far from the Pahartali Railway Station in chittagong. This lake is fairly big in size and was created by erecting an embankment across a narrow valley from one hill top to the other. Geologically, these hills are composed of dupi tila formation. There is another artificial lake close to the south of the Pahartali Railway Station, which was excavated by the same railway authority in 1920. Both the lakes are tourist spots of Chittagong City and are regularly visited by local and foreign tourists. In order to attract more tourist, a mini-zoo has been set up at the entrance of the Foy's Lake. Both the lakes are intended to serve as reservoirs for drinking water to the extensive railway areas of Chittagong.

French East India Company : The French East India Company (French Compagnie des Indes Orientales) was a commercial enterprise, founded in 1664 to compete with the British and Dutch East India companies. Planned by Jean Baptiste Colbert, it was chartered by King Louis XIV for the purpose of trading in the Eastern Hemisphere. The first Director General for the Company was François Caron, who had spent 30 years working for the Dutch East India Company, including 20 years in Japan.

The Company failed to found a colony on Madagascar but established ports on the nearby islands of Bourbon and Île-de-France (today's Réunion and Mauritius). By 1719, it had established itself in India but was near bankruptcy. In the same year it was combined under John Law with other French trading companies to form the Compagnie Perpétuelle des Indes. It resumed independence in 1723.

With the decline of the Mogul Empire, the French decided to intervene in Indian political affairs to protect their interests, notably by forging alliances with local rulers in south India. From 1741 the French under Joseph François Dupleix pursued an aggressive policy against both the Indians and the English until they ultimately were defeated by Robert Clive.

The Company was not able to maintain itself financially, and it was abolished in 1769, a few years before the French Revolution. Several Indian trading ports, including Pondicherry and Chandernagore, remained under French control until 1949.

French India : Following the British, the French also established trading bases in India. At the height of French power in the mid-18th century, the French occupied most of southern India and the area lying in today's northern Andhra Pradesh and Orissa. The French, however, suffered major military setbacks against the British, losing their possessions by the end of the 18th century. The enclaves of Pondicherry, Karaikal, Yanam, Mahé and Chandernagore were returned to France in 1816, and were integrated with India after independence.

Frontline : Frontline is a fortnightly English language magazine published by The Hindu group. The magazine is published in Chennai, India. The magazine reports world affairs in addition to domestic content.

Fulhar Building Complex : Fulhar Building Complex located on the right bank of the Karatoya in the village of Fulhar in Govindaganj upazila of Gaibandha district. It is not very far from the ancient Fort of Ghoraghat in Dinajpur district. The buildings of the complex are well arranged—a three-domed mosque in the west, a series of four small structures of varying dimensions in the east and another structure of considerable size in the north, while the southern side is now open.

Fumenie and Jagarana : This dance style is performed in Himachal by the ladies on the eve of groom's departure to inlaws house. Both the songs are sung by a group of females consisting 15-20 members. This traditional dance form depicts the feelings and emotions of women folk.